Teach Yourself
VISUALLY™
Flash™ MX

To download
the screen examples
used in this book, visit
www.maran.com/resources/flash

Visual

From
maranGraphics®

&

Wiley Publishing, Inc.

Teach Yourself VISUALLY™ Flash™ MX

Published by
Wiley Publishing, Inc.
909 Third Avenue
New York, NY 10022

Published simultaneously in Canada

Copyright © 2002 by maranGraphics Inc.
   5755 Coopers Avenue
   Mississauga, Ontario, Canada
   L4Z 1R9

Library of Congress Control Number: 2002103985

ISBN: 0-7645-3661-3

Manufactured in the United States of America

10 9 8 7 6 5 4 3 2

1K/SU/QW/QS/MG

Trademark Acknowledgments

Important Numbers

For U.S. corporate orders, please call maranGraphics at 800-469-6616 or fax 905-890-9434.

For general information on our other products and services or to obtain technical support, please contact our Customer Care Department within the U.S. at 800-762-2974, outside the U.S. at 317-572-3993 or fax 317-572-4002.

Permissions

Wiley Publishing, Inc.   is a trademark of Wiley Publishing, Inc.

U.S. Corporate Sales	U.S. Trade Sales
Contact maranGraphics at (800) 469-6616 or fax (905) 890-9434.	Contact Wiley at (800) 762-2974 or fax (317) 572-4002.

Some comments from our readers...

"I have to praise you and your company on the fine products you turn out. I have twelve of the *Teach Yourself VISUALLY* and *Simplified* books in my house. They were instrumental in helping me pass a difficult computer course. Thank you for creating books that are easy to follow."

—*Gordon Justin (Brielle, NJ)*

"I commend your efforts and your success. I teach in an outreach program for the Dr. Eugene Clark Library in Lockhart, TX. Your *Teach Yourself VISUALLY* books are incredible and I use them in my computer classes. All my students love them!"

—*Michele Schalin (Lockhart, TX)*

"Thank you so much for helping people like me learn about computers. The Maran family is just what the doctor ordered. Thank you, thank you, thank you."

—*Carol Moten (New Kensington, PA)*

"I would like to take this time to compliment maranGraphics on creating such great books. Thank you for making it clear. Keep up the good work."

—*Kirk Santoro (Burbank, CA)*

"I write to extend my thanks and appreciation for your books. They are clear, easy to follow, and straight to the point. Keep up the good work!"

—*Seward Kollie (Dakar, Senegal)*

"What fantastic teaching books you have produced! Congratulations to you and your staff. You deserve the Nobel prize in Education in the Software category. Thanks for helping me to understand computers."

—*Bruno Tonon (Melbourne, Australia)*

"Over time, I have bought a number of your 'Read Less-Learn More' books. For me, they are THE way to learn anything easily."

—*José A. Mazón (Cuba, NY)*

"I was introduced to maranGraphics about four years ago and YOU ARE THE GREATEST THING THAT EVER HAPPENED TO INTRODUCTORY COMPUTER BOOKS!"

—*Glenn Nettleton (Huntsville, AL)*

"Compliments To The Chef!! Your books are extraordinary! Or, simply put, Extra-Ordinary, meaning way above the rest! THANK YOU THANK YOU THANK YOU! for creating these."

—*Christine J. Manfrin (Castle Rock, CO)*

"I'm a grandma who was pushed by an 11-year-old grandson to join the computer age. I found myself hopelessly confused and frustrated until I discovered the Visual series. I'm no expert by any means now, but I'm a lot further along than I would have been otherwise. Thank you!"

—*Carol Louthain (Logansport, IN)*

"Thank you, thank you, thank you...for making it so easy for me to break into this high-tech world. I now own four of your books. I recommend them to anyone who is a beginner like myself. Now...if you could just do one for programming VCR's, it would make my day!"

—*Gay O'Donnell (Calgary, Alberta, Canada)*

"You're marvelous! I am greatly in your debt."

—*Patrick Baird (Lacey, WA)*

maranGraphics is a family-run business
located near Toronto, Canada.

At **maranGraphics**, we believe in producing great computer books—one book at a time.

Each maranGraphics book uses the award-winning communication process that we have been developing over the last 25 years. Using this process, we organize screen shots, text and illustrations in a way that makes it easy for you to learn new concepts and tasks.

We spend hours deciding the best way to perform each task, so you don't have to! Our clear, easy-to-follow screen shots and instructions walk you through each task from beginning to end.

Our detailed illustrations go hand-in-hand with the text to help reinforce the information. Each illustration is a labor of love—some take up to a week to draw!

We want to thank you for purchasing what we feel are the best computer books money can buy. We hope you enjoy using this book as much as we enjoyed creating it!

Sincerely,
The Maran Family

Please visit us on the Web at:
www.maran.com

CREDITS

Author:
Ruth Maran

Technical Consultant,
Illustrator and
Screen Examples:
Russ Marini

Copy Development Director:
Kelleigh Johnson

Copy Developer and Indexer:
Raquel Scott

Researcher and Editor:
Wanda Lawrie

Project Manager:
Judy Maran

Editing and
Screen Captures:
Roxanne Van Damme
Roderick Anatalio
Norm Schumacher
Megan Kirby

Layout Designer
and Illustrator:
Treena Lees

Illustrator:
Steven Schaerer

Screen Artist
and Illustrator:
Darryl Grossi

Wiley Vice President and
Executive Group Publisher:
Richard Swadley

Wiley Vice President
and Publisher:
Barry Pruett

Wiley Editorial Support:
Jennifer Dorsey
Sandy Rodrigues
Lindsay Sandman

Post Production:
Robert Maran

ACKNOWLEDGMENTS

Thanks to the dedicated staff of maranGraphics, including
Roderick Anatalio, Darryl Grossi, Kelleigh Johnson,
Megan Kirby, Wanda Lawrie, Treena Lees,
Jill Maran, Judy Maran, Robert Maran, Ruth Maran,
Russ Marini, Steven Schaerer, Norm Schumacher,
Raquel Scott, Roxanne Van Damme
and Paul Whitehead.

Finally, to Richard Maran who originated
the easy-to-use graphic format of this guide.
Thank you for your inspiration and guidance.

TABLE OF CONTENTS

Chapter 1

Chapter 2

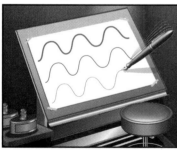

Chapter 3

WORK WITH OBJECTS

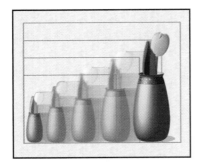

Chapter 4

ADD AND WORK WITH TEXT

TABLE OF CONTENTS

Chapter 5

USING SYMBOLS

Chapter 6

CREATE AND MANAGE LAYERS

Chapter 7

WORK WITH IMPORTED IMAGES

Chapter 8

CREATE ANIMATIONS

TABLE OF CONTENTS

Chapter 9

CREATE TWEENED ANIMATIONS

Chapter 10

ADD AND WORK WITH SCENES

Chapter 11

ADD BUTTONS AND SOUNDS

Chapter 12

Chapter 13

Chapter 14

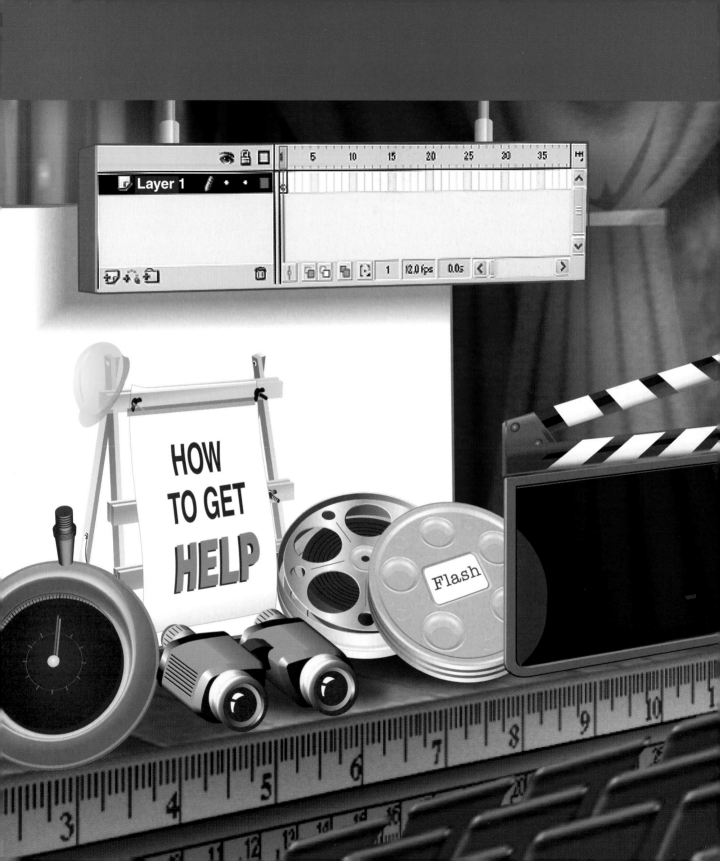

CHAPTER 1

Flash Basics

This chapter teaches you the basic skills you need to use Flash.

INTRODUCTION TO FLASH

Macromedia®
Flash™ MX allows
you to create
lively, colorful
and interactive
movies for the
Web. Flash movies
have relatively
small file sizes
so the movies
download and
play quickly.

Most people use movies created in Flash on the Internet. Flash allows you to create animated logos and banners, Web site navigation controls or entire Web sites.

You can also distribute movies you create in Flash to friends, family or colleagues in e-mail messages and on CDs or other media.

Create Movie Content

Flash includes many tools you can use to draw and paint the objects you want to include in your movies. After you create objects, you can make changes to the objects, such as resizing, rotating, aligning, erasing and changing the color of the objects. You can also add text to your movies and specify the font, size, alignment and orientation of the text. Flash also allows you to use images you created in other programs in your Flash movies.

Work With Symbols

Symbols are objects you create once in a movie and can reuse throughout the movie. Using symbols instead of individually drawn objects helps reduce your movie's file size. When you add a symbol to your movie, you are adding an instance of the symbol. Instances are linked to the original symbol so any changes you make to the symbol will affect all the instances of the symbol you added to the movie.

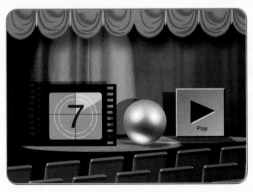

Work With Layers

Layers help you organize the artwork in a movie. Each layer is like a separate piece of transparent paper containing a specific part of a movie. You can add, delete and rename layers and lock a layer to prevent accidental changes to the objects on the layer. You can also create special layers, such as a guide layer that helps you position objects in a movie.

Create Animations

You can use the many tools included with Flash to create animations. Flash provides a Timeline that consists of frames, with each frame displaying the content for a specific location in your movie. You can create frame-by-frame animations by changing an object in each frame or you can create tweened animations where you specify the content of the first and last frames and have Flash automatically create the in-between frames. You can also add sounds to a movie to have sound effects, background music or narration play in the movie.

Create Interactive Elements

You can create interactive buttons that change in appearance when a user positions the mouse pointer over or clicks the button. You can assign actions to buttons that instruct Flash to perform specific tasks when a user clicks the buttons. For example, you can create an action to have a movie jump to another location in the movie, display a specific Web page, stop playing all sounds or stop playing the movie. You can also assign actions to specific frames in your movie.

Publish Movies

Flash provides many ways that you can publish your movies for others to view. You can publish a movie that will display on a Web page, publish a movie as a Flash movie file or publish a movie as a projector file so a computer that does not have Flash installed can play the movie. Before you publish a movie, you can preview how the movie will appear, print the movie and test the download performance of the movie.

START FLASH

When you start Flash, a blank document appears on your screen. You can immediately begin creating a new movie.

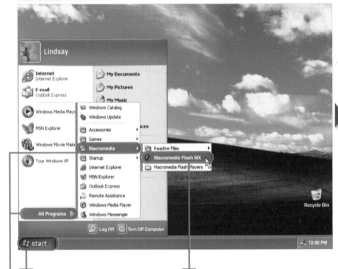

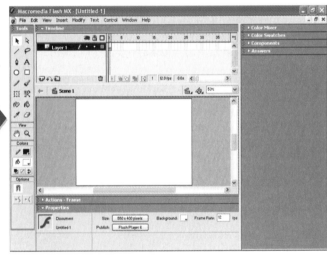

1 On a Windows computer, click **start**.

2 Click **All Programs**.

3 Click **Macromedia**.

4 Click **Macromedia Flash MX**.

Note: On a Macintosh computer, locate the folder that contains the Flash program file and then double-click the program file to start Flash.

■ The Macromedia Flash window appears, displaying a blank document.

The Flash window displays
many items you can use to
create and work with objects
and animations in Flash.

The items in the Flash
window may appear
differently on a Macintosh
computer.

Title Bar

Shows the name of
the program and the
displayed document.

Menu Bar

Provides
access to lists
of commands
available in
Flash.

Toolbox

Contains the tools
you can use to create
and work with objects
in Flash.

Stage

The location where
you create, change
and view the
content of a movie.

Work Area

The area surrounding
the Stage. Objects
you place in the work
area will not appear
in the movie.

Timeline

Allows you to organize
and control the content
of a movie. The Timeline
contains layers that help
organize the artwork in
a document and frames
that store the content
for specific locations in a
movie. The red playhead
indicates the frame that
is currently displayed on
the Stage.

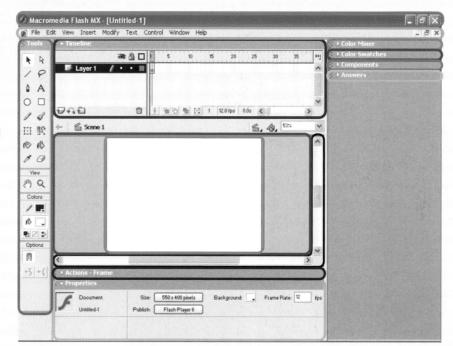

Actions Panel

Allows you to add
and work with actions
in a movie. An action
instructs Flash to
perform a specific task
when an event occurs.

Property Inspector

Allows you to view and
change the settings for
an object or movie.

Scroll Bar

Allows you to browse
through information
displayed in the area.

Color Mixer

Allows you to
create and
change colors
and gradients
that you can use
in a document.

Color Swatches Panel

Allows you to add and
delete colors from the
palette of available
colors that you can
use in a document.

Components Panel

Allows you to add
components that
provide simple
interactivity, such
as a check box (☑)
or radio button (⊙),
to a document.

Answers Panel

Allows you to
quickly access
help information.

CREATE A NEW DOCUMENT

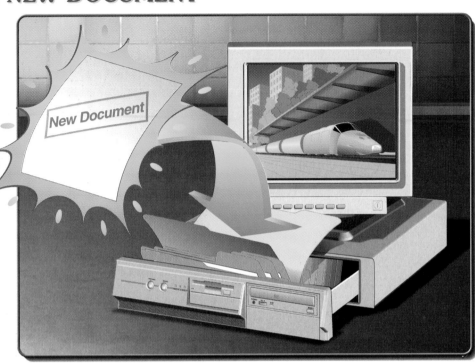

You can create a new Flash document at any time to start creating a new movie, animation or interactive feature.

CREATE A NEW DOCUMENT

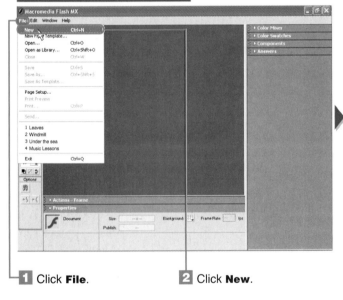

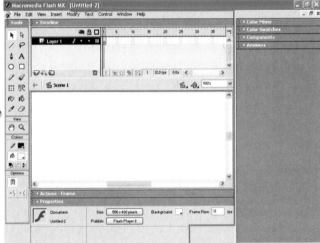

1 Click **File**.

2 Click **New**.

■ The new document appears on your screen.

■ Flash assigns the document a temporary name until you save the document. To save the document, see page 9.

You can save a Flash document to store it for future use. Saving a Flash document allows you to later review and make changes to the document.

You should regularly save changes you make to a Flash document to avoid losing your work.

SAVE A DOCUMENT

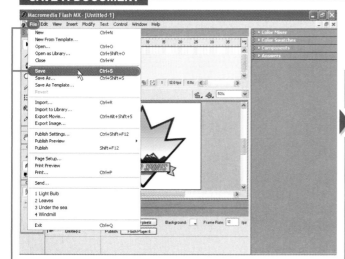

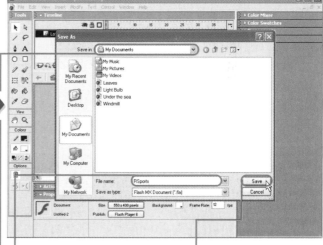

1 Click **File**.

2 Click **Save**.

■ The Save As dialog box appears.

Note: If you previously saved your document, the Save As dialog box will not appear since you have already named the document.

3 Type a name for your document.

■ This area shows the location where Flash will store your document. You can click this area to change the location.

4 Click **Save** to save the document.

CLOSE A DOCUMENT

When you finish working with a Flash document, you can close the document to remove the document from your screen.

CLOSE A DOCUMENT

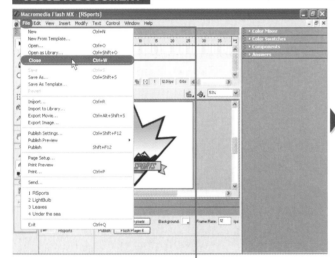

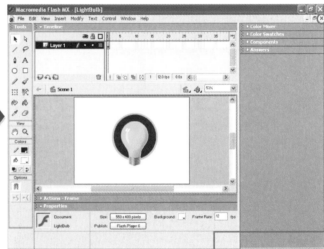

■ Before closing a document, make sure you save any changes you made to the document. To save a document, see page 9.

1 Click **File**.

2 Click **Close**.

■ The document disappears from your screen.

Note: If you have other documents open, the last document you worked with appears on your screen.

■ To quickly close a document on a Windows computer, you can click ☒.

OPEN A DOCUMENT

You can open a saved
Flash document to view
the document on your
screen. Opening a
Flash document allows
you to review and
make changes to the
document.

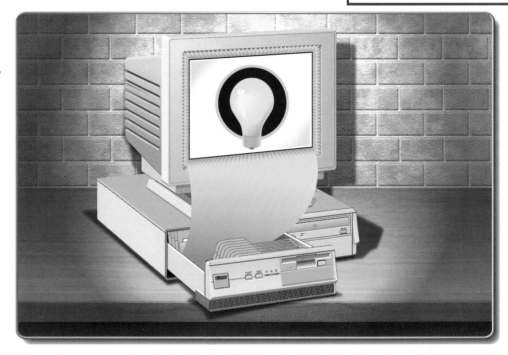

OPEN A DOCUMENT

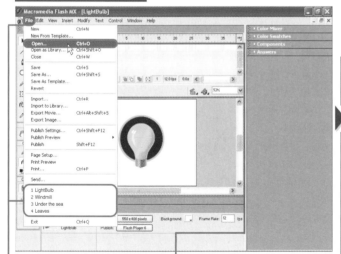
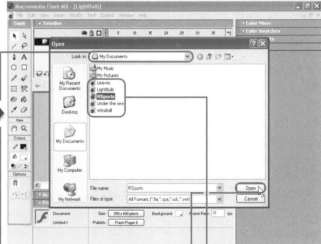

1 Click **File**.

■ This area displays the
names of the last four
documents you worked
with. To open one of these
documents, click the name
of the document.

*Note: On a Macintosh computer,
click **Open Recent** to display a
list of recently used documents.
Then click the name of the
document you want to open.*

2 If the document you
want to open does not
appear in the list, click
Open.

■ The Open dialog box
appears.

■ This area shows the
location of the displayed
documents. You can click
this area to change the
location.

3 Click the name of
the document you want
to open.

4 Click **Open** to open
the document.

SWITCH BETWEEN DOCUMENTS

Flash allows you to have several open documents at one time. You can easily switch from one open document to another.

SWITCH BETWEEN DOCUMENTS

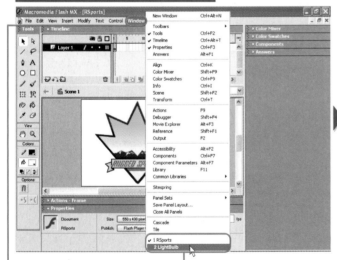

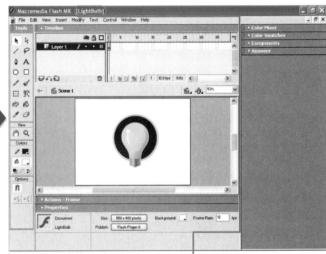

1 Click **Window** to display a list of all the documents you currently have open.

2 Click the name of the document you want to switch to.

Note: If the list of documents does not appear, click ▼ at the bottom of the menu to display the list.

■ The document you selected appears.

■ This area displays the name of the displayed document.

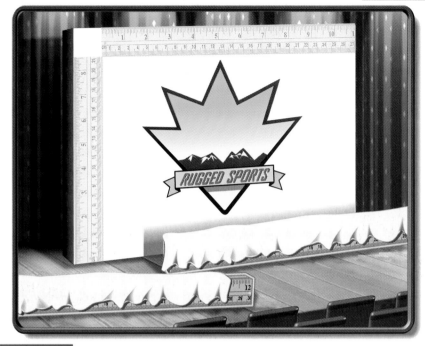

You can display or
hide the rulers at
any time. The rulers
can help you draw
and position objects
with more precision
on the Stage.

Hiding the rulers
can provide a
larger and less
cluttered working
area.

DISPLAY OR HIDE THE RULERS

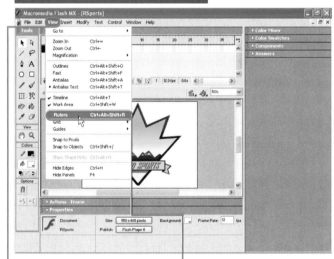

1 Click **View**.

■ A check mark (✔)
appears beside **Rulers**
when the rulers are
displayed.

2 Click **Rulers** to display
or hide the rulers.

■ The rulers appear or
disappear on the left and
top sides of the Stage.

*Note: To change the unit of
measurement for the rulers,
see page 20.*

DISPLAY OR HIDE THE TOOLBOX

You can display or hide the toolbox at any time. The toolbox contains tools that you can use to create and work with objects in Flash.

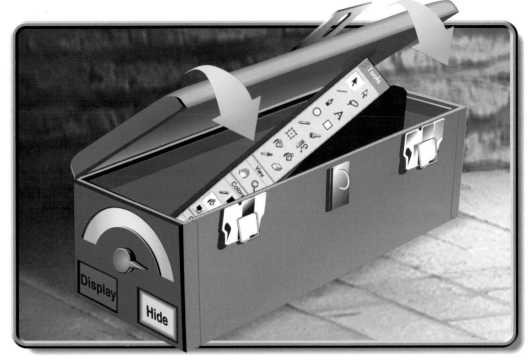

When you first start Flash, the toolbox appears on your screen.

DISPLAY OR HIDE THE TOOLBOX

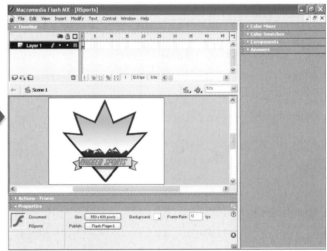

■1 Click **Window**.

■2 Click **Tools**.

■ A check mark (✔) appears beside Tools when the toolbox is displayed.

■ Flash displays or hides the toolbox.

Note: Hiding the toolbox provides a less cluttered and larger work area.

■ On a Macintosh computer, you can click 🖿 on the title bar of the toolbox to quickly display or hide the toolbox when the toolbox is displayed.

You can display
or hide the
Timeline at
any time. The
Timeline allows
you to organize
and control
the content
of a movie.

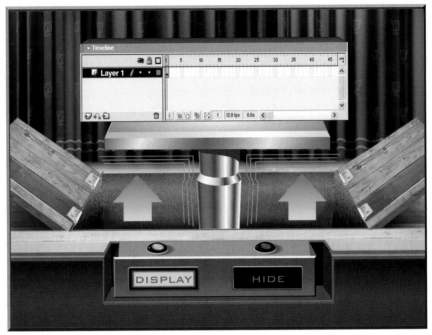

When you first start
Flash, the Timeline
appears on your
screen.

The Timeline contains
the layers and frames
for a movie. For
information on layers,
see page 132. For
information on frames,
see page 160.

DISPLAY OR HIDE THE TIMELINE

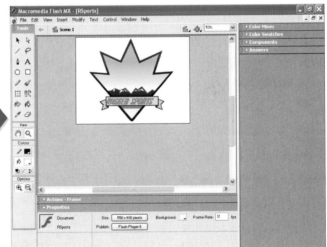

■1 Click **Window**.

■2 Click **Timeline**.

■ A check mark (✔)
appears beside Timeline
when the Timeline is
displayed.

■ Flash displays or
hides the Timeline.

*Note: Hiding the Timeline
provides a less cluttered
and larger work area.*

■ You can also display
or hide the contents of the
Timeline by clicking the
Timeline title bar when
the Timeline is displayed.

DISPLAY OR HIDE THE PROPERTY INSPECTOR

You can display or
hide the Property
inspector at any
time. The Property
inspector allows
you to view and
change settings
for an object or
your movie.

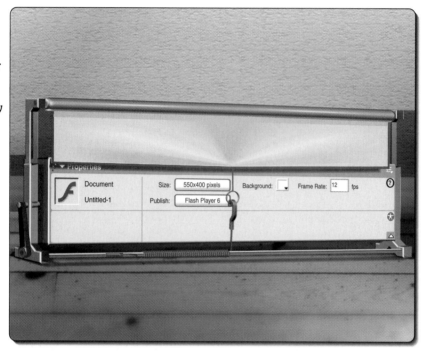

The options available
in the Property
inspector depend
on the item selected
in the toolbox, on
the Timeline or on
the Stage.

When you first start
Flash, the Property
inspector appears
on your screen.

DISPLAY OR HIDE THE PROPERTY INSPECTOR

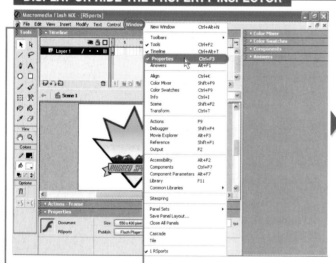

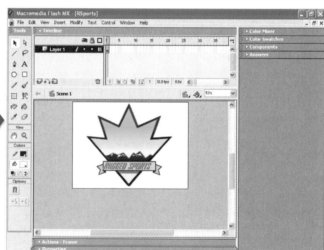

1 Click **Window**.

2 Click **Properties**.

■ A check mark (✔)
appears beside Properties
when the Property
inspector is displayed.

■ Flash displays or hides
the Property inspector.

*Note: Hiding the Property inspector
provides a less cluttered and larger
work area.*

■ To quickly display or
hide the contents of the
Property inspector on
a Windows computer,
click the **Properties** title
bar when the Property
inspector is displayed.

You can display
or hide the
Actions panel
at any time.
The Actions
panel allows
you to add
and work with
actions in a
movie.

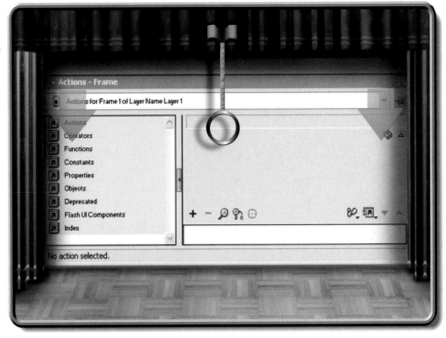

An action instructs
Flash to perform a
specific task when
an event occurs.
For example, you
can add an action
to a button to allow
users to click the
button to display a
specific Web page.
For more information
on actions, see
pages 250 to 265.

DISPLAY OR HIDE THE ACTIONS PANEL

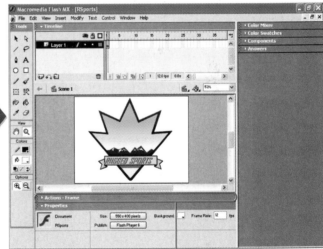

1 Click **Window**.

2 Click **Actions**.

■ A check mark (✔)
appears beside Actions
when the Actions panel
is displayed.

■ Flash displays or
hides the Actions panel.

*Note: Hiding the Actions panel
provides a less cluttered and
larger work area.*

■ To quickly display or hide
the contents of the Actions
panel on a Windows computer,
click the **Actions** title bar
when the Actions panel is
displayed.

UNDOCK OR DOCK A PANEL

You can undock and dock panels to position the panels in convenient locations on your screen.

Undocking a panel changes the panel to a floating panel that you can move on your screen. Docking a panel anchors the panel to a specific location on your screen.

Panels allow you to create and work with items in a document. Each panel allows you to perform specific tasks.

UNDOCK A PANEL

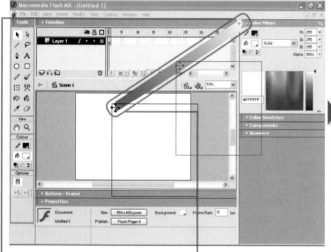

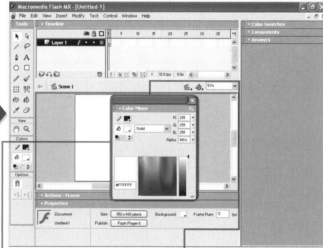

1 Position the mouse ⍟ over the top left edge of the panel you want to undock (⍟ changes to ✛ or ⍟).

2 Drag the panel away from its current position.

■ An outline indicates where the panel will appear.

■ Flash creates a floating panel.

■ To move the floating panel to a different location on your screen, position the mouse ⍟ over the title bar of the panel and then drag the panel to a new location.

How do I resize a floating panel?

To resize a floating panel on a Windows computer, position the mouse ⌖ over an edge of the panel (⌖ changes to ↕, ↔, ↖ or ↗). Then drag the mouse ⌖ until the panel displays the size you want. On a Macintosh computer, position the mouse ⬉ over ◰ in the bottom right corner of the floating panel and then drag the corner of the panel to a new position.

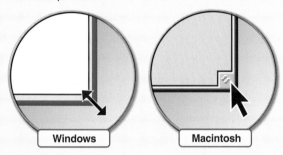

| Windows | Macintosh |

How do I quickly remove all the panels from the Flash window?

To quickly remove all the panels from the Flash window, press the `Tab` key. Removing all the panels creates a larger working area that contains only the Timeline and the Stage. You can press the `Tab` key again to redisplay all the panels.

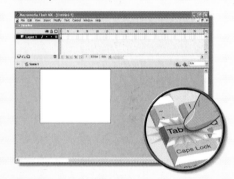

DOCK A PANEL

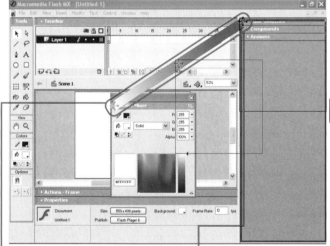

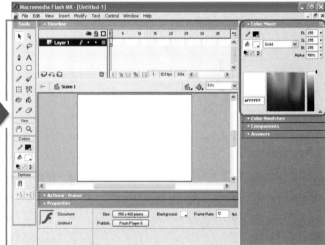

1 Position the mouse ⌖ over the top left edge of the panel you want to dock (⌖ may change to ✛ or ✋).

2 Drag the panel to where you want to dock the panel.

■ An outline indicates where the panel will appear.

■ Flash docks the panel in the location you specified and resizes the panel to fit the new location.

SET THE PROPERTIES FOR A DOCUMENT

You can set the properties for a document, such as the size and background color of the Stage and the speed of the movie.

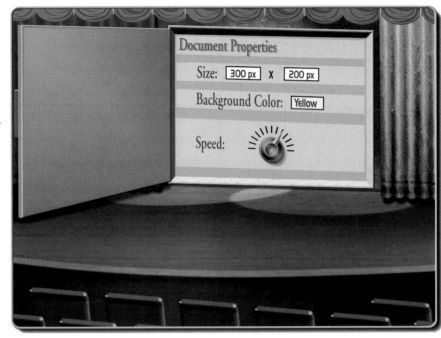

The Stage is the area that displays the objects in a movie.

SET THE PROPERTIES FOR A DOCUMENT

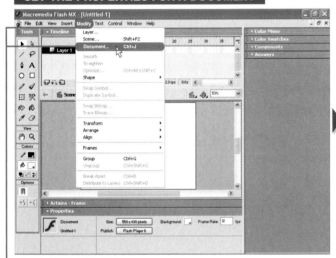

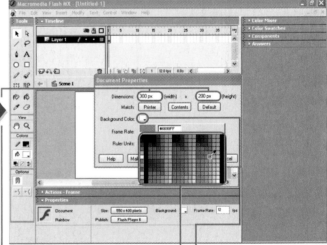

1 Click **Modify**.

2 Click **Document**.

■ The Document Properties dialog box appears.

3 To change the size of the Stage, double-click the current size in these areas and type a new width and height for the Stage in pixels.

Note: To use a different unit of measurement for the size of the Stage, perform steps 7 and 8 before performing step 3.

4 To select a background color for the Stage, click this area to display the available colors.

5 Click the background color you want to use.

What other ways can I adjust the size of the Stage?

You can click one of the following options in the Document Properties dialog box to adjust the size of the Stage.

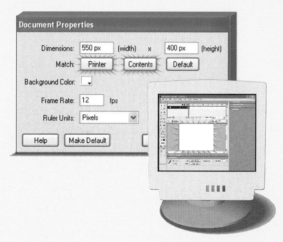

Printer

Changes the size of the Stage to match the maximum print area available to you. Flash uses your printer's paper size and margin information set in your computer to determine the size of the print area.

Contents

Changes the size of the Stage to fit its contents. Flash creates an equal amount of space between the objects on the Stage and the edges of the Stage.

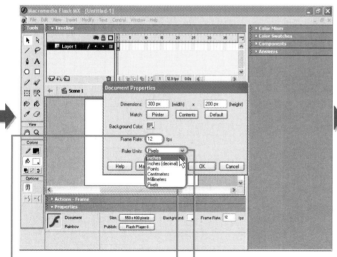

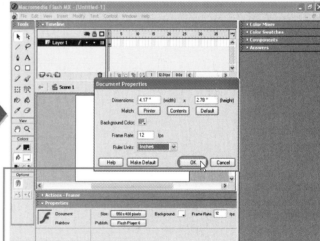

6 To specify a speed for the movie, double-click this area and type the number of frames per second (fps) for the movie.

Note: For most movies, a frame rate of 12 fps is usually sufficient.

7 To specify the unit of measurement for the rulers and the size of the Stage, click this area to display the available units.

Note: For information on the rulers, see page 13.

8 Click the unit of measurement you want to use.

9 Click **OK** to confirm your changes.

■ If you do not like the changes you made, repeat steps **1** and **2** to redisplay the Document Properties dialog box. Click **Default** and then click **OK** to restore the default settings.

*Note: On a Macintosh computer, clicking **Default** in the Document Properties dialog box restores the default settings only for the size of the Stage.*

21

GETTING HELP

If you do not know how to perform a task in Flash, you can obtain help information on the task.

HELP DESK

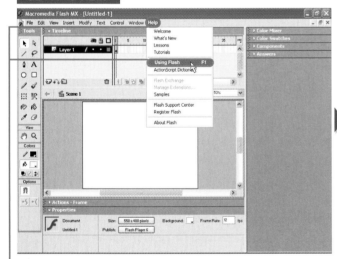

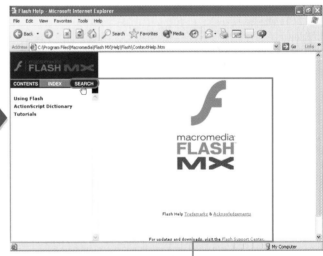

1 Click **Help**.

2 Click **Using Flash**.

Note: To quickly access Flash's help information on a Windows computer, you can press the **F1** *key instead of performing steps 1 and 2.*

■ Your Web browser opens, displaying Flash Help.

3 Click **Search** to search for help information.

What other ways can I obtain help in Flash?

In addition to the Search feature, Flash Help also offers the following options that you can use to obtain help information.

Contents

You can browse through help information by clicking a topic and subtopics until you find the information you need.

Index

The Index organizes help information like an index at the back of a book. You can click a letter to access an alphabetical list of all the help topics beginning with that letter.

Can I access up-to-date information on the Web?

Yes. If your computer is connected to the Internet, you can click the Flash logo in Flash Help to display the Macromedia Flash Support Center Web site in your Web browser. The Web site allows you to access the most up-to-date resources, such as news, articles, tutorials and online discussion groups about Flash.

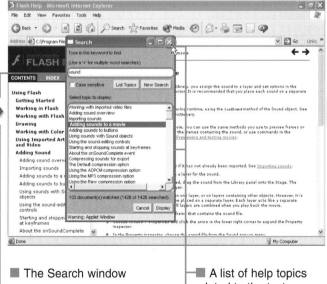

■ The Search window appears.

4 Click this area and type the word or phrase you want to get help information on. Then press the Enter key (Windows) or the Return key (Macintosh).

■ A list of help topics related to the text you typed appears.

5 Double-click the help topic of interest.

6 Click ☒ (Windows) or ☐ (Macintosh) to close the Search window.

■ The help topic you selected appears in this area.

*Note: To display another help topic, click **Search** again and then double-click the help topic of interest in the Search window.*

■ You can click text that appears underlined and in color to display a related help topic.

7 When you finish reviewing the help information, click ☒ (Windows) or ☐ (Macintosh) to close the Web browser window.

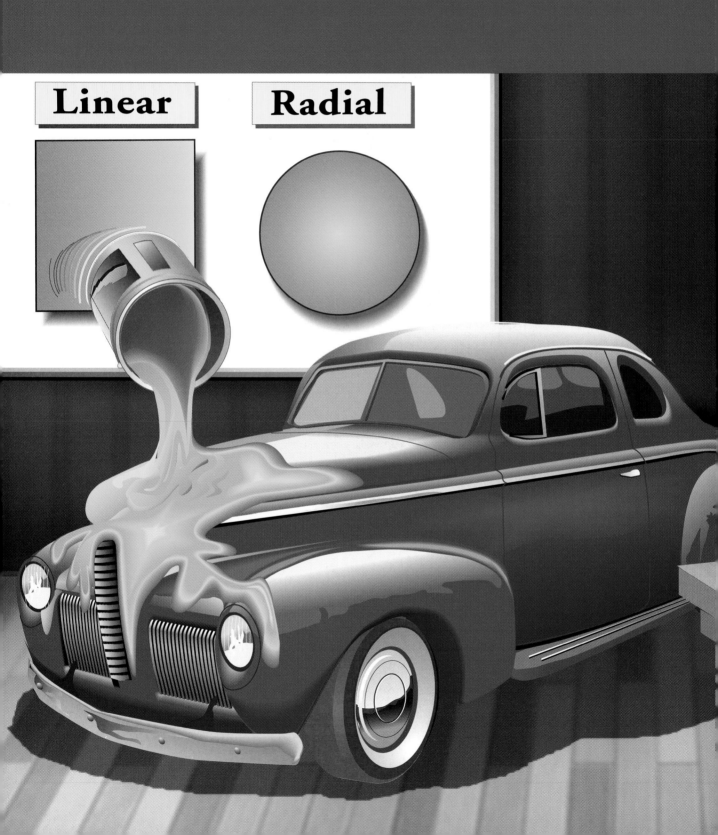

CHAPTER 2

Draw and Paint Objects

In this chapter, you will learn how to use the tools Flash provides to draw and paint objects. You will also find out how to work with the color palette, zoom in and out and use guides to place objects on the Stage.

DRAW LINES WITH THE LINE OR PENCIL TOOL

You can use the
Line and Pencil
tools to draw
lines and shapes
in various colors.

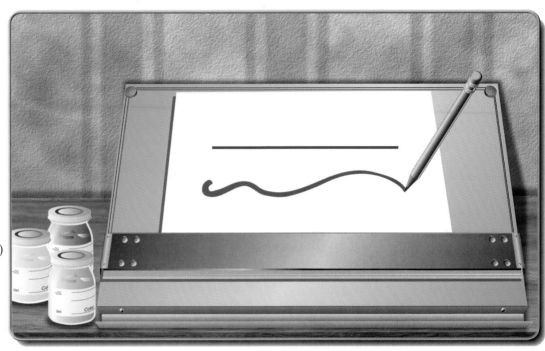

The Line tool ( ) draws straight lines. The Pencil tool ( ) works like a real pencil to draw straight lines, curvy lines and shapes.

In Flash, lines are called strokes.

DRAW LINES WITH THE LINE OR PENCIL TOOL

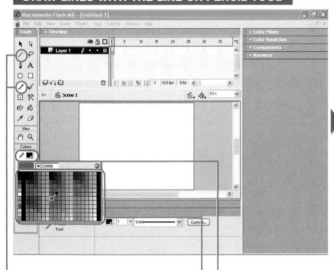

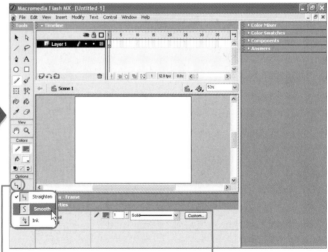

■ Before drawing lines, make sure you deselect all objects on the Stage. To deselect all objects, click and then click a blank area on the Stage.

1 Click the Line ( ) or Pencil ( ) tool.

2 To select a color for the line, click in this area to display the available colors.

3 Click the color you want to use.

4 If you selected the Pencil tool ( ) in step 1, click to display the available line options.

Note: On a Macintosh computer, click and hold down the mouse.

5 Click the line option you want to use.

Note: For information on the available line options, see the top of page 27.

When using the Pencil tool, what line options can I use?

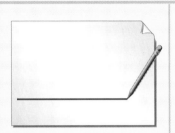

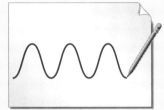

Straighten

Straightens lines you draw and automatically converts roughly drawn shapes such as circles, squares and triangles into neater shapes.

Smooth

Converts lines you draw into smooth lines.

Ink

Does not change lines you draw.

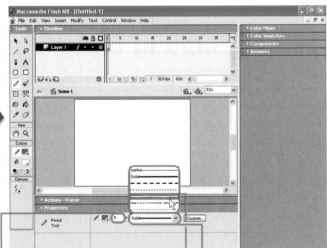

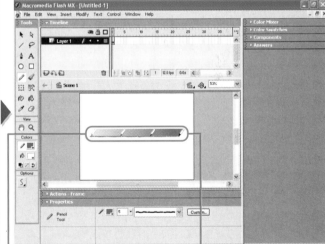

6 To specify a thickness for the line, double-click this area and type a new thickness in points.

Note: If the area is not displayed, see page 16 to display the Property inspector.

7 To select a line style, click this area to display the available styles.

8 Click the line style you want to use.

*Note: Selecting a line style other than **Solid** can increase the file size.*

9 Position the mouse ☐ where you want to begin drawing the line (☐ changes to + or ☐ on a Windows computer).

10 Drag the mouse ☐ until the line is the length you want.

Note: To draw a perfectly vertical or horizontal line, press and hold down the **Shift** *key as you perform step* **10***.*

DRAW LINES WITH THE PEN TOOL

You can use the Pen tool to draw straight lines in various colors and thicknesses.

DRAW STRAIGHT LINES

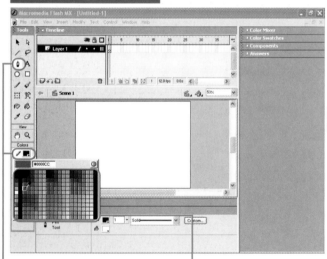

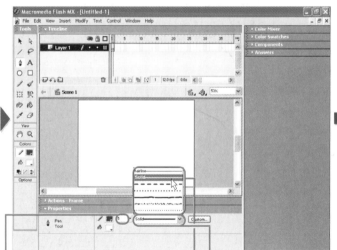

1 Click 🖊 to draw lines with the Pen tool.

2 To select a color for the line, click ■ in this area to display the available colors.

3 Click the color you want to use.

4 To specify a thickness for the line, double-click this area and type a thickness in points.

Note: If the area is not displayed, see page 16 to display the Property inspector.

5 To change the line style, click this area to display the available styles.

6 Click the line style you want to use.

*Note: Selecting a line style other than **Solid** can increase the file size.*

Can I draw perfectly vertical or horizontal lines with the Pen tool?

To draw a perfectly vertical, horizontal or 45-degree line with the Pen tool, press and hold down the Shift key as you create the line.

How do I create a closed shape with the Pen tool?

Perform steps 1 to 9 below to draw the lines for the shape. When drawing the last line for the shape, position the mouse ♣ᵒ over the beginning of the first line and then click to complete the shape. Flash closes the shape and uses the currently selected fill color to fill the shape. To change the fill color for the shape, select the fill area of the shape and then click 🔲 in the Fill Color area to select a new color. To select objects, see page 58.

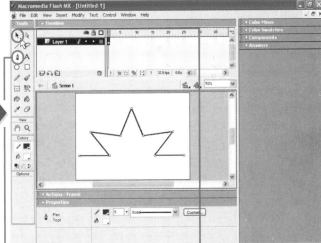

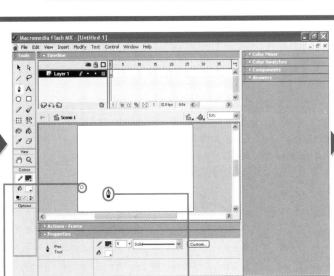

7 Click the location on the Stage where you want the line to begin. A small circle (○) appears on the Stage.

8 Click the location where you want the line to end.

■ Flash draws a line between the two locations on the Stage.

9 To continue drawing connected lines, repeat step 8 for each line you want to draw.

10 When you finish drawing connected lines, click ♣ to complete the line.

11 Click ▶ to see the finished line on the Stage.

CONTINUED ▶

DRAW LINES WITH THE PEN TOOL

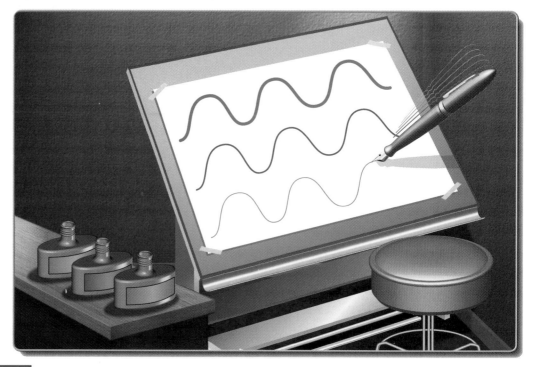

You can use the Pen tool to draw curved lines in various colors and thicknesses.

DRAW CURVED LINES

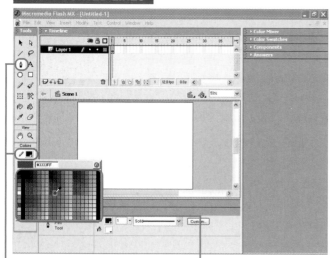

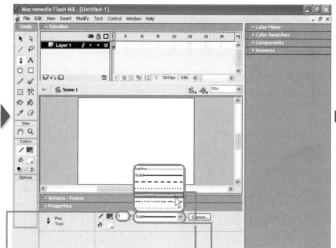

1 Click 🖋 to draw curved lines with the Pen tool.

2 To select a color for the curved line, click 🔲 in this area to display the available colors.

3 Click the color you want to use.

4 To specify a thickness for the curved line, double-click this area and type a thickness in points.

Note: If the area is not displayed, see page 16 to display the Property inspector.

5 To change the line style, click this area to display the available styles.

6 Click the line style you want to use.

*Note: Selecting a line style other than **Solid** can increase the file size.*

Why does the straight line appear when I draw a curved line with the Pen tool?

When you draw a curved line with the Pen tool, a straight line called a tangent handle appears, helping you draw the curve. Dragging this handle helps you shape the curved line the way you want. You can drag the handle in any direction to change the shape and angle of the curve. The length of the handle determines the depth of the curve.

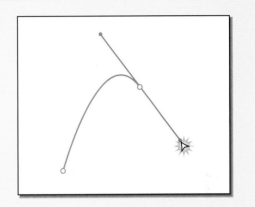

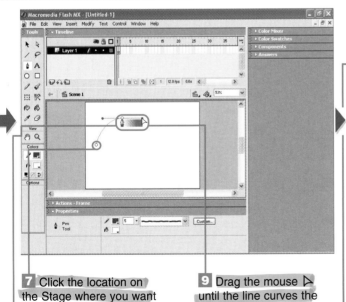

7 Click the location on the Stage where you want the curved line to begin. A small circle (○) appears on the Stage.

8 Position the mouse over the location where you want the curve to end.

9 Drag the mouse until the line curves the way you want.

Note: A straight line appears at the end of the curve as you drag the mouse. This line will disappear when you release the mouse button.

10 To continue drawing connected curved lines, repeat steps **8** and **9** for each curved line you want to draw.

11 When you finish drawing connected curved lines, click to complete the line.

12 Click to see the finished curved line on the Stage.

DRAW SHAPES WITH THE OVAL OR RECTANGLE TOOL

You can use the Oval and Rectangle tools to draw basic shapes, including ovals, circles, rectangles and squares.

You can control the color and size of a shape that you draw.

Flash allows you to draw an outline of a shape, a solid shape or a solid shape with an outline.

DRAW SHAPES WITH THE OVAL OR RECTANGLE TOOL

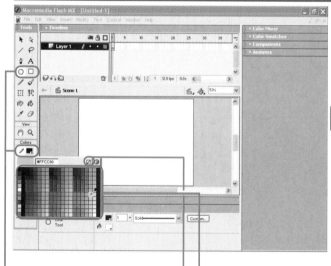

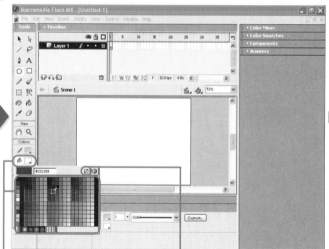

■1 Click the Oval (○) or Rectangle (□) tool.

■2 To select a color for the border of the shape, click ■ in this area to display the available colors.

■3 Click the color you want to use.

■ If you do not want the shape to display a border, click ☑.

■4 To select a color for the inside of the shape, click □ in this area to display the available colors and gradients.

■5 Click the color or gradient you want to use.

Note: A gradient is two or more colors that blend from one color to another.

■ If you do not want the shape to display an inside color, click ☑.

How can I create a rectangle with rounded corners?

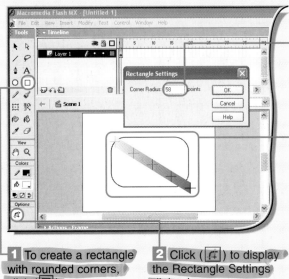

3 Type a value for the corners of the rectangle in points and then press the Enter key (Windows) or the Return key (Macintosh).

Note: A value of 0 creates square corners. Larger values create rounded corners.

4 To draw the rectangle, drag the mouse + until the rectangle is the size you want.

Note: To change the corners of a rectangle as you drag the mouse, press the ↓ or ↑ key to make the corners more or less rounded.

1 To create a rectangle with rounded corners, click (□).

2 Click (⬚) to display the Rectangle Settings dialog box.

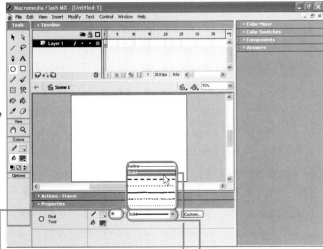

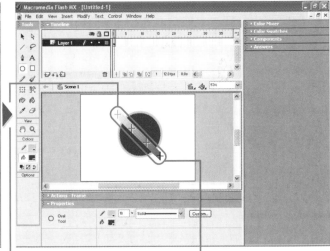

6 To specify a thickness for the border of the shape, double-click this area and type a new thickness in points.

Note: If the area is not displayed, see page 16 to display the Property inspector.

7 To select a border style, click this area to display the available styles.

8 Click the border style you want to use.

*Note: Selecting a border style other than **Solid** can increase the file size.*

9 Position the mouse ⬚ where you want to begin drawing the shape (⬚ changes to + on a Windows computer).

10 Drag the mouse + until the shape is the size you want.

Note: To draw a circle or square, press and hold down the Shift key as you perform step 10.

PAINT WITH THE BRUSH TOOL

You can use the Brush tool to draw brush strokes the same way you would use a paintbrush.

You can specify how you want the brush strokes to appear on the Stage as well as the color, size and shape of the brush.

When choosing a color for your brush stroke, you can select a solid color or a gradient. A gradient is two or more colors that blend from one color to another.

PAINT WITH THE BRUSH TOOL

■ Before painting with the Brush tool, make sure you deselect all objects on the Stage. To deselect all objects, click ▶ and then click a blank area on the Stage.

1 Click ✎ to paint with the Brush tool.

2 To select a color for the brush, click ⬜ in this area to display the available colors and gradients.

3 Click the color or gradient you want to use.

4 To specify how you want the brush strokes to appear, click ⊙ to display the available options.

Note: On a Macintosh computer, click ⊙ and hold down the mouse.

5 Click the way you want the brush strokes to appear.

Note: For information on the available options, see the top of page 35.

How can I have the brush strokes appear on the Stage?

Flash offers five different ways that brush strokes can
appear on the Stage.

Paint Normal	Paint Fills	Paint Behind	Paint Selection	Paint Inside
Paints over everything, including lines and filled areas.	Paints over filled areas, but does not paint over lines.	Paints behind objects.	Paints only the area you select. To select objects, see page 58.	Paints the inside of a filled area where you begin the brush stroke, but does not paint outside the area.

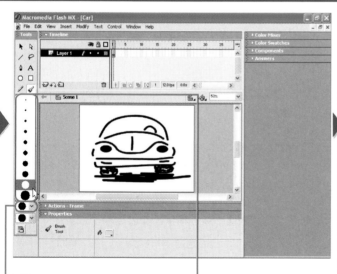

6 To select a brush size, click (Windows) or (Macintosh) in this area to display the available sizes.

7 Click the brush size you want to use.

8 To select a brush shape, click (Windows) or (Macintosh) in this area to display the available shapes.

9 Click the brush shape you want to use.

10 Position the mouse where you want to begin painting.

Note: The mouse pointer displays the brush size and shape you selected.

11 Drag the mouse until the brush stroke appears the way you want.

FILL OBJECTS WITH THE PAINT BUCKET TOOL

You can use the Paint Bucket tool to add a fill or change the fill of objects on the Stage.

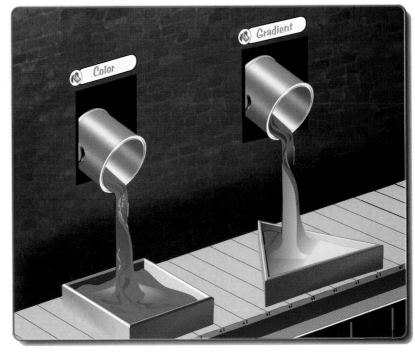

Flash allows you to fill objects with solid colors and gradients. A gradient is two or more colors that blend from one color to another.

FILL OBJECTS WITH A SOLID COLOR

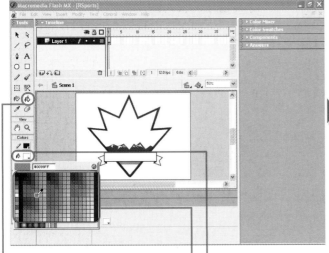

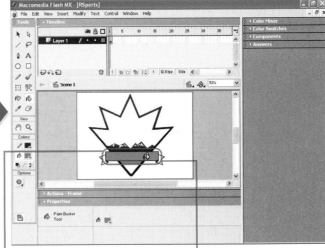

■ Before filling an object, make sure you deselect all objects on the Stage. To deselect all objects, click ▶ and then click a blank area on the Stage.

1 Click 🪣 to fill an object.

2 To select the color you want to use to fill an object, click ▢ in this area to display the available colors.

3 Click the color you want to use.

4 Click inside the object you want to fill with the color you selected.

■ The object displays the color you selected.

How can I fill an object that has a gap in its outline?

You can use the options the Paint Bucket tool provides to fill an object when the object's outline has a gap.

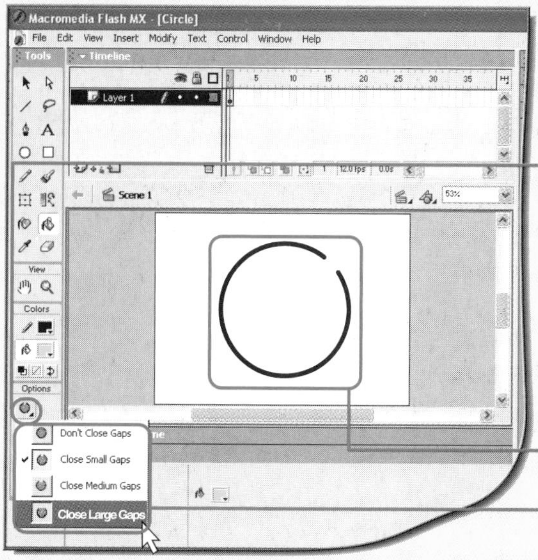

1 Perform steps **1** to **3** below.

2 Click to display the options you can use to fill an object.

Note: On a Macintosh computer, click and hold down the mouse.

3 Click the option you want to use to fill the object.

4 Click inside the object you want to fill.

■ The object displays the color you selected.

FILL OBJECTS WITH A GRADIENT

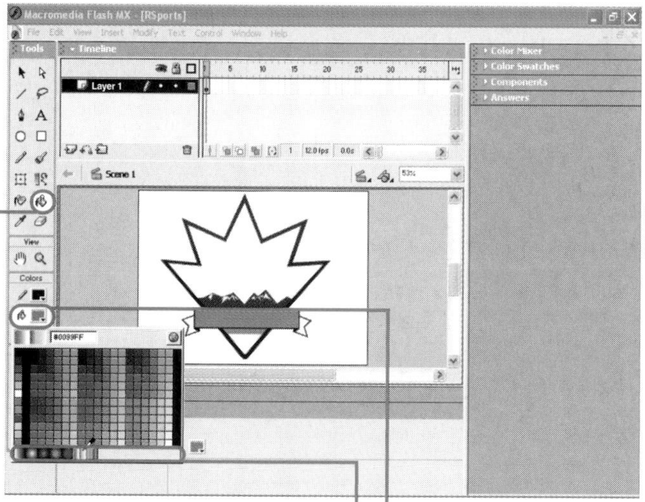

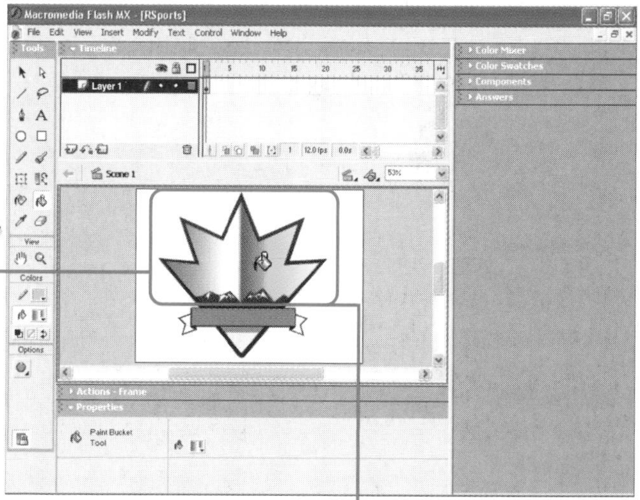

■ Before filling an object, make sure you deselect all objects on the Stage. To deselect all objects, click and then click a blank area on the Stage.

1 Click to fill an object.

2 To select the gradient you want to use to fill an object, click in this area to display the available colors and gradients.

3 Click the gradient you want to use.

4 Click inside the object you want to fill with the gradient you selected.

■ The object displays the gradient you selected.

USING THE ERASER TOOL

You can use the Eraser tool to erase parts of a drawing.

You can specify how you want the Eraser tool to erase objects. You can also choose a shape and size for the eraser.

USING THE ERASER TOOL

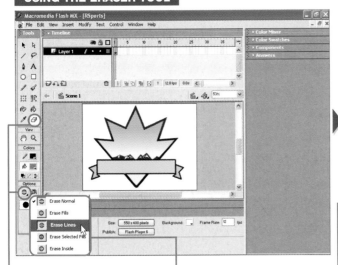

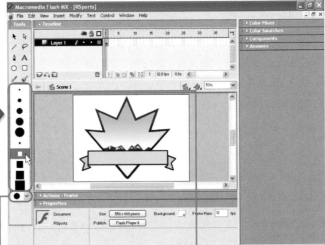

1 Click 🖉 to erase part of your drawing.

2 To specify how you want to erase objects, click 🔄 to display the available options.

Note: On a Macintosh computer, click 🔄 and hold down the mouse.

3 Click the way you want to erase objects.

Note: For information on the ways you can erase objects, see the top of page 39.

4 To select a shape and size for the eraser, click ⊽ (Windows) or ⬍ (Macintosh) in this area.

5 Click the shape and size you want to use for the eraser.

How can I erase objects?

Flash offers five different ways that you can erase objects.

Erase Normal	**Erase Fills**	**Erase Lines**	**Erase Selected Fills**	**Erase Inside**
Erases everything, including lines and filled areas.	Erases filled areas, but does not erase lines.	Erases lines, but does not erase filled areas.	Erases only the area you select. To select objects, see page 58.	Erases the inside of a filled area where you begin using the eraser, but does not erase outside the area.

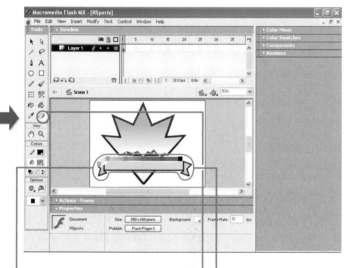

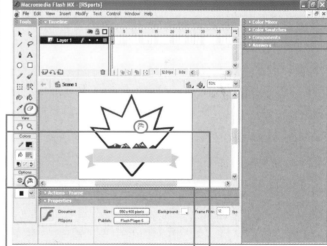

6 Position the mouse ■ where you want to begin erasing.

Note: The mouse pointer displays the eraser shape and size you selected.

7 Drag the mouse ■ over the objects you want to erase.

■ To instantly erase everything on the Stage, double-click [⌀].

QUICKLY ERASE LINES OR FILLED AREAS

1 Click [⌀] to erase a line or filled area.

2 Click [⚲].

3 Position the mouse ⚲ over the line or filled area you want to erase. Make sure the drop of water appears directly on the line or filled area.

4 Click the line or filled area you want to erase.

5 When you have finished erasing lines or filled areas, click [⚲] again.

CREATE A SOLID COLOR

You can create a custom color that you can use for lines and to fill shapes.

Creating a custom color is useful if you want to use a specific color in your drawing, but the color is not available in Flash's color palette.

CREATE A SOLID COLOR

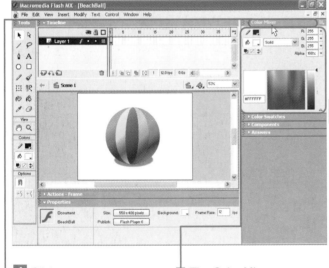

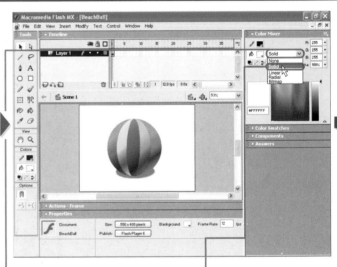

1 Click **Color Mixer** to display the Color Mixer.

■ The Color Mixer appears.

*Note: To hide the Color Mixer at any time, click **Color Mixer** again.*

2 Click this area to select the type of fill you want to create.

3 Click **Solid** to create a solid color.

How do I create a transparent color?

To create the color you want to make transparent, perform steps 1 to 5 below. To define the degree of transparency for the color, double-click the percentage value in the Alpha area of the Color Mixer and then enter the value you want to use. A value of 0 creates a fully transparent color, while a value of 100 creates a fully opaque color.

How can I quickly apply a new color in my drawing?

You can select the object that you want to display the new color in your drawing before you start creating the color. To select objects, see page 58. Perform steps 1 to 3 below and then click the Stroke Color ( ) or Fill Color ( ) icon in the Color Mixer to specify whether you want to create a line or fill color. Then perform steps 4 to 7 below to create the color. The object you selected will automatically display the new color.

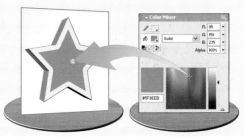

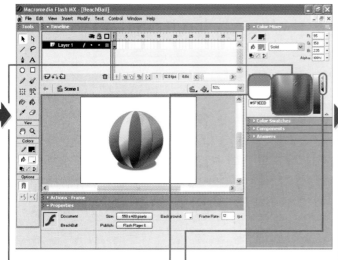

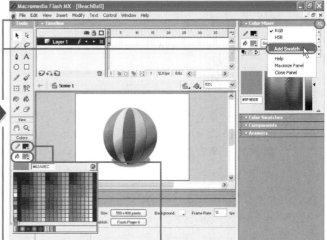

4 Click the color you want to use.

5 To change the brightness for the color you selected, drag this slider ( ) up or down to increase or decrease the brightness.

■ This area displays the color with the brightness you selected.

6 To save the color you created, click .

7 Click **Add Swatch**.

■ When you click ( ) in these areas to select the line or fill color for an object in the current document, the color you created will appear near the bottom of the palette. You can select the color you created as you would select any color in the palette.

CREATE A GRADIENT

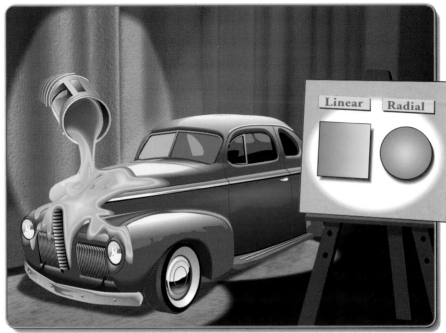

You can create a gradient to add interest and depth to your drawings. A gradient is two or more colors that blend from one color to another.

Flash allows you to create a linear gradient or a radial gradient. A **linear** gradient blends colors from one side of a shape to another. A **radial** gradient blends colors from the center point of a shape to the outer edges.

CREATE A GRADIENT

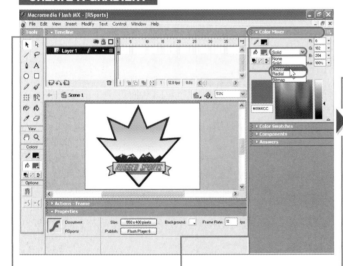

1 Click **Color Mixer** to display the Color Mixer.

■ The Color Mixer appears.

*Note: To hide the Color Mixer at any time, click **Color Mixer** again.*

2 Click this area to select the type of gradient you want to create.

3 Click **Linear** or **Radial**.

■ Each pointer (⌂) in this area defines a color and the color's location in the gradient.

4 To change a color in the gradient, click the pointer (⌂) for the color.

5 Click the color you want to use.

How do I add another color to a gradient?

2 Perform steps **4** to **6** below to define the color for the pointer.

■ To remove a color from the gradient, position the mouse over the pointer for the color and then drag the pointer away from the gradient bar.

1 Click the location on the gradient bar where you want the new color to appear.

■ A pointer (⌂) for the color appears below the gradient bar.

How do I change the location of a color in a gradient?

You can move the pointer (⌂) for a color to change where the color appears in the gradient. To move a pointer, position the mouse ⌖ over the pointer and then drag the pointer along the gradient bar to the location where you want the color to appear. Moving a pointer closer to another pointer shortens the transition between the colors, while moving a pointer further away lengthens the transition.

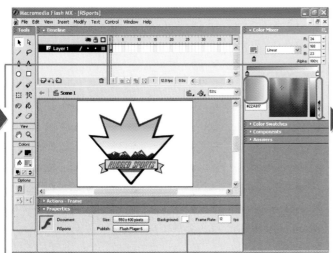

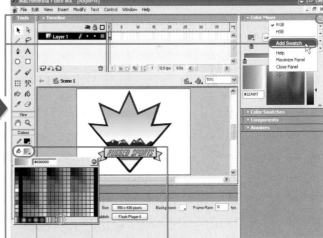

6 To change the brightness for the color you selected, drag this slider (◀) up or down to increase or decrease the brightness.

7 To specify the color and brightness for other pointers (⌂), repeat steps **4** to **6** for each pointer.

■ This area displays a preview of the gradient.

8 To save the gradient you created, click ▤.

9 Click **Add Swatch**.

■ When you click (▦) in this area to select the fill color for an object in the current document, the gradient you created will appear at the bottom of the palette. You can select the gradient as you would select any fill color in the palette.

CUSTOMIZE A COLOR PALETTE

You can duplicate a color you often use in the color palette so you can easily access the color at any time. You can also remove a color you do not need from the color palette.

Each Flash document provides a color palette of 216 colors. Changes you make to a color palette will affect the color palette for only the current document.

DUPLICATE A COLOR

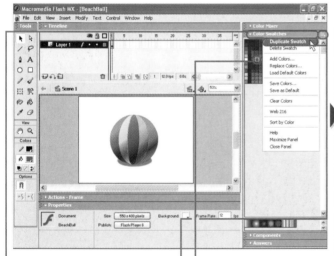

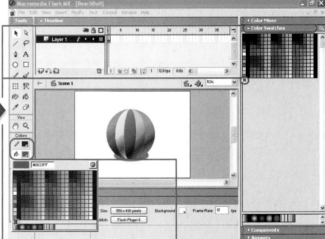

1 Click **Color Swatches** to display the Color Swatches panel.

■ The Color Swatches panel appears.

2 Click the color you want to duplicate.

3 Click in this area to display options for the Color Swatches panel.

4 Click **Duplicate Swatch**.

■ The color you selected appears at the bottom of the palette for easy access.

■ To hide the Color Swatches panel, click **Color Swatches**.

■ When you click in these areas to select the line or fill color for an object in the current document, the color you duplicated will appear near the bottom of the palette. You can select the color you duplicated as you would select any color in the palette.

The Color Swatches panel is not available on my screen. How do I display the panel?

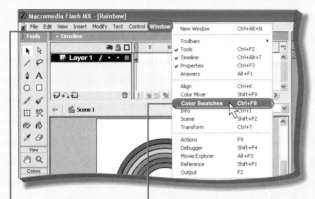

1 To display the Color Swatches panel on your screen, click **Window**.

2 Click **Color Swatches**.

■ A check mark (✔) appears beside Color Swatches when the panel is displayed.

Can I add customized colors or gradients to the color palette?

When you create and save a customized color or gradient in the Color Mixer, Flash automatically adds the new color or gradient to the color palette for you. To create a solid color, see page 40. To create a gradient, see page 42.

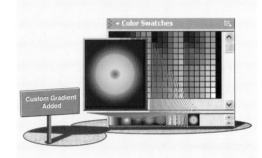

REMOVE A COLOR

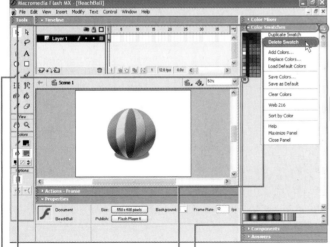

1 Click **Color Swatches** to display the Color Swatches panel.

■ The Color Swatches panel appears.

2 Click the color you want to remove.

3 Click ▦ in this area to display options for the Color Swatches panel.

4 Click **Delete Swatch**.

■ The color you selected disappears from the color palette.

■ To hide the Color Swatches panel, click **Color Swatches**.

■ When you click ▦ in these areas to select the line or fill color for an object in the current document, the color you removed will no longer appear in the palette.

SAVE AND OPEN A COLOR PALETTE

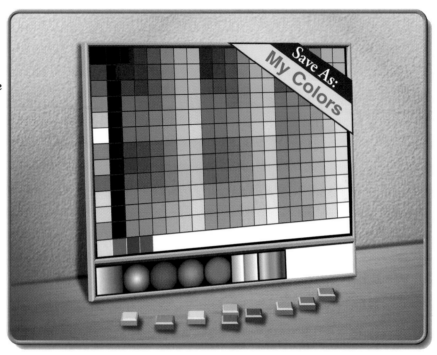

You can save a color palette you have customized so you can use the color palette in other Flash documents.

Using the same color palette in multiple documents allows you to keep the colors consistent in your documents.

You can create a custom color palette by adding, duplicating and deleting colors in the palette. To add colors, see pages 40 and 42. To duplicate colors, see page 44. To delete colors, see page 45.

SAVE A COLOR PALETTE

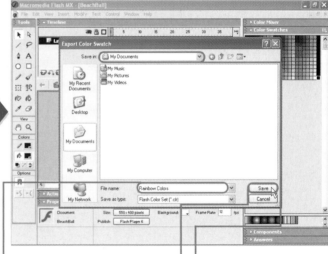

1 Click **Color Swatches** to display the Color Swatches panel.

■ The Color Swatches panel appears, displaying the custom color palette you want to save.

2 Click ▦ in this area to display options for the Color Swatches panel.

3 Click **Save Colors** to save the displayed color palette.

■ The Export Color Swatch dialog box appears.

4 Type a name for the color palette.

■ This area shows the location where Flash will store the color palette. You can click this area to change the location.

5 Click **Save** to save the color palette.

How can I redisplay Flash's default color palette?

If you no longer want to use a custom color palette, you can redisplay the default color palette at any time. Perform steps **1** and **2** on page 47 and then click **Web 216** to display the default color palette in your document.

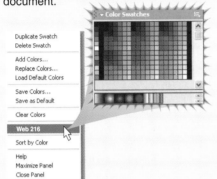

Can I add colors and gradients from a custom color palette to another color palette?

Yes. If you do not want to replace the entire color palette in a document with a custom color palette you have saved, you can add only the custom colors and gradients from the saved color palette. To add custom colors and gradients from a saved color palette, perform steps **1** to **5** on page 47, except select **Add Colors** in step **3**.

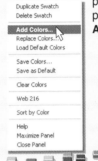

OPEN A COLOR PALETTE

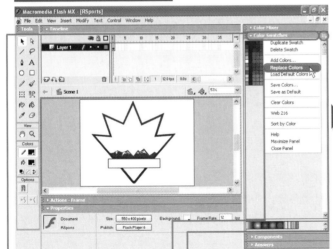

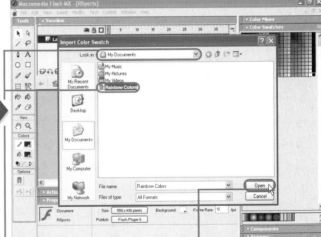

1 Click **Color Swatches** to display the Color Swatches panel.

■ The Color Swatches panel appears.

2 Click 📋 in this area to display options for the Color Swatches panel.

3 Click **Replace Colors** to replace the current color palette with a custom color palette you have saved.

■ The Import Color Swatch dialog box appears.

■ This area shows the location of the displayed files. You can click this area to change the location.

4 Click the name of the color palette you want to use in the current document.

5 Click **Open** to replace the current color palette with the color palette you selected.

■ The Color Swatches panel displays the new color palette.

ZOOM IN OR OUT

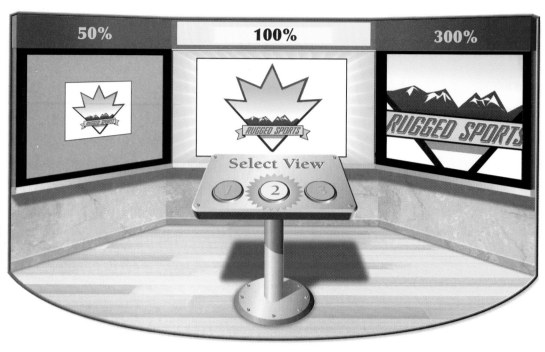

You can zoom in or out to magnify or reduce the display of the Stage on your screen.

You can zoom in to view objects on the Stage in more detail or zoom out to see more objects on the Stage at once.

Zooming in or out will not affect the way objects appear in your movie.

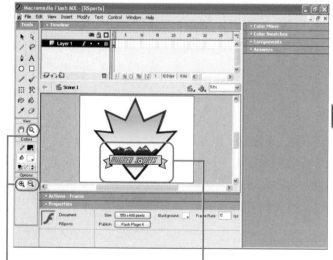

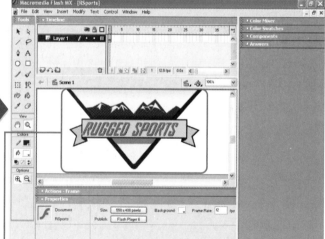

1 Click 🔍 to magnify or reduce the display of the Stage.

2 Click an option to specify if you want to magnify (🔍) or reduce (🔍) the display of the Stage.

3 Click the area of the Stage you want to magnify or reduce.

■ The area you selected is magnified or reduced.

■ To further magnify or reduce the display of the Stage, repeat step **3**.

How can I quickly zoom in to a specific area?

To quickly magnify a specific area on the Stage, click 🔍 and then drag the mouse ⊕ or ⊖ over the area on the Stage you want to magnify until a rectangle surrounds the area. Flash will magnify the area you selected.

How can I quickly view another area on the Stage after I zoom in or out?

To quickly display a different area on the Stage after you zoom in or out, click ✋. Then use the mouse ✋ to drag the Stage in any direction until the area you want to view appears.

SELECT A ZOOM PERCENTAGE

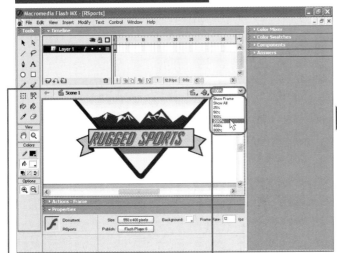

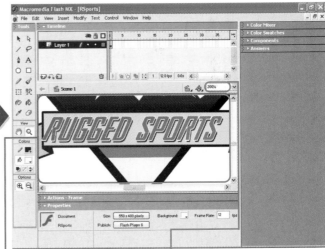

■ This area displays the current zoom percentage.

1 To use a different zoom percentage, click ⯆ (Windows) or ⬍ (Macintosh) in this area to display the available zoom percentages.

2 Click the zoom percentage you want to use.

Note: To display the entire Stage, click Show Frame. To display only the objects on the Stage, click Show All.

■ The Stage appears in the zoom percentage you selected.

■ To use a specific zoom percentage, click (Windows) or double-click (Macintosh) this area and type the percentage you want to use. Then press the Enter key (Windows) or the Return key (Macintosh).

USING GUIDES

You can add guides to a document to help you draw and position objects more precisely on the Stage.

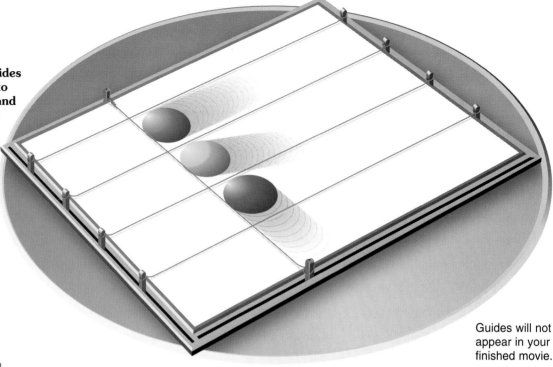

Guides will not appear in your finished movie.

ADD A GUIDE

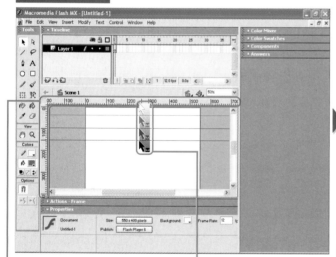

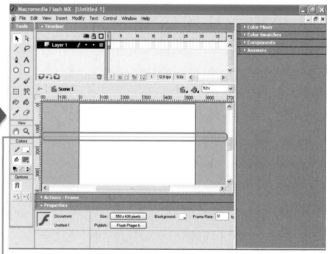

1 Position the mouse ▷ over the vertical or horizontal ruler.

Note: To display the rulers, see page 13.

2 Drag the mouse ⬏ or ⬏ until the guide appears in the position you want on the Stage.

Note: A black line indicates where the guide will appear.

■ The guide appears on the Stage. You can now use the guide to help you draw and position objects on the Stage.

■ To add more guides to the Stage, repeat steps **1** and **2** for each guide.

Can I use guides to position objects in an irregular pattern on the Stage?

If you want to create an irregular or custom guide, you can use a guide layer. A guide layer allows you to draw the guide you want to use to position your objects on the Stage. For example, you can draw a triangle on your guide layer to help you position objects in a triangular pattern on the Stage. To create a guide layer, see page 146.

After positioning the guides on the Stage, how do I avoid moving the guides accidentally?

You can lock the guides into place on the Stage.

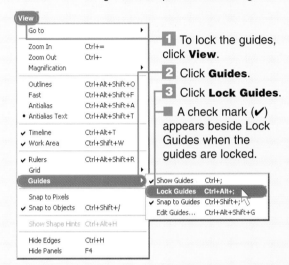

■ **1** To lock the guides, click **View**.

■ **2** Click **Guides**.

■ **3** Click **Lock Guides**.

■ A check mark (✔) appears beside Lock Guides when the guides are locked.

MOVE A GUIDE

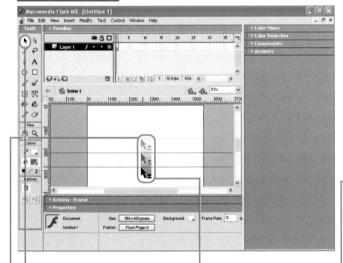

1 Click 🔖 to be able to select the guide you want to move.

2 Position the mouse ↘ over the guide you want to move (↘ changes to ↘▪ or ↘▪).

3 Drag the guide to a new location on the Stage.

Note: A black line indicates the new location of the guide.

REMOVE A GUIDE

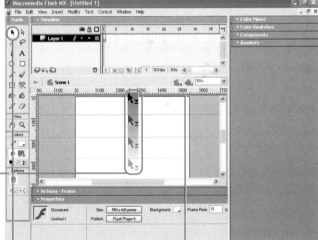

1 Click 🔖 to be able to select the guide you want to remove from the Stage.

2 Position the mouse ↘ over the guide you want to remove (↘ changes to ↘▪ or ↘▪).

3 Drag the guide to the horizontal or vertical ruler.

■ The guide disappears.

CONTINUED ▶

USING GUIDES

You can display or hide the guides you added to the Stage at any time. You can also change the color of the guides.

Changing the color of the guides can help you more clearly see the guides on the Stage.

DISPLAY OR HIDE GUIDES

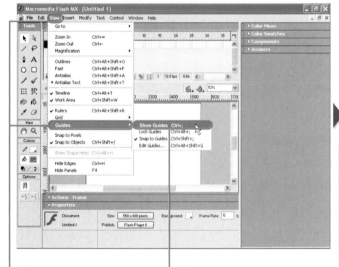

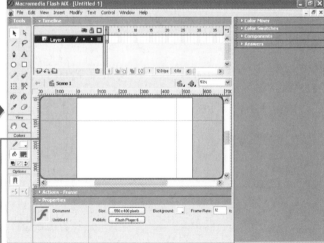

1 Click **View**.

2 Click **Guides**.

3 Click **Show Guides**.

■ A check mark (✔) appears beside Show Guides when the guides are displayed.

■ The guides appear or disappear from the Stage.

Note: Hiding guides is useful if you want to reduce the amount of clutter on the Stage.

How can I stop Flash from automatically aligning my objects with the guides?

To help you line up objects on the Stage, Flash automatically aligns the edge or center of an object with a guide when you position the object near the guide. If you do not want Flash to automatically align objects with the guides, perform steps **1** and **2** below and then click **Snap to Guides** to turn the option off. A check mark (✔) appears beside Snap to Guides when the option is turned on.

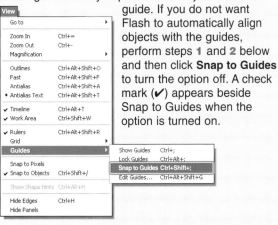

How can I quickly remove all the guides I added to the Stage?

To quickly remove all the guides from the Stage, perform steps **1** to **3** below to display the Guides dialog box. Then click **Clear All** to remove all the guides.

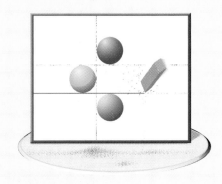

CHANGE GUIDE COLOR

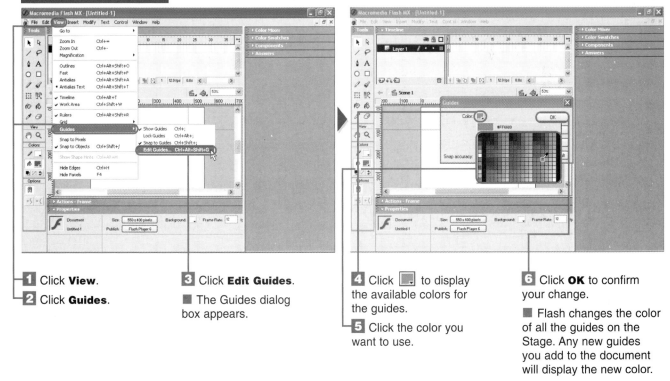

1 Click **View**.

2 Click **Guides**.

3 Click **Edit Guides**.

■ The Guides dialog box appears.

4 Click to display the available colors for the guides.

5 Click the color you want to use.

6 Click **OK** to confirm your change.

■ Flash changes the color of all the guides on the Stage. Any new guides you add to the document will display the new color.

USING THE GRID

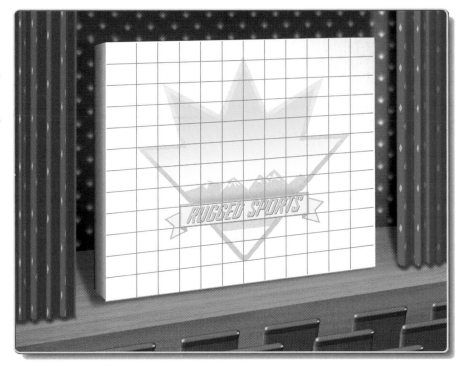

You can display the grid to help you draw and position objects more precisely on the Stage.

The grid is a set of horizontal and vertical lines that appear on the Stage. The grid will not appear in your finished movie.

DISPLAY THE GRID

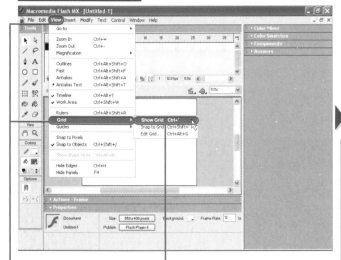

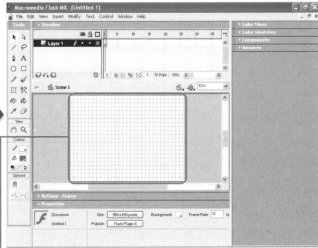

1 Click **View**.

2 Click **Grid**.

3 Click **Show Grid**.

■ A check mark (✔) appears beside Show Grid when the grid is displayed.

■ The grid appears on the Stage to help you draw and position objects more precisely.

■ To remove the grid, repeat steps **1** to **3**.

How can I quickly align objects with the grid?

You can have Flash automatically align the edge or center of an object with a grid line when you position the object close to the grid line. Perform steps 1 and 2 below and then click **Snap to Grid**. A check mark (✓) appears beside **Snap to Grid** when the option is turned on.

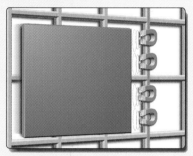

Can I save the settings I specify for the grid?

Yes. After performing steps 1 to 6 below to customize the settings for the grid, click **Save Default** in the Grid dialog box to save the settings. Each new document you open will automatically display the grid with the settings you specified.

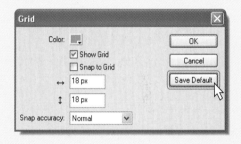

CUSTOMIZE THE GRID

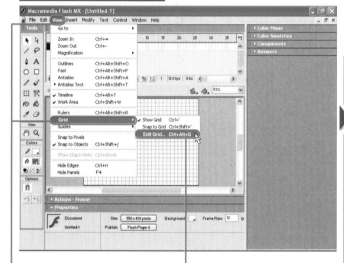

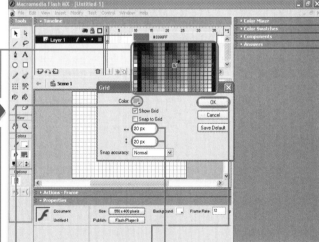

1 Click **View**.

2 Click **Grid**.

3 Click **Edit Grid**.

■ The Grid dialog box appears.

4 To change the color of the grid lines, click 🔲 to display the available colors.

5 Click the color you want to use.

6 To change the spacing of the grid lines, double-click the number in these areas and type the number of horizontal and vertical pixels of space you want to appear between each grid line.

7 Click **OK** to confirm your changes.

CHAPTER 3

Work With Objects

Read this chapter to find out how to make changes to the objects in your movie, such as moving, copying, deleting, rotating, flipping and skewing objects. You will also learn how to change the stacking order of objects and reshape lines and objects.

SELECT OBJECTS

Before working with objects, you need to select the objects you want to work with.

You can use the Arrow tool to quickly select any object.

SELECT OBJECTS USING THE ARROW TOOL

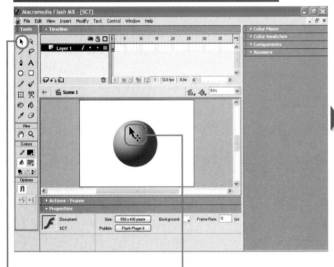

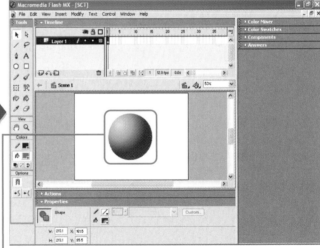

SELECT AN OBJECT BY CLICKING

1 Click ▶ to select an object.

2 Click the object you want to select.

■ To select a filled area and the outline of the area, double-click the filled area.

■ The object you selected appears highlighted with a pattern.

■ To deselect an object, click a blank area on the Stage.

When I click to select an outline, why isn't the entire outline selected?

Flash may treat an outline as a series of separate line segments, so clicking the outline may select only one segment of the outline. To quickly select the entire outline, click the Arrow tool ( ) and then double-click the outline.

How do I select multiple objects?

Selecting multiple objects allows you to work with the objects as a single unit. To select multiple objects, select the first object you want to work with. Then press and hold down the Shift key as you select the other objects you want to work with.

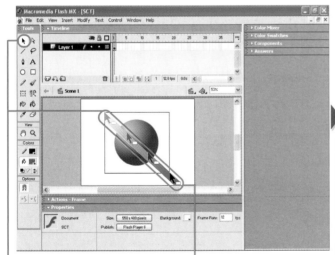

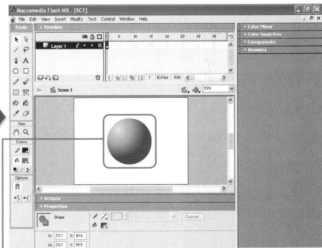

SELECT AN OBJECT BY DRAGGING

1 Click to select an object.

2 Position the mouse outside a corner of the object you want to select.

3 Drag the mouse until a black line surrounds the object.

Note: You can select an entire object or only part of an object in step 3.

■ The object you selected appears highlighted with a pattern.

■ To deselect an object, click a blank area on the Stage.

CONTINUED

SELECT OBJECTS

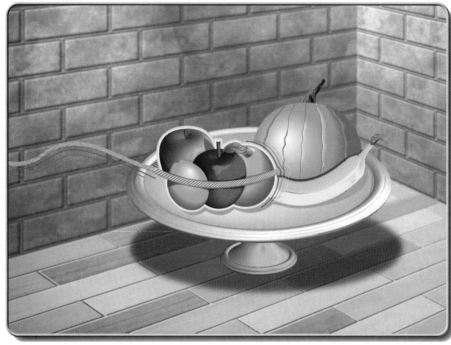

You can use the Lasso tool to select irregularly shaped objects.

When using the Lasso tool to select objects, you can draw freehand lines or straight lines to surround the object you want to select.

SELECT OBJECTS USING THE LASSO TOOL

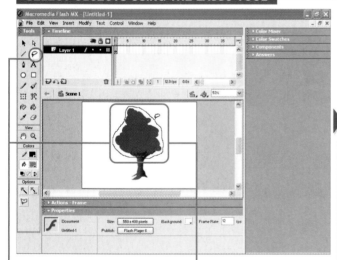

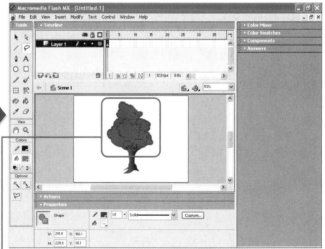

LASSO AN OBJECT USING FREEHAND LINES

1 Click 🖉 to select an object.

2 Position the mouse ⍩ outside the object you want to select (⍩ changes to ⌇).

3 Drag the mouse ⌇ around the object until a black line surrounds the object.

Note: You can select an entire object or part of an object in step 3.

■ The object you selected appears highlighted with a pattern.

■ To deselect an object, click a blank area on the Stage.

I accidentally clicked an area of the Stage when using the Lasso tool with straight lines. How do I deselect?

You can double-click the mouse at any time to deselect the area of the Stage and start over.

Can I switch between freehand lines and straight lines when selecting an object?

Yes. Perform steps 1 to 3 on page 60 to use the Lasso tool with freehand lines. To start using straight lines, press and hold down the Alt key (Windows) or Option key (Macintosh) and then perform steps 3 and 4 below to continue selecting the object. To complete your selection, double-click the mouse.

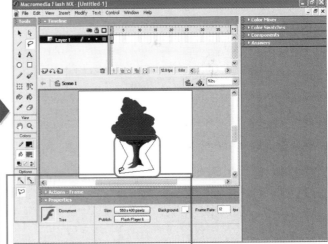

LASSO AN OBJECT USING STRAIGHT LINES

1 Click 🔗 to select an object.

2 Click 🔗 to use straight lines to select an object.

3 Click the location where you want to start selecting the object.

4 Click the location where you want the line to end.

5 Repeat step 4 until you finish drawing all the lines around the object you want to select.

6 To complete the selection, double-click the mouse.

■ The object appears highlighted with a pattern.

■ To deselect an object, double-click a blank area on the Stage.

MOVE AND COPY OBJECTS

You can move or copy an object to a new location on the Stage.

Moving objects allows you to rearrange objects on the Stage. Copying objects allows you to repeat objects on the Stage without having to recreate the objects.

MOVE AN OBJECT

1 Select the object you want to move. To select objects, see page 58.

2 Click ↖.

3 Position the mouse ↖ over the selected object (↖ changes to ↖⁺).

4 To move the object, drag the object to where you want to place the object.

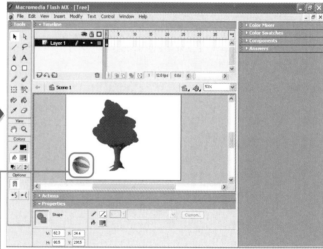

■ The object moves to the new location.

Note: To move an object only horizontally, vertically or at a 45-degree angle, press and hold down the **Shift** *key as you perform step* **4**.

How can I precisely control where I move an object?

Use the Arrow Keys

Select the object you want to move and then press the ↑, ↓, ← or → key to move the object one pixel at a time.

Note: To move the object 10 pixels at a time, press and hold down the Shift *key as you press an arrow key.*

Specify Coordinates

Select the object you want to move. In the Property inspector, double-click the X box and type a new coordinate to move the object horizontally, relative to the left edge of the Stage. Double-click the Y box and type a new coordinate to move the object vertically, relative to the top edge of the Stage. Then press the Enter key (Windows) or the Return key (Macintosh) to move the object to the new location.

Note: If the Property inspector is not displayed, see page 16 to display the Property inspector.

X: 100.0

Y: 100.0

COPY AN OBJECT

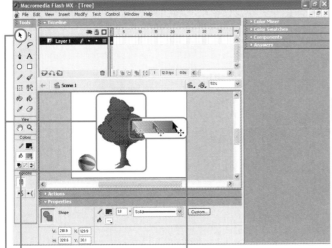

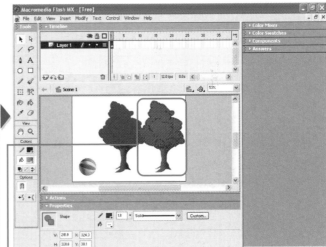

1 Select the object you want to copy. To select objects, see page 58.

2 Click ▶.

3 Position the mouse ▷ over the selected object (▷ changes to ⊹).

4 To copy the object, press and hold down the Ctrl key (Windows) or the Option key (Macintosh) as you drag the object to where you want to place the copy of the object.

■ A copy of the object appears in the new location.

RESIZE OBJECTS

You can increase
or decrease the
size of an object.
Resizing an object
is also known as
scaling an object.

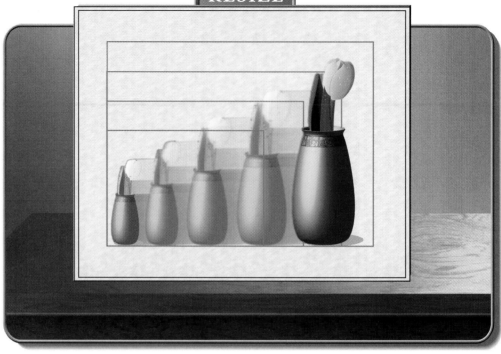

RESIZE AN OBJECT BY DRAGGING

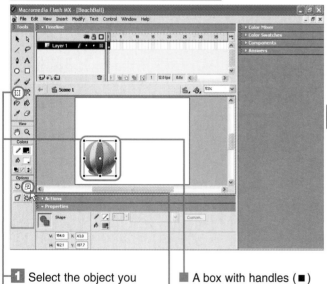

1 Select the object you
want to resize. To select
objects, see page 58.

2 Click ⊞.

■ A box with handles (■)
appears around the object.

3 Click 🔲 to resize the
object.

4 Position the mouse ▷
over a handle (▷ changes
to ↗, ↔, ↘ or ↕).

5 Drag the handle
until the object is the
size you want.

■ Flash displays an
outline of the object as
you resize the object.

What handle (■) should I use to resize an object?

WIDTH | HEIGHT | WIDTH/HEIGHT

■ To change only the width of an object, use a side handle. The object will be distorted.

■ To change only the height of an object, use the top or bottom handle. The object will be distorted.

■ To change the width and height of an object at the same time, use a corner handle. The width and height of the object will remain in proportion so the object will not be distorted.

How can I quickly undo a change when using the Transform panel?

When using the Transform panel to resize an object, you can click in the Transform panel to quickly undo changes you made to the object's size.

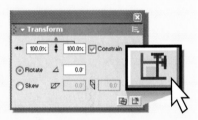

RESIZE AN OBJECT USING THE TRANSFORM PANEL

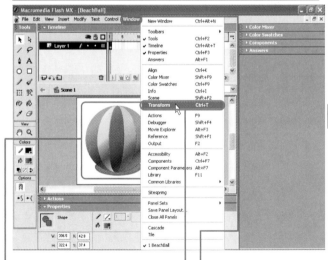

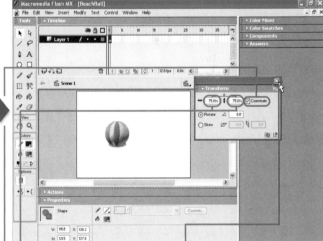

■ The Transform panel allows you to specify percentages less than 100% to shrink an object or percentages greater than 100% to enlarge an object.

1 Select the object you want to resize. To select objects, see page 58.

2 Click **Window**.

3 Click **Transform**.

■ The Transform panel appears.

4 Double-click each area and type a percentage for the width and height of the object.

5 This option maintains the object's proportions. You cannot change the width and height separately when this option is on. To turn the option on (☑) or off (☐), click the option.

6 To confirm your change, press the Enter key (Windows) or the Return key (Macintosh).

7 Click ☒ (Windows) or ☐ (Macintosh) to close the Transform panel.

DELETE AN OBJECT

You can delete an object that you no longer want to appear in your document.

DELETE AN OBJECT

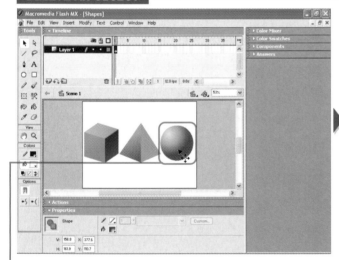

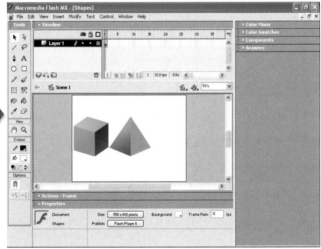

1 Select the object you want to delete. To select objects, see page 58.

2 Press the Delete key to delete the object.

■ The object disappears from the Stage.

UNDO CHANGES

Flash remembers the last changes you made to your document. If you regret these changes, you can cancel them by using the Undo feature.

UNDO CHANGES

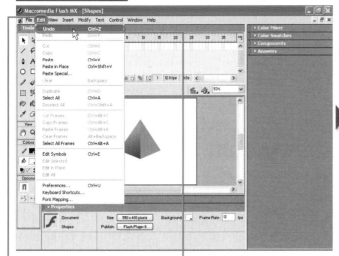

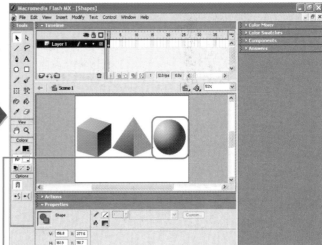

1 Click **Edit**.

2 Click **Undo** to cancel the last change you made to your document.

■ Flash cancels the last change you made to your document.

■ To cancel previous changes you made, repeat steps **1** and **2**.

■ To reverse the results of canceling your changes, perform steps **1** and **2**, except select **Redo** in step **2**.

ROTATE AN OBJECT

You can rotate objects to turn the objects in another direction.

Flash allows you to rotate objects by dragging or by specifying a rotation angle.

Rotating an object is useful when creating animations. For example, you can rotate an object to create an animation that shows the hands of a clock moving, a ball rolling or the tires of a car spinning.

ROTATE AN OBJECT BY DRAGGING

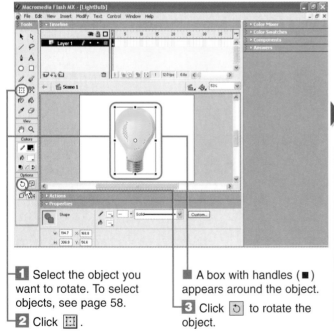

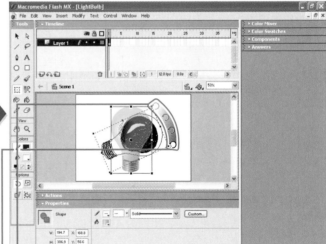

■1 Select the object you want to rotate. To select objects, see page 58.

■2 Click ⊞.

■ A box with handles (■) appears around the object.

■3 Click ⟳ to rotate the object.

■4 Position the mouse ⟨ over a corner handle (⟨ changes to ↻).

■5 Drag the handle until the object appears the way you want.

Note: To rotate the object 45 degrees at a time, press and hold down the Shift *key as you perform step 5.*

■ Flash displays an outline of the object as you rotate the object.

Can I rotate an object in a different way?

Yes. By default, Flash rotates an object around the object's center, but you can have the object rotate around a corner instead. Perform steps **1** to **3** on page 68. Position the mouse ↖ over the corner handle opposite the corner you want to rotate the object around (↖ changes to ↻). Then press and hold down the `Alt` key (Windows) or the `Option` key (Macintosh) as you drag the handle until the object appears the way you want.

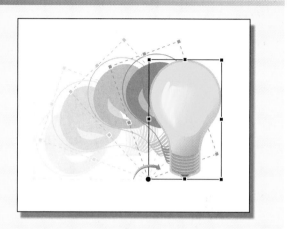

ROTATE AN OBJECT USING THE TRANSFORM PANEL

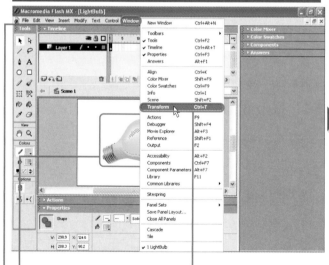

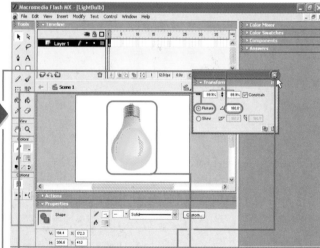

1 Select the object you want to rotate. To select objects, see page 58.

2 Click **Window**.

3 Click **Transform**.

■ The Transform panel appears.

4 Click **Rotate** (○ changes to ◉).

5 Double-click this area and type a rotation angle for the object. Then press the `Enter` key (Windows) or the `Return` key (Macintosh).

■ Flash rotates the object by the angle you specified.

6 Click ✕ (Windows) or ■ (Macintosh) to close the Transform panel.

Note: To rotate the object counterclockwise, type a negative value.

FLIP AN OBJECT

You can flip an object vertically or horizontally.

Flipping an object is useful when you want to use the mirror image of the object.

FLIP AN OBJECT

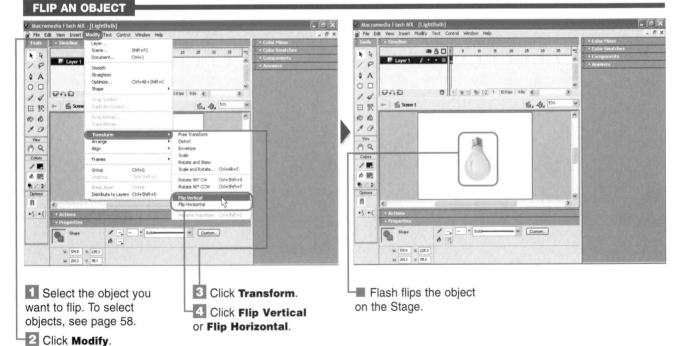

1 Select the object you want to flip. To select objects, see page 58.

2 Click **Modify**.

3 Click **Transform**.

4 Click **Flip Vertical** or **Flip Horizontal**.

■ Flash flips the object on the Stage.

You can skew an object
to slant the object
along the horizontal
or vertical axis.

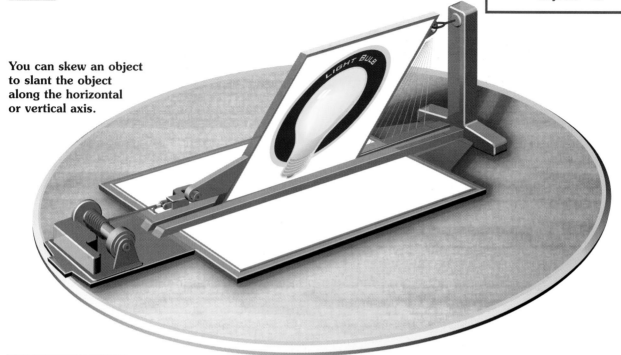

SKEW AN OBJECT

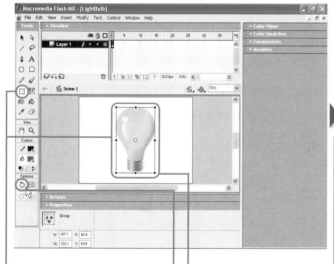

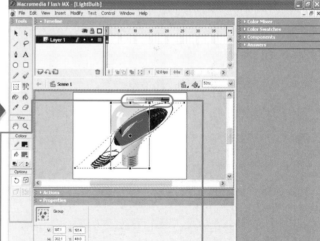

1 Select the object you
want to skew. To select
objects, see page 58.

2 Click 🔳 to be able
to transform the object.

■ A box with handles (■)
appears around the object.

3 Click 🔁 to be able to
skew the object.

4 Position the mouse ⊾
over a middle handle
on a side of the box that
surrounds the object
(⊾ changes to ↔ or ↕).

5 Drag the handle until
the object appears the
way you want.

■ Flash displays an
outline of the object as
you skew the object.

ALIGN OBJECTS

You can change the way objects line up on the Stage.

Flash allows you to align objects by their left, right, top or bottom edges or by their centers. You can align objects with each other or with the Stage. For example, you can align the bottom edges of objects with each other or with the bottom edge of the Stage.

ALIGN OBJECTS

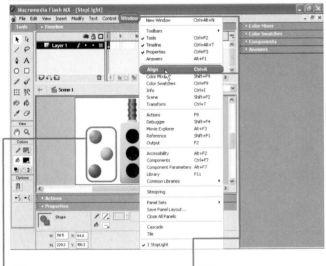

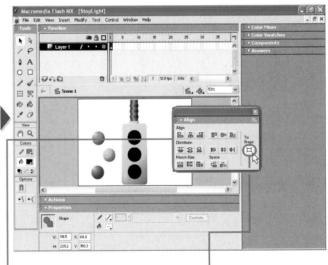

1 Select the objects you want to align. To select objects, see page 58.

2 Click **Window**.

3 Click **Align**.

■ The Align panel appears.

■ Flash will automatically align objects with each other.

4 To align objects with the Stage, click [▣].

What other options does the Align panel provide for aligning objects?

Distribute

These buttons allow you to arrange the selected objects evenly from the point you specify on the objects. You can distribute the objects vertically or horizontally from their edges or centers. If the To Stage button ( ) is selected, Flash distributes the objects across the entire Stage.

Match Size

These buttons allow you to make the selected objects the same width, the same height or the same width and height. Flash resizes smaller objects to match the size of the largest object. If the To Stage button ( ) is selected, the size of each object changes to match the height or width of the Stage.

Space

These buttons allow you to arrange the selected objects vertically or horizontally to create the same amount of space between all the objects. If the To Stage button ( ) is selected, Flash spaces the objects across the entire Stage.

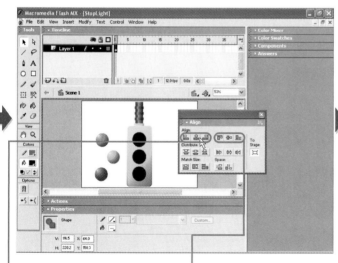

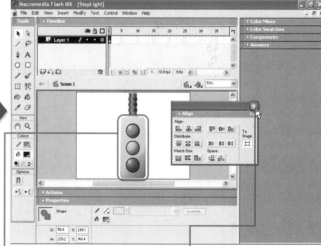

5 To vertically align the objects, click one of these buttons to align the left edges ( ), centers ( ) or right edges ( ) of the objects.

■ To horizontally align the objects, click one of these buttons to align the top edges ( ), centers ( ) or bottom edges ( ) of the objects.

■ Flash aligns the objects the way you specified.

6 Click (Windows) or (Macintosh) to close the Align panel.

Note: If the objects do not appear the way you want, see page 67 to undo your last change.

GROUP OBJECTS

If you want to work with several objects at the same time, you can group the objects. Grouping objects allows you to work with the objects as a single unit.

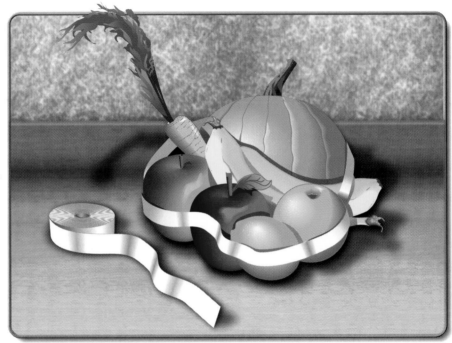

For example, grouping objects allows you to easily move several related objects at the same time, such as the parts of a face.

GROUP OBJECTS

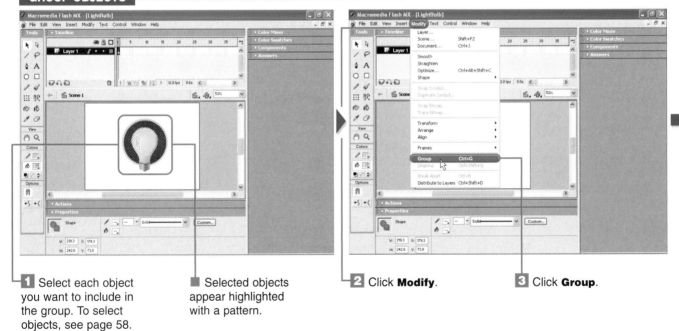

■1 Select each object you want to include in the group. To select objects, see page 58.

■ Selected objects appear highlighted with a pattern.

■2 Click **Modify**.

■3 Click **Group**.

How will grouping objects affect the way objects interact with each other on the Stage?

When two ungrouped objects overlap, the area covered by the top object is deleted from the bottom object. When a grouped object overlaps another object, no part of the bottom object is deleted.

Grouped objects always appear on top of ungrouped objects. Flash also always displays the most recently created group on top of any other grouped objects on the Stage.

Can I make changes to objects in a group?

Yes. Click ![arrow] and then double-click the group you want to change. Everything on the Stage becomes dim, except for the objects in the group. You can now edit the objects in the group in the same way you would edit any object. When you finish making changes to the objects in the group, click ![arrow] and then double-click a blank area of the Stage.

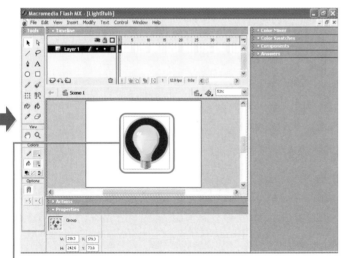

■ Flash groups the objects and surrounds the objects with a blue box.

■ Tasks you perform with the objects will now affect the entire group. For example, moving an object in the group will move all the objects in the group at the same time.

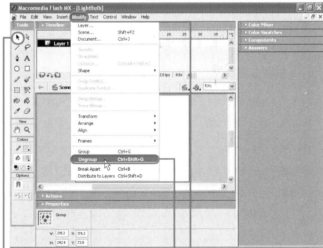

UNGROUP OBJECTS

1 Click ![arrow] to select objects.

2 Click the group that contains the objects you no longer want to include in a group.

3 Click **Modify**.

4 Click **Ungroup**.

■ The objects are now ungrouped.

CHANGE THE STACKING ORDER OF OBJECTS

When objects overlap on the Stage, you can change the stacking order to change which object appears on top.

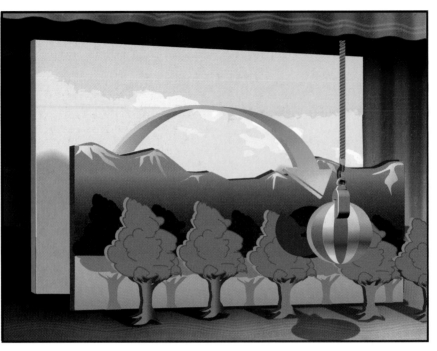

You can move an object to the front or back of the stack. You can also move an object forward or backward one level in the stack.

You can change the stacking order only of symbols and grouped objects. To convert an object to a symbol, see page 114. To group objects, see page 74.

CHANGE THE STACKING ORDER OF OBJECTS

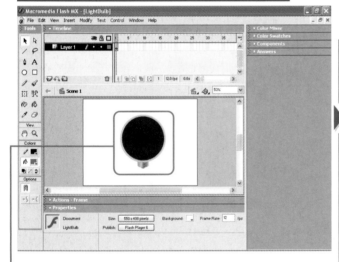

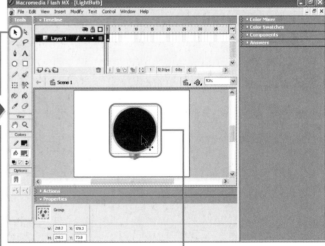

■ Flash stacks symbols and grouped objects on the Stage based on the order in which you created the objects. The most recently created object appears at the top of the stack.

■ Non-symbols and ungrouped objects always appear at the bottom of the stack.

1 Click ![cursor] to be able to select an object on the Stage.

2 Click the symbol or grouped object you want to appear in a different location in the stack.

Is there another way to change the stacking order of objects on the Stage?

You can also use layers to control how the objects are stacked in your drawing. Layers are like separate pieces of transparent paper stacked on top of each other on the Stage. You can place your objects on separate layers and then arrange the layers in the order you want the objects to appear. To create a layer, see page 132. To rearrange layers, see page 136.

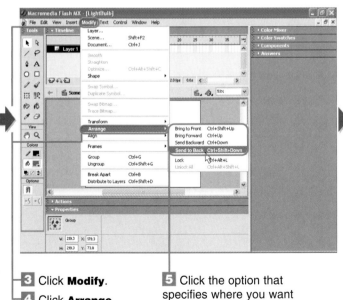

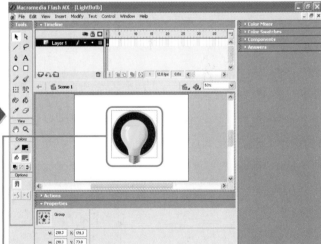

3 Click **Modify**.

4 Click **Arrange**.

5 Click the option that specifies where you want the object to appear in the stack.

■ The object appears in the new position in the stack.

■ In this example, the circle moved to the back of the stack.

CHANGE OR ADD LINES TO SHAPES

You can use
the Ink Bottle
tool to change
or add a line
to a shape on
the Stage.

Flash allows you
to select the color,
thickness and
style of lines.

You can also use
the Ink Bottle tool
to change the
attributes of any
line or curve on
the Stage.

CHANGE OR ADD LINES TO SHAPES

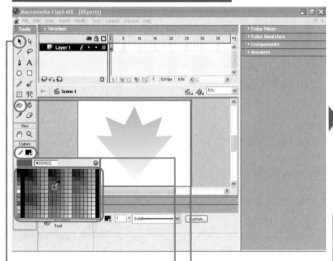

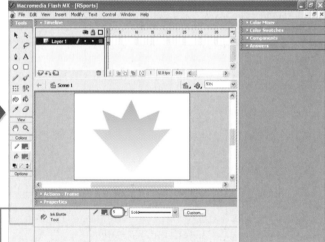

■ Before changing or
adding lines to shapes,
make sure you deselect
all objects on the Stage.
To deselect all objects,
click ▶ and then click a
blank area on the Stage.

1 Click 🕭 to change
or add a line to a shape.

2 To select a color for
the line, click ■ in
this area to display the
available colors.

3 Click the color you
want to use.

4 To specify a thickness
for the line, double-click
this area and type a line
thickness in points.

*Note: If the area is not
displayed, see page 16 to
display the Property inspector.*

How do I change or add a line to multiple areas of a shape at the same time?

Changing or adding a line to multiple areas of a shape is useful when a shape encloses another shape and you want to make the same changes to the outline of both shapes. Perform steps 1 to 6 below to specify the attributes for the line. Then click anywhere between the areas of the shape that you want to change or add the line to.

Is there another way to change the attributes of an existing line?

Yes. To change an existing line, you can select the line and then use the Property inspector to change the color, thickness or style of the line. To change the attributes for a segment of a line, select only the line segment you want to change. To select objects, see page 58.

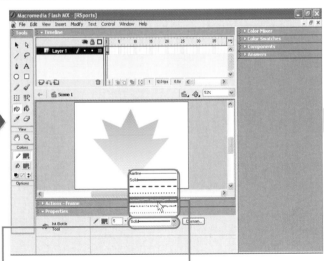

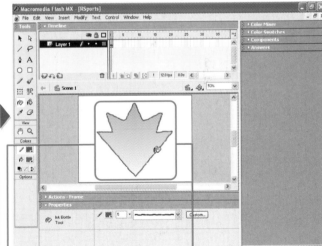

5 To specify a line style, click this area to display the available styles.

6 Click the line style you want to use.

*Note: Selecting a line style other than **Solid** can increase the file size.*

7 Click the outside edge of the shape you want to change or add a line to.

Note: You can also click a line on the Stage to change the line.

■ The shape displays the change.

■ To change or add the same line to other shapes, repeat step 7 for each shape.

COPY A FILLED AREA OR LINE

You can use the Eyedropper tool to quickly copy a filled area or line from one object to another object.

Copying filled areas and lines can save you time when creating and changing objects.

When you copy a filled area, Flash copies the color of the filled area. When you copy a line, Flash copies the color, thickness and style of the line.

COPY A FILLED AREA

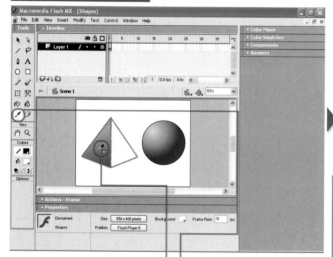

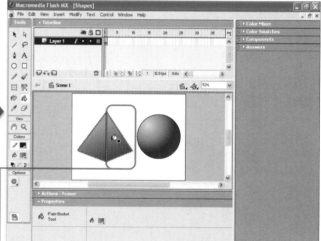

■ Before copying a filled area, make sure you deselect all objects on the Stage. To deselect all objects, click 🅡 and then click a blank area on the Stage.

1 Click 🖋 to be able to copy the filled area of an object to another object.

2 Position the mouse 🗘 over the filled area of the object you want to copy (🗘 changes to 🖋).

3 Click the filled area to copy the filled area (🖋 changes to 🪣).

4 Click the filled area of the object you want to display the same fill color.

■ Flash applies the same fill color to the object you selected.

■ To copy the fill color to other objects, repeat step **4** for each object.

When I copy a gradient to an object, why doesn't the object display the entire gradient?

By default, when you copy a gradient each object that contains the gradient will display only part of the gradient. To display the entire gradient in each object, perform steps **1** to **3** on page 80 and click 🖼 at the bottom of the toolbox. Then click each object you want to display the entire gradient.

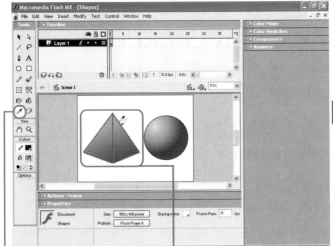

Can I use the Eyedropper tool to add a line to an object?

Yes. You can use the Eyedropper tool to quickly copy a line from one object and then add the line to another object that does not have a line. Perform steps **1** to **3** below to select the line you want to copy. Then click the object you want to add the same line to.

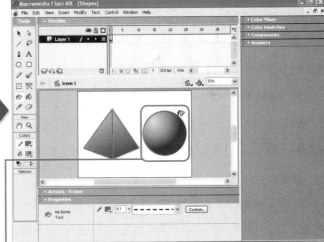

COPY A LINE

■ Before copying a line, make sure you deselect all objects on the Stage. To deselect all objects, click ▶ and then click a blank area on the Stage.

1 Click ✏ to be able to copy a line to another object.

2 Position the mouse ▷ over the line you want to copy (▷ changes to ✐).

3 Click the line to copy the line (✐ changes to ✐).

4 Click the line you want to display the same line color, thickness and style.

■ Flash applies the same line color, thickness and style to the line you selected.

■ To copy the line color, thickness and style to other lines, repeat step **4** for each line.

CHANGE HOW A GRADIENT FILLS AN OBJECT

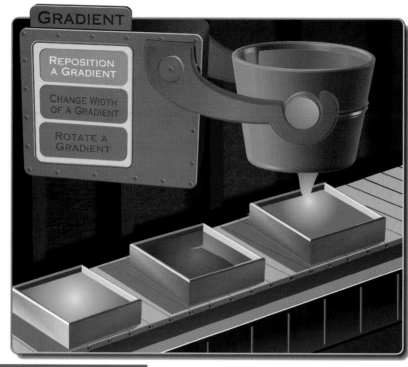

You can change how a gradient fills an object. Flash allows you to reposition a gradient, change the width of a gradient or rotate a gradient within an object.

A gradient is two or more colors that blend from one color to another.

CHANGE HOW A GRADIENT FILLS AN OBJECT

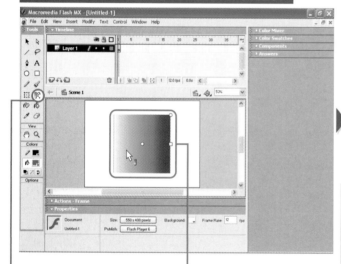

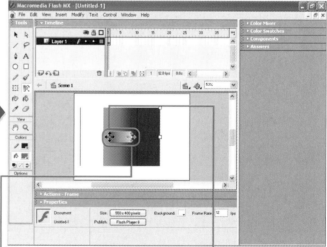

1 Click 🔲 to be able to change how a gradient fills an object.

Note: To fill an object with a gradient, see page 37.

2 Click the object that displays the gradient you want to change. An outline with handles that allow you to make changes to the gradient appears.

REPOSITION A GRADIENT

3 To reposition the gradient within the object, position the mouse ⬚ over the round handle (○) at the center of the gradient (⬚ changes to ✥).

4 Drag the gradient to a new location.

■ A black outline indicates the new position of the gradient.

82

Is there another way to change the size of a radial gradient?

A radial gradient blends colors from the center point of an object to the outer edges of the object. You can change the size of an entire radial gradient instead of just the width.

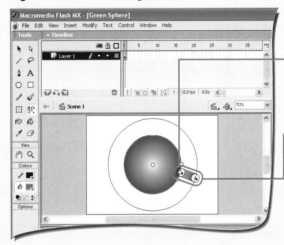

1 Perform steps **1** and **2** below to be able to change a radial gradient.

2 Position the mouse ⌖ over the middle round handle (○) on the outline at the edge of the object (⌖ changes to (⊙)).

3 Drag the handle until the gradient displays the size you want.

■ A black outline indicates the new size of the gradient.

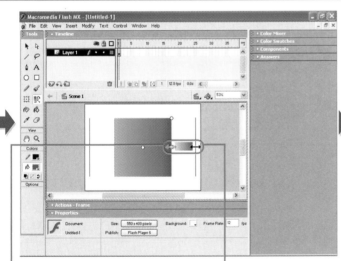

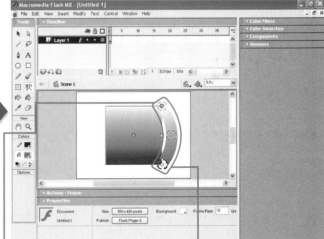

CHANGE THE WIDTH OF A GRADIENT

5 To change the width of the gradient within the object, position the mouse ⌖ over the square handle (□) on the outline at the edge of the object (⌖ changes to ↔).

6 Drag the handle until the gradient is the width you want.

■ A black outline indicates the new width of the gradient.

ROTATE A GRADIENT

7 To rotate the gradient within the object, position the mouse ⌖ over the round handle (○) on the outline at the edge of the object (⌖ changes to ↻).

8 Drag the handle until the gradient appears the way you want.

■ A black outline indicates the new rotation of the gradient.

RESHAPE LINES OR OBJECTS WITH THE ARROW TOOL

You can reshape
lines and objects
with the Arrow
tool.

You can reshape the
middle of a line or a
side of an object. You
can also reposition
the end of a line or a
corner of an object.

RESHAPE A LINE OR OBJECT

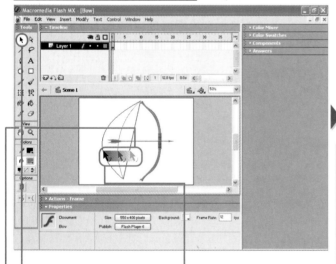

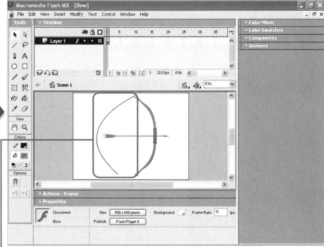

1 Click ![arrow icon] to be able to reshape a line or object.

2 Position the mouse ![cursor] over the middle of the line or the side of the object you want to reshape (![cursor] changes to ![cursor]).

3 Drag the mouse ![cursor] until the line or the side of the object appears the way you want.

Note: To create a corner on a line or side of an object, press and hold down the **Ctrl** *key (Windows) or the* **Option** *key (Macintosh) as you perform step 3.*

■ Flash reshapes the
line or the side of the
object.

Are there other options I can use to reshape a line or object?

The Arrow tool offers additional options that you can use to reshape a line or object.

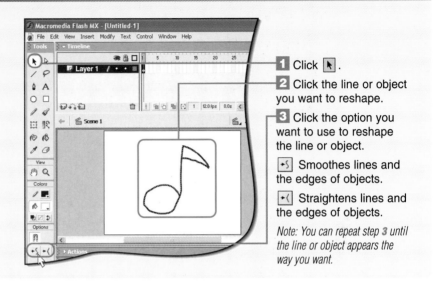

1 Click .

2 Click the line or object you want to reshape.

3 Click the option you want to use to reshape the line or object.

Smoothes lines and the edges of objects.

Straightens lines and the edges of objects.

Note: You can repeat step 3 until the line or object appears the way you want.

REPOSITION THE END OF A LINE OR CORNER OF AN OBJECT

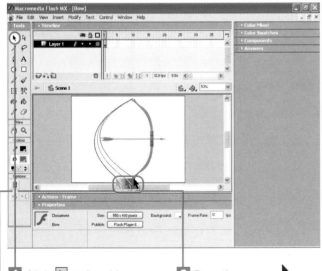

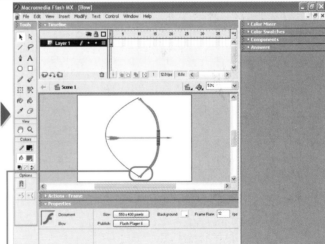

1 Click to be able to reposition the end of a line or the corner of an object.

2 Position the mouse over the end of the line or the corner of the object you want to reposition (changes to).

3 Drag the mouse until the line or the corner of the object appears the way you want.

■ Flash changes the position of the end of the line or corner of the object.

RESHAPE LINES OR OBJECTS
WITH THE SUBSELECTION TOOL

You can use the
Subselection tool
to reshape lines
and objects in
your Flash movie.

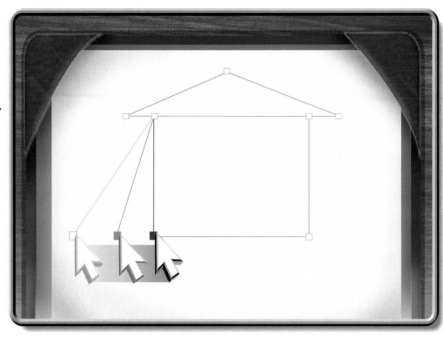

The Subselection
tool allows you to
reveal and move
the anchor points
that define the
position and
shape of lines
and objects.

REPOSITION THE END OF A LINE OR CORNER OF AN OBJECT

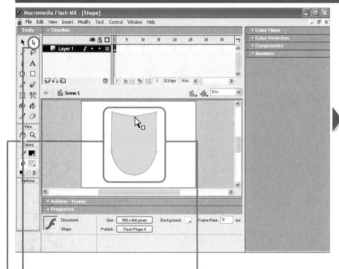

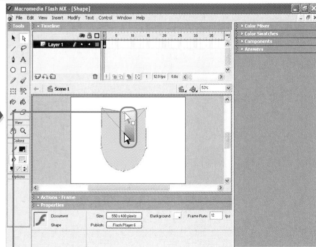

1 Click ▸ to be able to
reposition the end of a line
or the corner of an object.

2 Click the line or the edge of
the object you want to change.
Anchor points (□) appear
around the line or object.

3 Position the mouse ▸
over the anchor point (□)
at the end of the line or
the corner of the object
you want to reposition
(▸ changes to ▸□).

4 Drag the mouse ▸
until the line or the corner
of the object appears the
way you want.

*Note: A line indicates the new
position of the end of the line
or the corner of the object.*

How can I add anchor points to a curve?

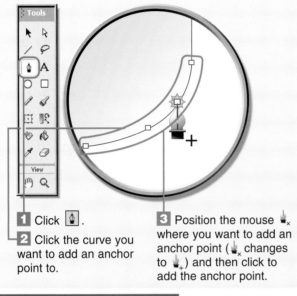

1 Click .

2 Click the curve you want to add an anchor point to.

3 Position the mouse where you want to add an anchor point (changes to) and then click to add the anchor point.

Can I change a corner on a line or object to a curve?

Yes. Perform steps **1** and **2** on page 86. Click the anchor point at the corner you want to change and then press and hold down the Alt key (Windows) or the Option key (Macintosh) as you drag the anchor point. Tangent handles (●) appear. You can drag the handles to create the curve you want.

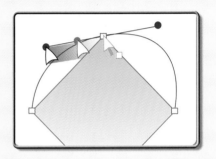

RESHAPE A CURVED LINE OR OBJECT

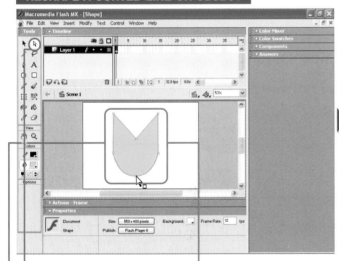

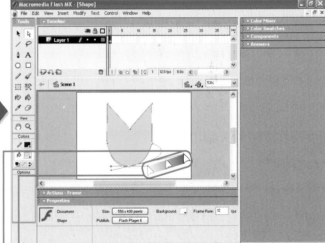

1 Click to be able to reshape a curved line or object.

2 Click the curved line or the edge of the object you want to reshape. Anchor points (□) appear around the curved line or object.

3 Click the anchor point (□) on the curve you want to change. Tangent handles (●) appear.

4 Position the mouse over a tangent handle (changes to).

5 Drag the tangent handle until the curved line or the side of the object appears the way you want.

Note: A line indicates the new curve of the line or the side of the object.

RESHAPE LINES OR OBJECTS WITH THE FREE TRANSFORM TOOL

You can distort and warp lines and objects on the Stage to create interesting effects.

You cannot distort symbols, grouped objects or text.

DISTORT AN OBJECT

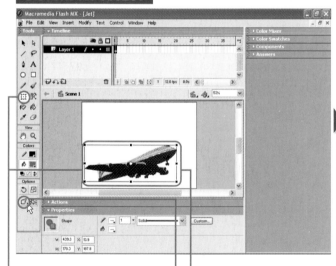

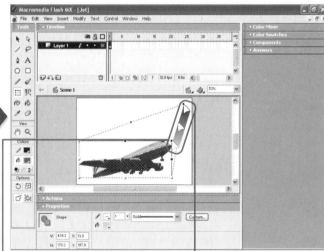

1 Select the line or object you want to distort. To select objects, see page 58.

2 Click ⊞ to be able to transform a line or object.

■ A box with handles (■) appears around the line or object.

3 Click 🗗 to be able to distort the line or object.

4 Position the mouse ▷ over the handle you want to use to distort the line or object (▷ changes to ▷).

5 Drag the handle until the line or object appears the way you want.

■ A dashed line indicates the new shape of the line or object.

88

TEACH YOURSELF

Can I distort two corners of an object at the same time?

Yes. Perform steps 1 to 4 on page 88, positioning the mouse over a corner handle in step 4. To distort the corresponding corner of the object at the same time, press and hold down the Shift key as you drag the corner handle.

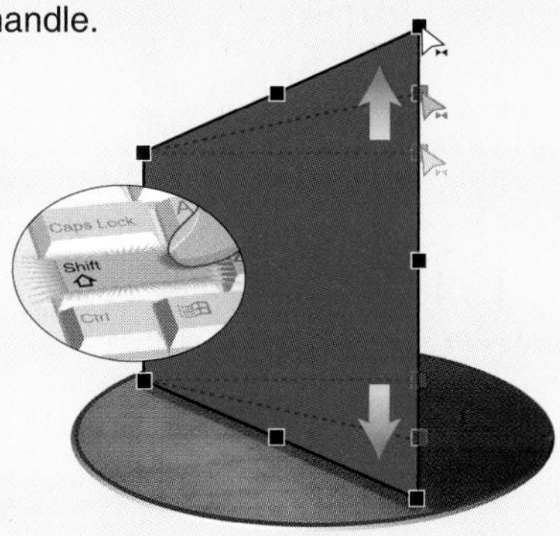

TEACH YOURSELF

When warping an object, why does a straight line appear when I drag a round handle?

When you drag a round handle, a straight line called a tangent handle appears. Dragging this handle helps you shape the edge of the object the way you want. You can drag the handle in any direction to change the curve and angle of the edge of the object.

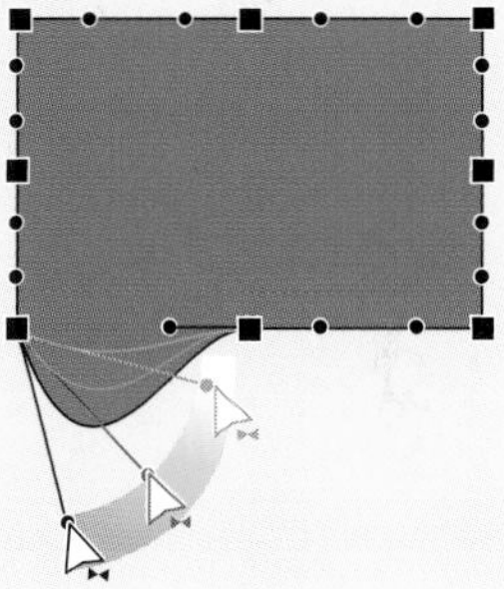

WARP AN OBJECT

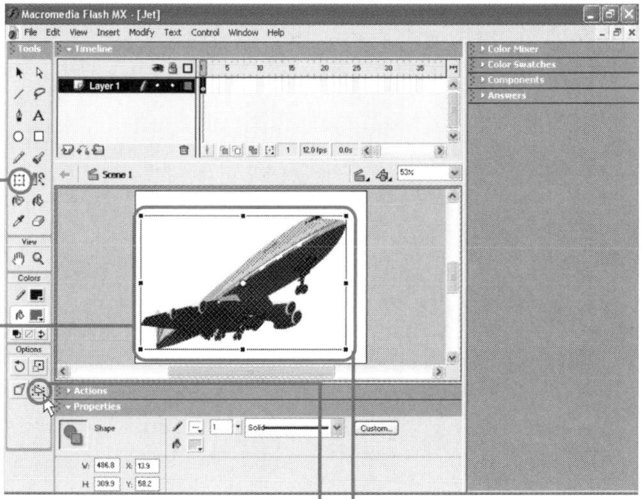

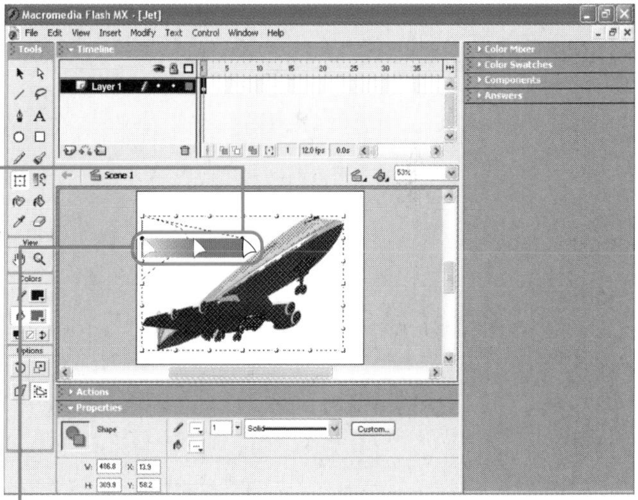

1 Select the line or object you want to warp. To select objects, see page 58.

2 Click to be able to transform a line or object.

■ A box with handles (■) appears around the line or object.

3 Click to be able to warp the line or object.

4 Position the mouse over the handle you want to use to warp the line or object (changes to).

5 Drag the handle until the line or object appears the way you want.

■ A dashed line indicates the new shape of the line or object.

Note: Dragging a square handle (■) changes the location of the point on the line or object. Dragging a round handle (●) changes the shape of that part of the line or object.

SOFTEN THE EDGES OF AN OBJECT

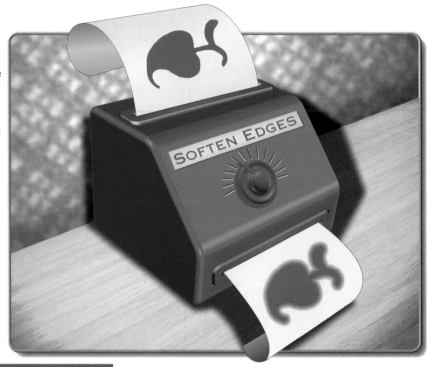

You can soften the edges of an object on the Stage to add an interesting visual effect to the object.

Softening the edges of an object is useful when you want to create a shadow effect around the object or when you want to have the object blend into the background of your drawing.

SOFTEN THE EDGES OF AN OBJECT

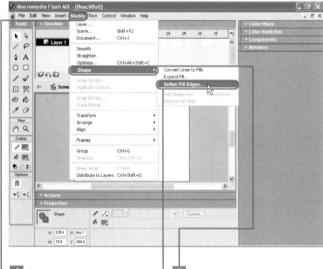

■ Select the object you want to change. To select objects, see page 58.

■ Click **Modify**.

■ Click **Shape**.

■ Click **Soften Fill Edges**.

■ The Soften Fill Edges dialog box appears.

■ To specify a width for the softened edges of the object, double-click the number in this area and then type a width in pixels.

■ To specify how many steps Flash will use to soften the edges of the object, double-click this area and then type a number.

Note: A higher number of steps will create smoother edges but can increase the file size.

How can I get the best results when softening the edges of an object?

For the best results, you should soften the edges of small, simple shapes that do not have outlines. Softening the edges of an object with a lot of detail may produce unexpected results and can increase the file size of your document. If you soften the edges of an object that has an outline, the outline will not increase or decrease in size to match the new size of the object.

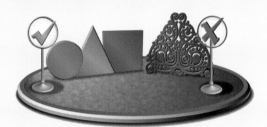

 How does Flash create the softening effect?

When you soften the edges of an object, Flash uses the number of steps you specify to create a series of concentric shapes around the object. The shapes get progressively lighter towards the edge of the object to produce a fading out effect. You can zoom into an object to view the steps Flash uses to soften the edges of the object. To zoom in or out, see page 48.

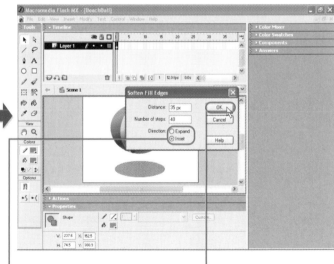

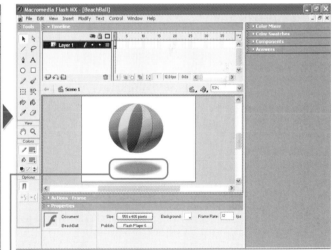

7 Click an option to specify whether Flash will increase or decrease the size of the object to soften the edges of the object (○ changes to ◉).

8 Click **OK** to confirm your changes.

■ Flash softens the edges of the object.

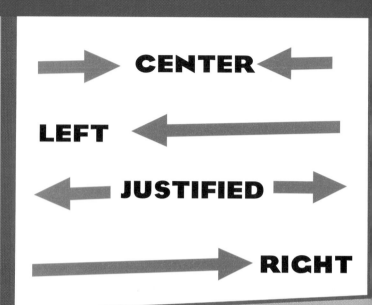

CHAPTER 4

Add and Work With Text

This chapter teaches you how to work with text in your Flash movie. Learn how to add text and change the font, size, letter spacing and orientation of text.

ADD TEXT

You can use the Text tool to add text to the Stage.

When adding text to the Stage, you can type words or phrases on a single line or on multiple lines.

TYPE TEXT ON A SINGLE LINE

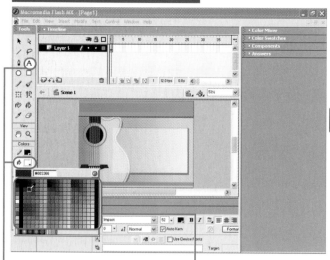

1 Click **A** to add text.

2 To select a color for the text, click ☐ in this area to display the available colors.

3 Click the color you want to use.

4 Click the location on the Stage where you want the text to appear.

5 Type the text. The text box expands to display the text on one line.

■ To start a new line, press the **Enter** key (Windows) or the **Return** key (Macintosh).

6 When you finish typing the text, click outside the text box.

How can I later change the color of text?

To change the color of text in your document, click A. To select the text you want to change, drag the mouse I over the text. To select a color for the text, click ☐ in the Fill Color area and then click the color you want to use.

Can I edit the text in a text box?

Yes. Click A to work with the text. To select the text you want to change, drag the mouse I over the text. You can then make changes to the text.

TYPE TEXT ON MULTIPLE LINES

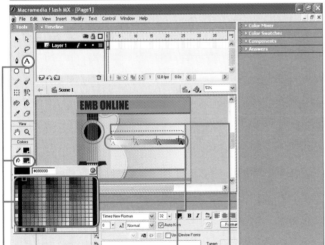

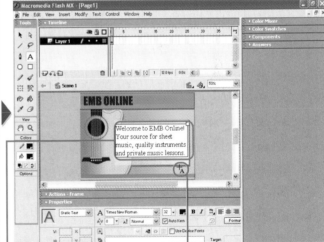

1 Click A to add text.

2 To select a color for the text, click ■ in this area to display the available colors.

3 Click the color you want to use.

4 Position the mouse ⬚ where you want the top left corner of the text to appear (⬚ changes to ⁺ₐ).

5 Drag the mouse ⁺ₐ until the text box is the width you want.

6 Type the text. When the text you type reaches the end of the text box, the text automatically wraps to the next line.

7 When you finish typing the text, click outside the text box.

SELECT TEXT

Before you can change text in a text box, such as changing the font or alignment of the text, you must first select the text you want to change.

You can drag the mouse to select some of the text in a text box. You can also select a text box to select all the text in the text box.

SELECT TEXT

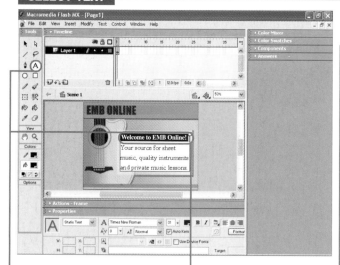

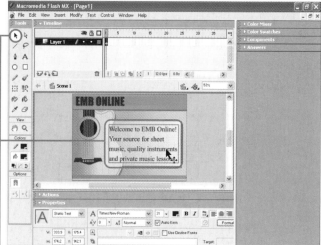

SELECT SOME TEXT

1 Click **A** to work with text.

2 Position the mouse I to the left of the text you want to select.

3 Drag the mouse I over the text you want to select until the text is highlighted.

Note: To quickly select a word, double-click the word.

■ To deselect text, click outside the selected area.

SELECT ALL TEXT

1 Click **▶** to select text.

2 Click the text in the text box that you want to select. A box appears around the text, indicating that the text is selected.

■ To select all the text in another text box, press and hold down the **Shift** key as you click the text in each text box that you want to select.

■ To deselect text, click outside the selected area.

You can bold
or italicize text
to emphasize
information in
your document.

BOLD OR ITALICIZE TEXT

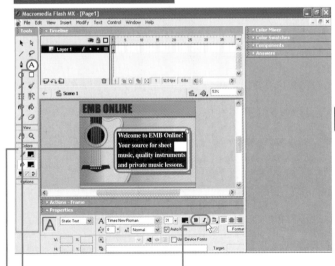

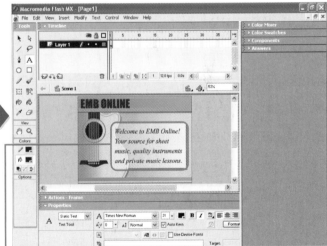

1 Click **A** to work with text.

2 Select the text you want to bold or italicize. To select text, see page 96.

3 Click one of these buttons to bold (**B**) or italicize (**I**) the text.

*Note: If **B** and **I** are not displayed, see page 16 to display the Property inspector.*

■ The text you selected appears in bold or italics.

■ To remove a bold or italic style from text, repeat steps **1** to **3**.

CHANGE THE FONT OF TEXT

You can change
the font of text to
enhance the text
in a text box.

CHANGE THE FONT OF TEXT

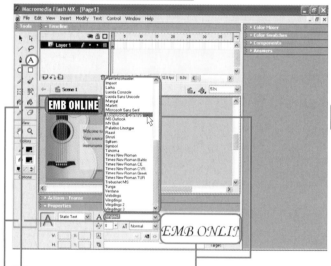

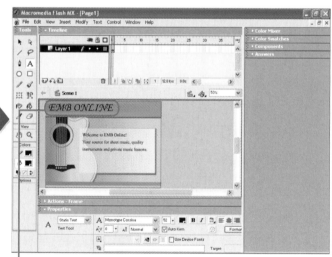

1 Click ▲ to work with text.

2 Select the text you want
to change. To select text, see
page 96.

3 Click ☐ (Windows) or
☐ (Macintosh) in this area
to display the available fonts.

*Note: If the area is not
displayed, see page 16 to
display the Property inspector.*

4 Click the font you
want to use.

■ A preview of the
highlighted font
appears in a window.

■ The text changes to
the font you selected.

98

CHANGE THE SIZE OF TEXT

You can increase
or decrease the
size of text in a
text box.

Larger text is
easier to read,
but smaller text
allows you to fit
more information
on the Stage.

CHANGE THE SIZE OF TEXT

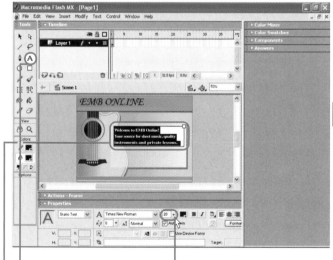

1 Click **A** to work
with text.

2 Select the text you
want to change. To
select text, see page 96.

3 To select a different font
size, click ▼ in this area
and hold down the mouse.

*Note: If the area is not displayed,
see page 16 to display the Property
inspector.*

4 Drag the slider (◁)
up or down to increase
or decrease the size of
the text.

■ The text appears in
the size you selected.

■ To quickly specify an
exact size for the selected
text, double-click this area
and type the size in points.
Then press the **Enter** key
(Windows) or the **Return** key
(Macintosh).

ALIGN TEXT

You can align
text to specify
the position of
the text within
the text box.

Center

Right align

Justify

Left align

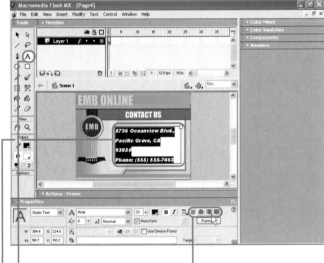

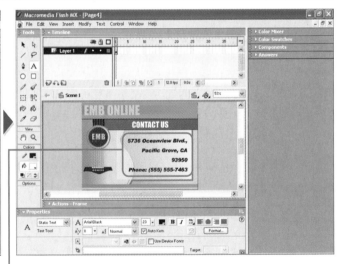

1 Click A to work with
text.

2 Select the paragraph or
the text box that contains
the text you want to align
differently. To select text,
see page 96.

3 Click one of the
following buttons.

▤ Left align

▤ Center

▤ Right align

▤ Justify

*Note: If the buttons are not
displayed, see page 16 to
display the Property inspector.*

■ The text displays the
new alignment.

You can increase or decrease the amount of space that appears between letters in a text box.

CHANGE LETTER SPACING OF TEXT

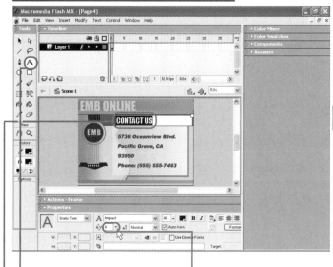

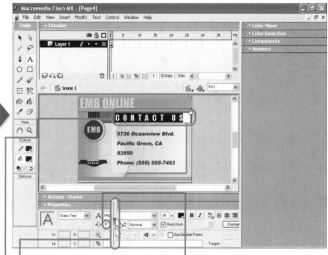

1 Click A to work with text.

2 Select the text you want to change. To select text, see page 96.

3 To select a different letter spacing, click ▼ in this area and hold down the mouse.

Note: If the area is not displayed, see page 16 to display the Property inspector.

4 Drag the slider (◄) up or down to increase or decrease the amount of space between the characters.

■ The text displays the letter spacing you selected.

■ To quickly specify an exact letter spacing for text, double-click this area and type the amount of spacing you want to use. Then press the Enter key (Windows) or the Return key (Macintosh).

CHANGE THE ORIENTATION OF TEXT

You can change the orientation of a single line of text in a document.

CHANGE THE ORIENTATION OF TEXT

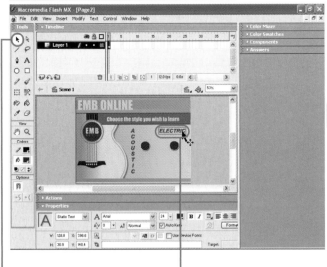

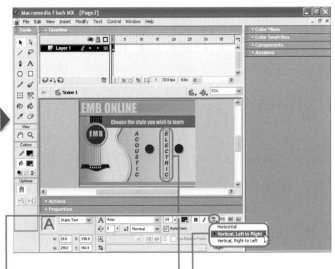

■1 Click 🅺 to be able to select a text box.

■2 Click the text box that contains the single line of text you want to display in a different orientation. A blue border appears around the text box.

Note: To add a single line of text to the Stage, see page 94.

■3 Click 🔡 to change the orientation of the text.

Note: If 🔡 is not displayed, see page 16 to display the Property inspector.

■4 Click the text orientation you want to use.

■ Flash changes the orientation of the text.

You can create a link
that connects a word or
phrase in a document
to a page on the Web.
When a user clicks the
text, the Web page will
appear.

LINK TEXT TO A WEB PAGE

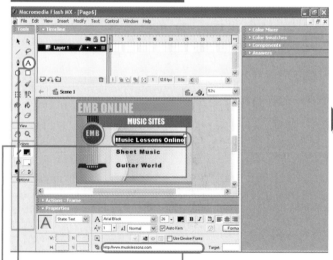

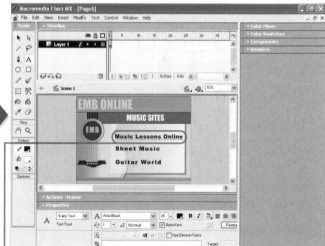

1 Click A to work with
text.

2 Select the text you want
to link to a Web page. To
select text, see page 96.

3 Click this area and type
the address of the Web page
you want to link the text to.
Then press the Enter key
(Windows) or the Return key
(Macintosh).

*Note: If the area is not displayed,
see page 16 to display the Property
inspector.*

■ A dashed line appears
under the text you selected
to indicate that the text is
a link.

■ When a user clicks the
text in the published movie,
the Web page you specified
will appear.

*Note: To test the link you added to
the text, see page 171 to preview
the movie in the Flash Player.*

■ To remove a link from
text, perform steps **1** to **3**,
except drag the mouse I
over the Web page address
in step **3**. Then press the
Delete key.

CHANGE INDENTATION, LINE SPACING AND MARGINS

You can change
the indentation,
line spacing and
margins of text
in a text box.

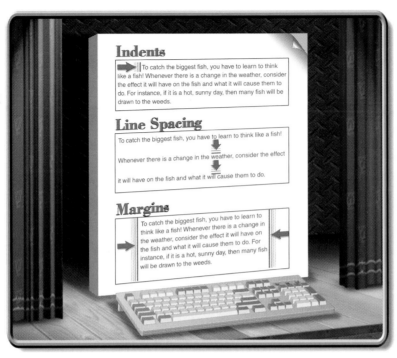

Indents

An indent determines the
amount of space between
the left edge of the text box
and the first line of text in a
paragraph.

Line Spacing

Line spacing determines the
amount of space between
lines in a paragraph.

Margins

Left and right margins
determine the amount of
space between the edges
of the text box and the
lines of text in a paragraph.

CHANGE INDENTATION, LINE SPACING AND MARGINS

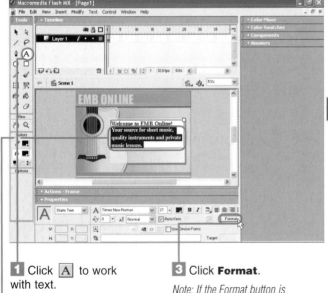

1 Click A to work
with text.

2 Select the text you
want to change. To
select text, see page 96.

3 Click **Format**.

*Note: If the Format button is
not displayed, see page 16 to
display the Property inspector.*

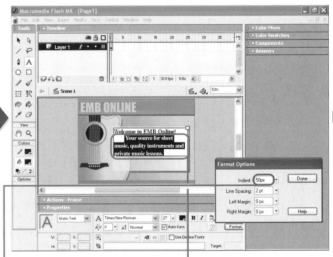

■ The Format Options
dialog box appears.

4 To indent the first
line of every paragraph,
double-click the number
in this area and type a
value for the indentation
in pixels.

■ The first line of every
paragraph you selected
is indented.

How do I create a hanging indent?

A hanging indent moves all but the first line of a paragraph farther from the left edge of the text box. To create a hanging indent, perform steps **1** to **3** below. Double-click the number in the Left Margin area and type the number of pixels you want to indent the lines in the paragraph, such as 30 pixels. Then double-click the number in the Indent area and type the corresponding negative number, such as -30 pixels.

> ### Hanging Indent
>
> To catch the biggest fish, you have to learn to think like a fish! Whenever there is a change in the weather, consider the effect it will have on the fish and what it will cause them to do.

Can I reset my indents, line spacing or margins to the default settings?

After you change the settings for a text box, the settings you specified will be used for all new text boxes you create. To return to the default indent, line spacing or margin settings, repeat the steps below to change each option back to its original value. By default, the indent is set at 0 pixels, the line spacing is set at 2 points and the left and right margins are set at 0 pixels.

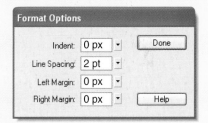

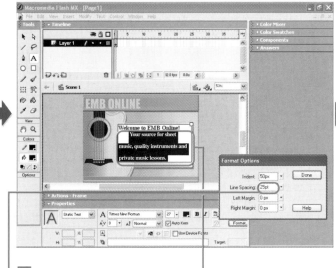

5 To change the line spacing of the text, double-click the number in this area and type a new line spacing in points.

■ The text you selected displays the new line spacing.

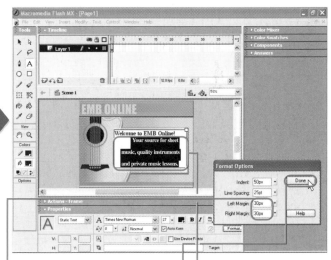

6 To change the left or right margin of the text, double-click the number in the area beside the margin you want to change and then type a new margin in pixels.

■ The text you selected displays the new margin.

7 Click **Done** to confirm your changes.

MOVE, RESIZE OR DELETE A TEXT BOX

You can move a text box or change the size of a text box on the Stage. You can also delete a text box you no longer want to appear in your document.

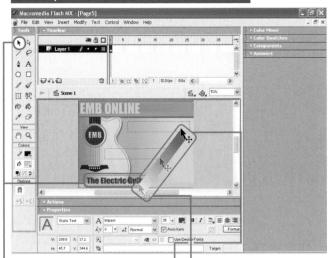

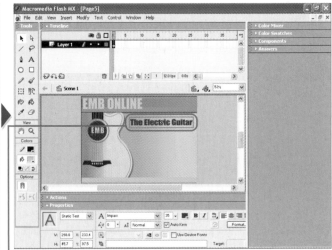

MOVE A TEXT BOX

1 Click ![cursor] to be able to select a text box.

2 Click the text box you want to move. A blue border appears around the text box.

3 Position the mouse ▷ over the selected text box (▷ changes to ![move cursor]).

4 To move the text box, drag the text box to where you want to place the text box.

■ The text box moves to the new location.

Note: To move a text box only horizontally, vertically or at a 45-degree angle, press and hold down the **Shift** *key as you perform step* **4**.

106

How do I copy a text box to another location on the Stage?

Click 🡅 and then click the text box you want to copy to select the text box. To copy the text box, position the mouse ⬚ over the text box (⬚ changes to 🡅₊). Then press and hold down the `Ctrl` key (Windows) or the `Option` key (Macintosh) as you drag the text box to a new location. Flash copies the text box to the new location.

What handle (■) should I use to resize a text box?

■ To change only the width of a text box, use a side handle.

■ To change only the height of a text box, use the top or bottom handle.

■ To change the width and height of a text box at the same time, use a corner handle.

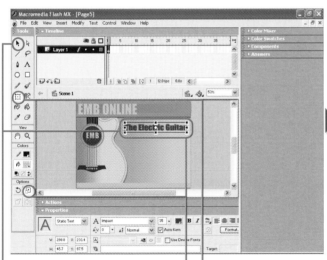

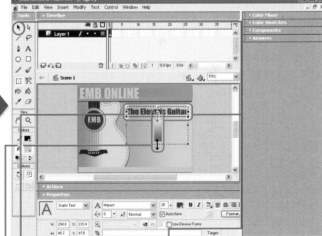

RESIZE A TEXT BOX

1 Click 🡅 to be able to select a text box.

2 Click the text box you want to resize. A blue border appears around the text box.

3 Click ⊞ to be able to resize the text box.

4 Click 🔲.

■ A black border with handles (■) appears around the text box.

5 Position the mouse ⬚ over a handle (⬚ changes to ↕, ↔, ⬊ or ⬈).

6 Drag the handle until the text box is the size you want.

DELETE A TEXT BOX

1 Click 🡅 to be able to select a text box.

2 Click the text box you want to delete. A blue border appears around the text box.

3 Press the `Delete` key to delete the text box.

BREAK APART TEXT

You can break apart text on the Stage to place each character in a separate text box.

Breaking apart text allows you to make changes to individual characters without affecting the other characters.

After you break apart a block of text, you can break apart each character to convert the characters to shapes. Converting characters to shapes is useful if the text uses an uncommon font that other computers may not be able to display.

BREAK APART TEXT

1 Click ![arrow] to be able to select the text you want to break apart.

2 Click the text you want to break apart. A blue box appears around the text.

3 Click **Modify**.

4 Click **Break Apart** to break apart the text.

After I convert characters to shapes, how can I work with all the shapes at once?

You can group all the shapes to be able to work with all the shapes as one unit. Grouping shapes allows you to easily perform tasks such as moving, resizing and rotating all the shapes at once. When you finish working with the shapes, you can ungroup the shapes at any time. To group and ungroup objects, see page 74.

How can I quickly place each character on a different layer?

After you break apart text, you may want to place each character on a different layer of your document. Placing each character on a different layer allows you to animate each character separately. To quickly distribute the characters to separate layers, see page 141.

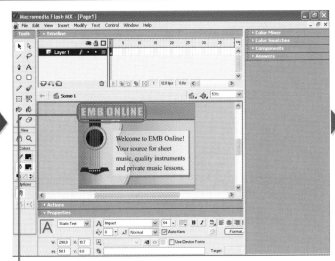

■ Flash places each character in a separate text box.

■ You can make changes to each character as you would make changes to any text.

5 To convert the characters to shapes, repeat steps **3** and **4**.

Note: Each character you want to convert to shapes must be selected. A blue box appears around a selected character. To select characters, see page 96.

■ Flash converts each character to shapes. You can no longer work with the characters as text.

■ You can work with the shapes as you would work with any shape in Flash.

CHAPTER 5

Using Symbols

This chapter shows you how to use symbols and symbol instances in your movie to help save time and reduce your movie's file size. You can create a new symbol, convert an object to a symbol, edit a symbol and more.

CREATE A NEW GRAPHIC SYMBOL

You can create a new graphic symbol that you can reuse throughout a document.

Flash stores each symbol you create in the library of the current document.

CREATE A NEW GRAPHIC SYMBOL

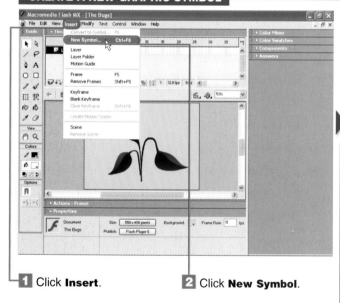

1 Click **Insert**.

2 Click **New Symbol**.

■ The Create New Symbol dialog box appears.

3 Type a name for the new symbol.

4 Click **Graphic** to create a graphic symbol (○ changes to ⊙).

5 Click **OK** to add the new symbol to the document's library.

Why would I use a symbol instead of copying an object?

Creating multiple copies of an object can increase the file size of your document since each copy of the object is stored separately in the document. Using symbols reduces a document's file size by allowing you to store an object only once as a symbol and then use instances of the symbol throughout your document.

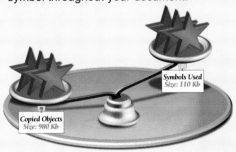

Why does a cross (+) appear on the Stage when I am creating a new symbol?

The cross (+) on the Stage indicates the center of your drawing. Flash uses this center point to determine how to position or change your symbol on the Stage. To help ensure that your symbol will appear the way you expect on the Stage, you should make sure the cross (+) appears at the center of your drawing when creating the symbol.

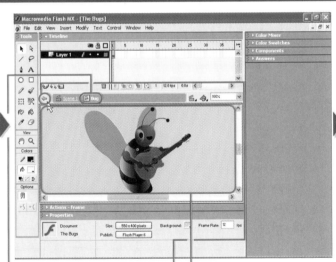

■ Flash switches to symbol-editing mode so you can create the graphic symbol.

■ The name of the symbol you are creating appears in this area.

6 Draw the graphic for the symbol on the Stage.

Note: To draw objects, see pages 26 to 37.

7 When you finish creating the symbol, click ⬑ to return to the document.

■ The document reappears on the screen.

Note: The symbol does not appear on the Stage.

■ You can now add the symbol to your document. To add a symbol to a document, see page 116.

CONVERT AN OBJECT TO A GRAPHIC SYMBOL

You can convert any object on the Stage to a graphic symbol. A symbol is an object that you create once in a document and can reuse throughout the document.

Flash stores each symbol you create in the library of the current document. When you add a symbol to the Stage, you are adding an instance of the symbol that is stored in the library.

You can use graphic symbols to create items such as company logos or advertising banners in your document.

CONVERT AN OBJECT TO A GRAPHIC SYMBOL

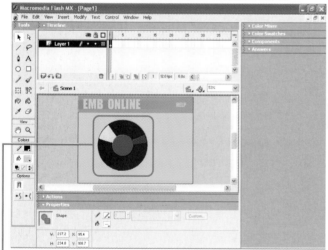

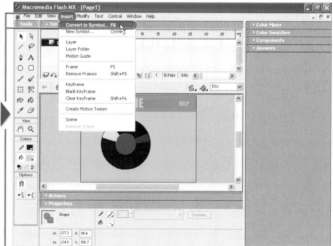

1 Select the object(s) you want to convert to a symbol on the Stage. To select objects, see page 58.

2 Click **Insert**.

3 Click **Convert to Symbol**.

Note: You can also press the **F8** *key instead of performing steps 2 and 3.*

What other types of symbols can I create?

In addition to graphic symbols, you can also create movie clips and button symbols.

Movie Clips

Movie clips are reusable animations that act like mini-movies in your document. When you play a movie, the movie clips within the movie will play in their own timeline. For more information on creating movie clips, see page 182.

Buttons

Buttons are interactive objects that change in appearance or perform an action when you position the mouse pointer over the button or click the button. For more information on creating buttons, see page 226.

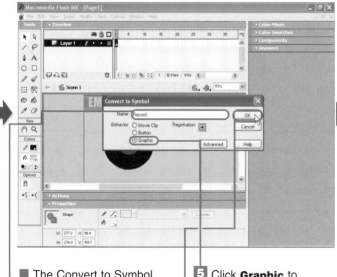

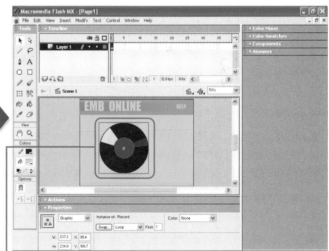

■ The Convert to Symbol dialog box appears.

4 Type a name for the symbol.

5 Click **Graphic** to create a graphic symbol (○ changes to ⊙).

6 Click **OK** to convert the object(s) to a symbol.

■ Flash converts the object(s) to a symbol and adds the symbol to the document's library.

Note: To use the library, see page 116.

■ The object(s) you selected on the Stage become an instance of the symbol. A blue box appears around the instance to indicate that the instance is selected.

Note: You can edit a symbol to change all instances of the symbol in your document. To edit a symbol, see page 118.

CREATE AN INSTANCE OF A SYMBOL

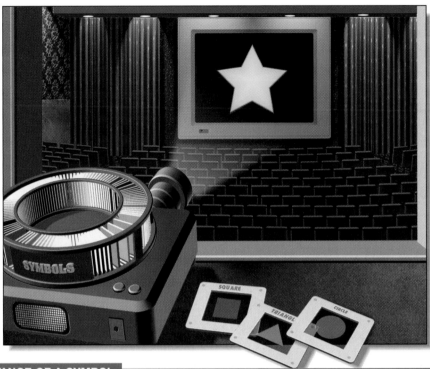

You can create an instance of a symbol on the Stage. Creating instances of a symbol allows you to use the symbol throughout your document.

Flash stores each symbol you create in the library of the current document. When you add a symbol to the Stage, you are adding an instance of the symbol that is stored in the library. To create a symbol, see pages 112 and 114.

CREATE AN INSTANCE OF A SYMBOL

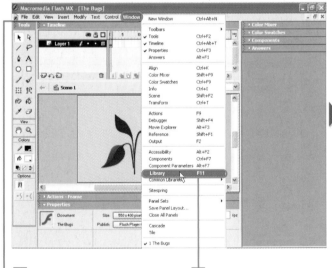

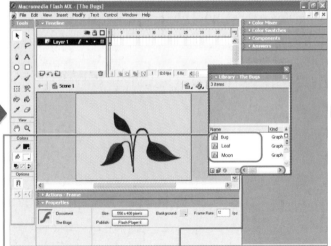

1 To display the library for the current document, click **Window**.

2 Click **Library**.

■ The Library panel appears.

■ This area displays the name of each symbol you can use in the document.

■ The library displays information about each symbol, such as the kind of symbol and the date the symbol was last changed.

■ You can use this scroll bar to scroll through the information.

How can I quickly find a symbol in the Library panel?

Flash lists the symbols in the Library panel alphabetically, from A to Z. If you have many symbols in the library, you can reverse the order of the symbols to quickly locate a symbol that appears near the bottom of the list. To reverse the order of the symbols, click ▲ in the Library panel.

How do I remove an instance of a symbol from the Stage?

To remove an instance of a symbol from the Stage, click ▶ and then click the instance. Then press the Delete key.

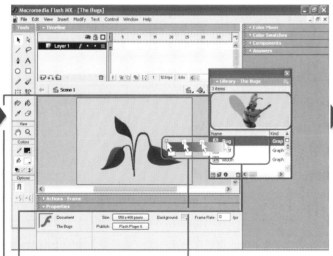

3 Click the name of the symbol you want to appear on the Stage. The symbol is highlighted.

■ This area displays a preview of the symbol.

4 To create an instance of the symbol on the Stage, position the mouse ▷ over the name of the symbol and then drag the symbol to the location where you want the instance of the symbol to appear.

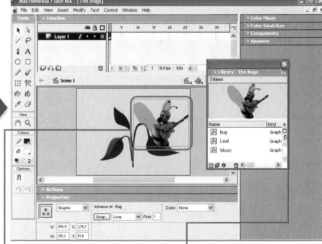

■ An instance of the symbol appears on the Stage.

■ To close the Library panel, click ☒ (Windows) or ☐ (Macintosh).

EDIT A SYMBOL

You can make changes to a symbol. Flash will automatically update all instances of the symbol throughout your document.

EDIT A SYMBOL

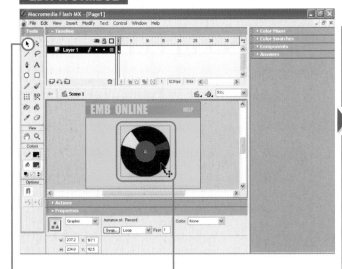

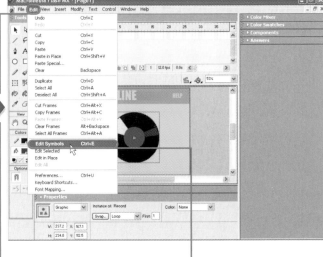

1 Click ![cursor] to be able to select a symbol on the Stage.

2 Click an instance of the symbol that you want to change on the Stage.

■ A blue border appears around the instance of the symbol.

3 Click **Edit**.

4 Click **Edit Symbols**.

How can I see the other objects on the Stage while I edit a symbol?

To see the other objects on the Stage while you edit a symbol, click ▶ and then double-click the symbol you want to edit. The document appears in symbol-editing mode. All the objects on the Stage remain visible, but appear dim. The symbol appears in full color. When you finish editing the symbol, click ▶ and then double-click a blank area of the Stage to exit symbol-editing mode.

Can I edit only one instance of a symbol?

You can make some changes to the appearance of one instance of a symbol without affecting the other instances in your document. For example, you can change the brightness, transparency or color of a symbol instance. For more information, see pages 120 to 123. To be able to fully edit one symbol instance without affecting other instances, you must first break the link between the instance and the symbol. For more information, see page 124.

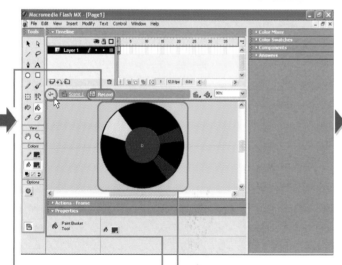

■ The symbol appears in symbol-editing mode.

■ In symbol-editing mode, the name of the symbol you are editing appears in this area.

5 Make the desired changes to the symbol. For example, you can change the color or add new shapes to the symbol.

6 When you finish making changes to the symbol, click ↵ to return to the document.

■ The document reappears on the screen.

■ Flash automatically updates each instance of the symbol in your document.

CHANGE THE BRIGHTNESS OF A SYMBOL INSTANCE

You can change the brightness of a symbol instance on the Stage to make the instance darker or lighter.

Changing the brightness of a symbol instance on the Stage will not affect the original symbol stored in the library or other instances of the symbol in the document.

CHANGE THE BRIGHTNESS OF A SYMBOL INSTANCE

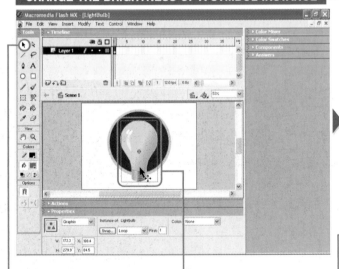

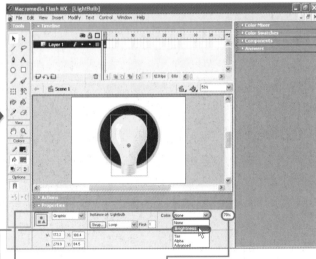

1 Click ![cursor] to be able to select an item on the Stage.

2 Click the instance of the symbol you want to change on the Stage.

■ A blue border appears around the instance.

3 Click this area to display a list of options.

Note: If the area is not displayed, see page 16 to display the Property inspector.

4 Click **Brightness**.

5 Double-click this area and type a percentage to darken or lighten the instance. Then press the [Enter] key (Windows) or the [Return] key (Macintosh).

Note: You can enter a percentage between -100 (black) and 100 (white). A percentage of 0 maintains the original brightness.

CHANGE THE TRANSPARENCY OF A SYMBOL INSTANCE

You can change the transparency of a symbol instance on the Stage to make the instance more or less transparent.

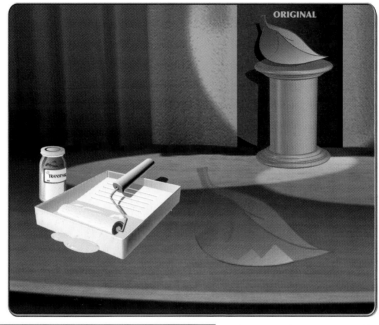

Changing the transparency of a symbol instance on the Stage will not affect the original symbol stored in the library or other instances of the symbol in the document.

CHANGE THE TRANSPARENCY OF A SYMBOL INSTANCE

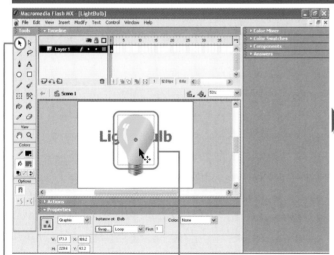

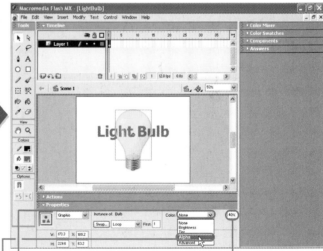

1 Click ► to be able to select an item on the Stage.

2 Click the instance of the symbol that you want to change on the Stage.

■ A blue border appears around the instance.

3 Click this area to display a list of options.

Note: If the area is not displayed, see page 16 to display the Property inspector.

4 Click **Alpha**.

5 Double-click this area and type a percentage to make the instance more or less transparent. Then press the Enter key (Windows) or the Return key (Macintosh).

Note: You can enter a percentage between 0 (completely transparent) and 100 (not transparent).

121

CHANGE THE COLOR OF A SYMBOL INSTANCE

You can change the color of a symbol instance on the Stage.

Flash allows you to blend the original color of the instance with another color.

Changing the color of a symbol instance on the Stage will not affect the original symbol stored in the library or other instances of the symbol in the document.

CHANGE THE COLOR OF A SYMBOL INSTANCE

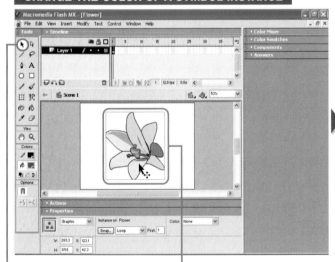

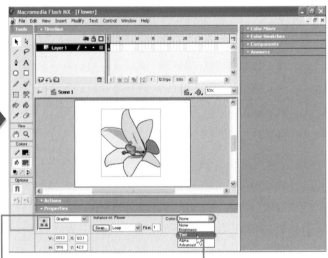

1 Click ![cursor] to be able to select an item on the Stage.

2 Click the instance of the symbol you want to change on the Stage.

■ A blue border appears around the instance.

3 Click this area to display a list of options.

Note: If the area is not displayed, see page 16 to display the Property inspector.

4 Click **Tint** to change the color of the instance.

The color I want to use is not displayed in the palette. What can I do?

If the palette does not display a color you want to use for the symbol instance, you can create a new color. To create a color, see page 40. After you create a color, the color will appear at the bottom of the palette when you click [ ] on the Property inspector. You can select the color you created as you would select any color in the palette.

Can I change the color of part of a symbol instance?

When you change the color of a symbol instance, the entire instance displays the new color. To change only a specific part of the symbol instance, you must edit the original symbol. Editing the original symbol will affect all the instances of the symbol in the document. To edit a symbol, see page 118. To be able to edit the instance without affecting other instances of the symbol, you must break the link between the symbol instance and the original symbol. For more information, see page 124.

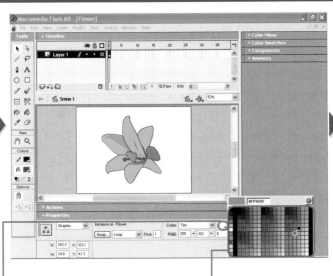

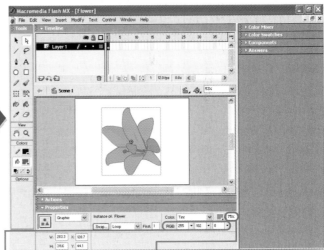

5 Click [ ] to display the available colors.

Note: As you position the mouse over a color in the palette, the instance on the Stage displays a blend of the color and the original color of the instance.

6 Click the color you want to use.

■ This area displays the red, green and blue values of the color you selected. You can double-click these areas to type new values.

7 To specify how much of the selected color you want to blend with the original color, double-click this area and type a percentage between 0 and 100. Then press the Enter key (Windows) or the Return key (Macintosh).

Note: A percentage of 100 changes the instance to the selected color.

BREAK APART A SYMBOL INSTANCE

You can break apart an instance of a symbol on the Stage to break the link between the instance and the symbol stored in the library.

Breaking apart a symbol instance allows you to make changes to the instance without affecting other instances in the document. Changes you make to the symbol in the library will also no longer affect the symbol instance on the Stage.

BREAK APART A SYMBOL INSTANCE

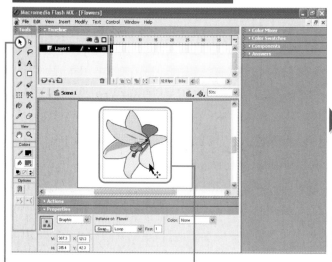

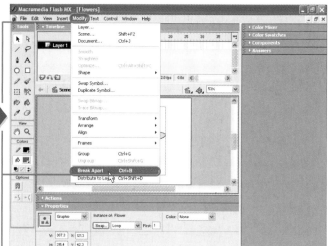

1 Click ▶ to be able to select the symbol instance that you want to break apart from the symbol stored in the library.

2 Click the symbol instance that you want to break apart.

3 Click **Modify**.

4 Click **Break Apart**.

■ Flash breaks the link between the symbol instance and the symbol stored in the library.

■ You can now make changes to the symbol instance without affecting other instances of the symbol in the document.

If you no longer need a symbol in a document, you can delete the symbol from the document's library. Deleting symbols helps keep the library from becoming cluttered.

When you delete a symbol from the library, Flash will also delete all the instances of the symbol from the document.

DELETE A SYMBOL FROM THE LIBRARY

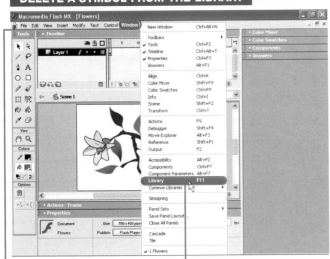

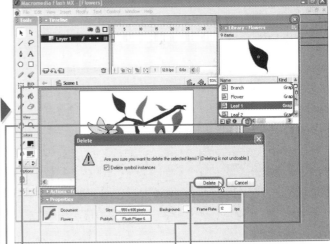

1 To display the library for the current document, click **Window**.

2 Click **Library**.

■ The Library panel appears, displaying the name of each symbol you can use in the document.

3 Click the name of the symbol you want to delete. Flash highlights the symbol and displays a preview at the top of the Library panel.

4 Click 🗑 to delete the symbol.

■ A confirmation dialog box appears.

5 Click **Delete** to delete the symbol from the library and remove all instances of the symbol from the document.

6 To close the Library panel, click ☒ (Windows) or ▢ (Macintosh).

ADD A FOLDER TO THE LIBRARY

You can create folders to help you better organize and manage the symbols in a document's library.

Each Flash document has a library that stores all the symbols in the document.

ADD A FOLDER TO THE LIBRARY

1 To display the library for the current document, click **Window**.

2 Click **Library**.

■ The Library panel appears.

3 Click 📁 to create a new folder.

■ The new folder appears. Folders display the 📁 icon.

4 Type a name for the new folder and then press the Enter key (Windows) or the Return key (Macintosh).

Can I rename a folder I created?

Yes. To rename a folder in the library, perform steps **1** and **2** on page 126 to display the Library panel. Double-click the name of the folder you want to change and type a new name for the folder. Then press the `Enter` key (Windows) or the `Return` key (Macintosh).

How do I delete a folder from the library?

Perform steps **1** and **2** on page 126 to display the Library panel. Click the folder you want to delete and click 🗑. Then click **Delete** in the confirmation dialog box that appears. Deleting a folder also deletes all the symbols stored in the folder and all the instances of the symbols in your document.

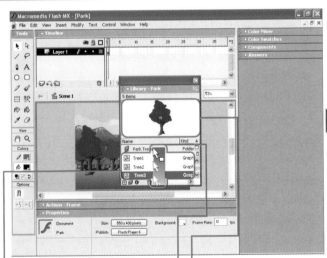

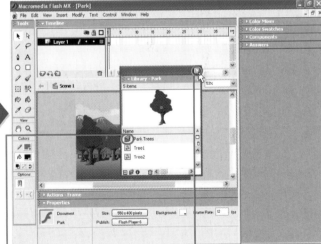

MOVE A SYMBOL TO A FOLDER

■ **1** Click the name of the symbol you want to move to a folder. The symbol is highlighted.

■ This area displays a preview of the symbol.

■ **2** Position the mouse over the name of the symbol and then drag the symbol to the folder you want to contain the symbol.

■ The symbol moves to the folder.

■ To add other symbols to the folder, repeat steps **1** and **2** for each symbol.

■ To hide or display the contents of a folder, double-click the folder icon (📁) beside the folder.

■ **3** When you finish working with the library, click ⊠ (Windows) or ▢ (Macintosh) to close the Library panel.

USE SYMBOLS FROM ANOTHER DOCUMENT

When working in a document, you can use symbols from another document's library.

When you add a symbol stored in another document's library to the Stage, Flash creates an instance of the symbol on the Stage and adds the symbol to the current document's library.

USE SYMBOLS FROM ANOTHER DOCUMENT

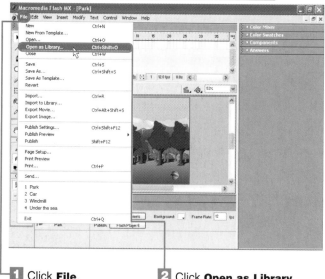

1 Click **File**.

2 Click **Open as Library**.

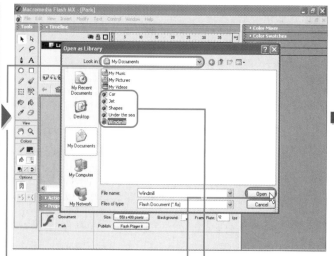

■ The Open as Library dialog box appears.

■ This area shows the location of the displayed documents. You can click this area to change the location.

3 Click the name of the document that contains the symbols you want to use.

4 Click **Open** to open the document's library.

How do I remove an instance of a symbol I added to the Stage?

To remove an instance of a symbol from the Stage, click ![pointer] and then click the symbol instance. Then press the Delete key.

Why can't I make changes to the contents of the other document's library?

You can only make changes to the library for the current document. To make changes to the library for another document, you must first open the document that contains the library. To open a document, see page 11. To display the library for the current document, see page 116.

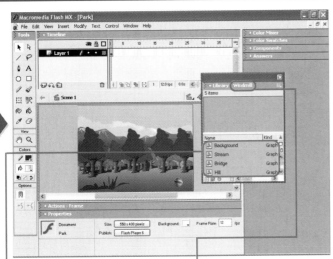

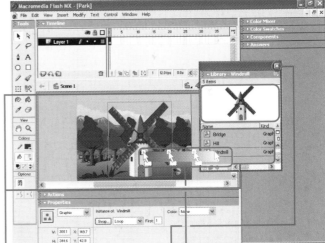

■ The Library panel from the document you selected opens.

■ This area displays the symbols from the document you selected.

■ This area displays the name of the document.

CREATE AN INSTANCE OF A SYMBOL

1 Click the name of the symbol you want to appear on the Stage. The symbol is highlighted.

■ This area displays a preview of the symbol.

2 Position the mouse ![pointer] over the name of the symbol and then drag the symbol to the location on the Stage where you want the instance of the symbol to appear.

3 To close the Library panel, click ![X] (Windows) or ![box] (Macintosh).

CHAPTER 6

Create and Manage Layers

Layers help you organize the content of your movie. This chapter shows you how to create and work with regular layers as well as layers that help you create special effects and animations in your movies.

SELECT A LAYER

Before you can make changes to objects on a layer, you need to select the layer you want to work with. Objects you add to the Stage will be added to the currently selected layer.

SELECT A LAYER

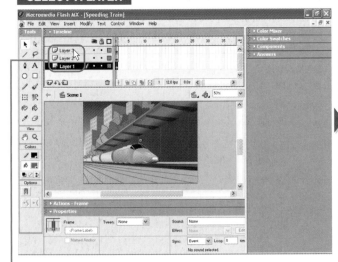

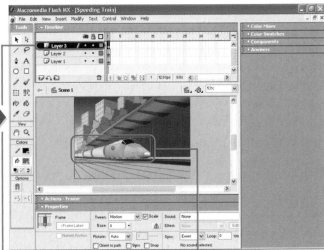

1 Click the name of a layer you want to select.

■ The layer is highlighted and displays the pencil icon (🖉) to indicate that the layer is active.

■ Flash automatically selects every object on the layer.

Note: You can also click an object on the Stage to select the layer that contains the object.

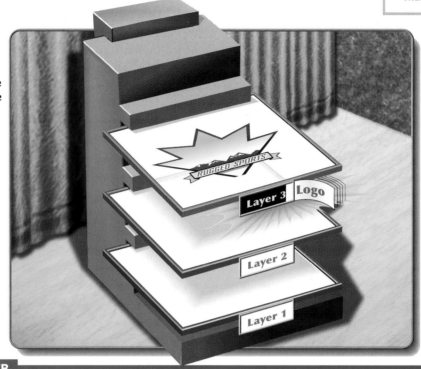

You can give a
layer a new name
to better describe
the contents of
the layer.

Flash automatically
names the first layer
in each document
Layer 1. Additional
layers are numbered
sequentially, such as
Layer 2 and Layer 3.

RENAME A LAYER

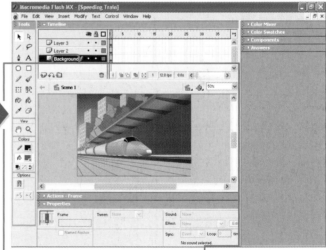

1 Double-click the
name of the layer you
want to change.

■ The name of the layer
is highlighted.

2 Type a new name for
the layer and then press
the Enter key (Windows) or
the Return key (Macintosh).

■ The layer displays
the new name.

REARRANGE LAYERS

You can change
the order of
layers to control
the way objects
appear on the
Stage.

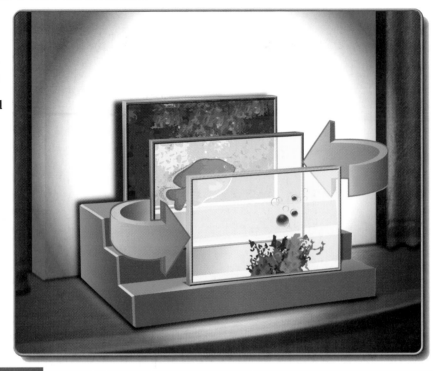

Each layer has
priority based on its
position in the list of
layers. Objects on a
higher layer in the list
of layers will appear
on top of objects on
a lower layer.

You may want to
rearrange the layers
in your drawing to
ensure that all the
objects are displayed
properly.

REARRANGE LAYERS

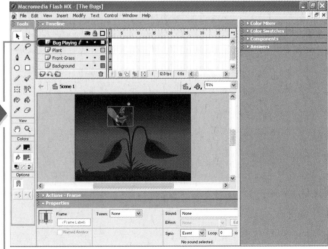

1 Click the name of the
layer you want to move.
The layer is highlighted.

2 Position the mouse ⫯
over the layer name and
then drag the layer to a
new location in the list of
layers.

■ A thick gray line shows
where the layer will appear.

■ The layer appears
in the new location.

LOCK A LAYER

You can lock a layer to prevent accidental changes to the layer.

LOCK A LAYER

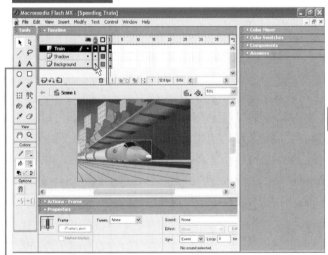

1 Below the lock icon (🔒), click the dot (●) beside the name of the layer you want to lock (● changes to 🔒).

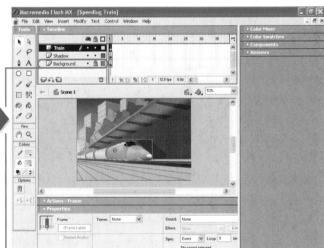

■ The layer is locked so you cannot make changes to the layer.

■ To unlock a layer, click the lock icon (🔒) beside the name of the layer (🔒 changes to ●).

Note: To quickly lock all the layers except one, press and hold down the **Alt** *key (Windows) or the* **Option** *key (Macintosh) as you click the dot (●) below the lock icon (🔒) beside the name of the layer you do not want to lock.*

VIEW A LAYER AS OUTLINES

You can view the objects on a layer as colored outlines. This allows you to focus on the contents of the layer you are currently working with but still see the position of objects on other layers.

Viewing objects on layers as outlines will not affect the appearance of the objects in the finished movie.

VIEW A LAYER AS OUTLINES

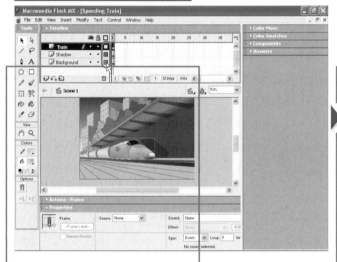

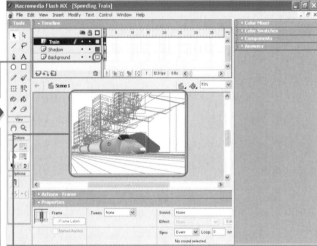

■1 To display all the objects on a layer as outlines, click the colored square beside the name of the layer (■ changes to □).

■ The color of the square beside the name of a layer indicates the outline color the objects on the layer will display.

■ All the objects on the layer appear as outlines.

■ To redisplay the objects on a layer as solid objects, click the square beside the name of the layer (□ changes to ■).

Note: To quickly display all the layers except one as outlines, press and hold down the Alt *key (Windows) or the* Option *key (Macintosh) as you click the colored square (■) beside the name of the layer containing the objects you do not want to view as outlines.*

CHANGE OUTLINE COLOR FOR A LAYER

You can change the color Flash uses when you view the objects on a layer as colored outlines. Changing the outline color for a layer can make the objects on the layer stand out more clearly on the Stage.

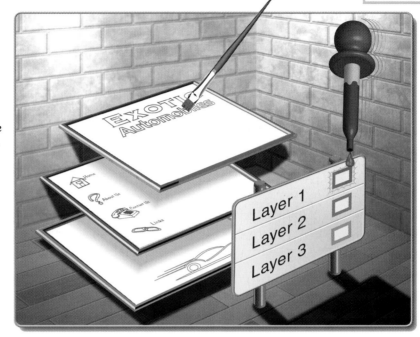

To view the objects on a layer as colored outlines, see page 138.

CHANGE OUTLINE COLOR FOR A LAYER

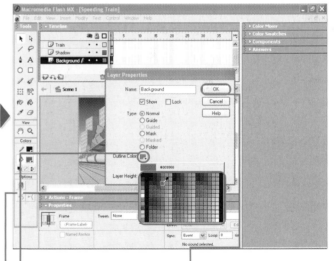

■ The color of the square beside the name of a layer indicates the outline color the layer uses.

1 To use a different outline color for the objects on a layer, double-click the icon beside the name of the layer.

■ The Layer Properties dialog box appears.

2 Click to display the available outline colors for the layer.

3 Click the outline color you want to use.

Note: Do not select a color that another layer currently uses.

4 Click **OK** to confirm your change.

HIDE A LAYER

You can temporarily hide a layer to hide all the objects on the layer. Hiding a layer is useful when you want to focus on the objects on other layers.

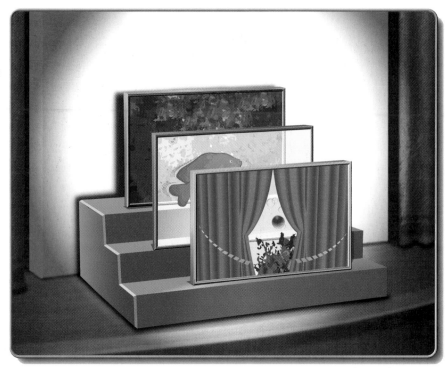

Hiding layers will not affect the finished movie.

HIDE A LAYER

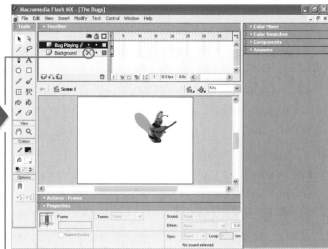

1 Below the eye icon (👁), click the dot (●) beside the name of the layer you want to hide (● changes to ✕).

■ All the objects on the layer are temporarily hidden.

■ To once again display all the objects on a layer, click ✕ beside the name of the layer (✕ changes to ●).

Note: To quickly hide all the layers except one, press and hold down the **Alt** *key (Windows) or the* **Option** *key (Macintosh) as you click the dot (●) below the eye icon (👁) beside the name of the layer you do not want to hide.*

You can place each object on the Stage on its own layer.

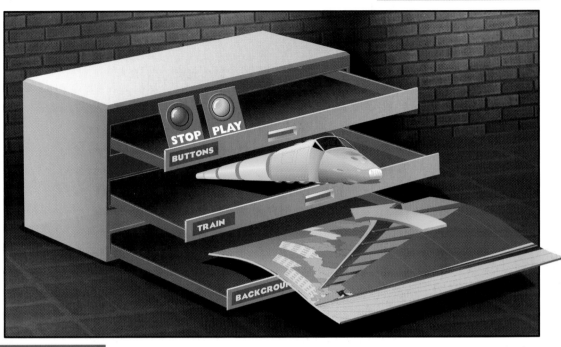

Placing each object on the Stage on its own layer can help you organize the artwork in your document and can allow you to animate each object separately.

DISTRIBUTE OBJECTS TO LAYERS

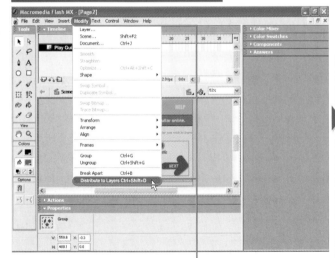

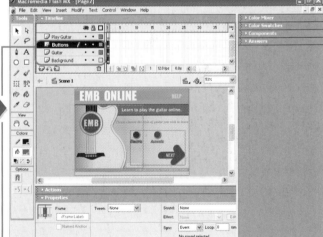

1 Select each object you want to place on its own layer. To select objects, see page 58.

2 Click **Modify**.

3 Click **Distribute to Layers**.

■ Flash places each object you selected on its own layer.

Note: To rename the new layers, see page 135.

ADD A FOLDER

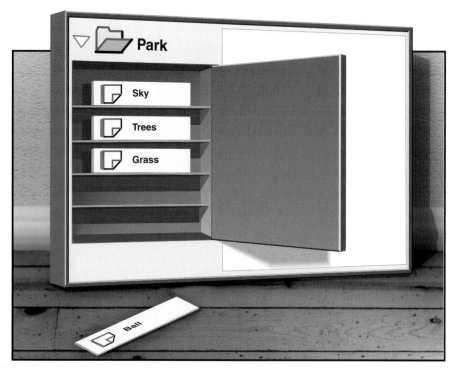

You can create folders to help you better organize and manage your layers.

Folders can contain layers as well as other folders.

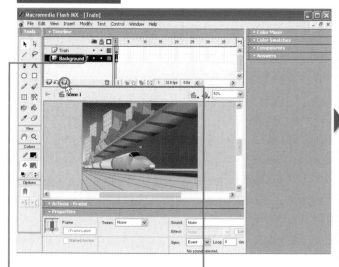

1 Click the name of the layer you want to appear below the new folder.

2 Click ➕ to add a new folder.

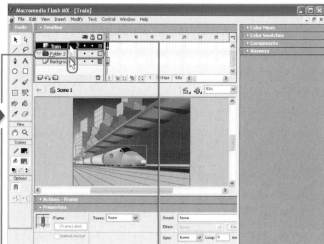

■ The new folder appears. Folders display the 📁 icon.

Note: You can rename the folder as you would rename a layer. To rename a layer, see page 135.

MOVE A LAYER TO A FOLDER

1 Position the mouse ⟋ over the name of the layer you want to move and then drag the layer to the folder you want to contain the layer.

■ A thick gray line shows where the layer will appear.

142

Can I work with the folders I create?

Yes. You can work with folders the same way you would work with layers. When you perform tasks with a folder, all the layers in the folder will be affected. For example, you can delete, lock, or hide a folder to delete, lock or hide all the layers in the folder. When you display objects in a folder as outlines, the objects on all the layers in the folder will appear as outlines.

How do I move a layer out of a folder?

To move a layer out of a folder, position the mouse ▷ over the name of the layer you want to move. Then drag the layer until the thick gray line for the layer no longer appears below the folder in the list.

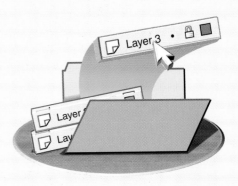

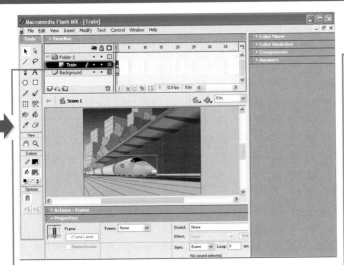

■ The layer appears indented below the folder.

■ To move other layers to the folder, repeat step 1 for each layer.

Note: You can also move a folder to another folder the same way you move a layer.

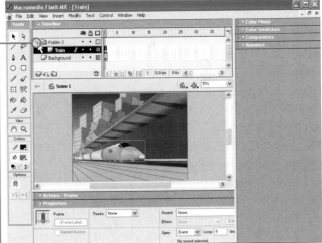

HIDE OR DISPLAY FOLDER CONTENTS

1 To hide the layers within a folder, click ▽ beside the name of the folder (▽ changes to ▷).

■ The layers in the folder are hidden.

Note: To once again display the layers in a folder, click ▷ beside the name of the folder (▷ changes to ▽).

CREATE A MASK LAYER

You can create a mask layer to hide parts of an underlying layer.

The mask layer determines which parts of the underlying layer will be displayed and which parts will be masked, or hidden.

CREATE A MASK LAYER

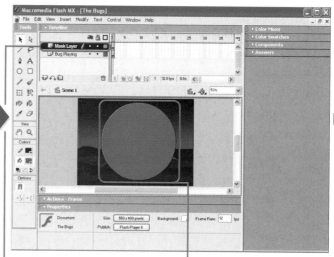

1 Click the name of the layer that contains the objects you want to mask.

2 Click 🔂 to create a new layer.

■ A new layer appears.

Note: To rename the new layer, see page 135.

3 Draw a filled shape on the Stage over the area you want to display. All objects outside the shape will be hidden.

Note: To draw a filled shape, see page 32.

Can I mask additional layers using the same mask layer?

Yes. To mask another layer, position the mouse over the name of the layer you want to mask and then drag the layer directly below the mask layer in the list of layers. To see the mask effect on the new layer you masked, you must lock the mask layer and all the layers you masked. To lock a layer, see page 137.

I no longer want to hide objects on the Stage. How do I remove a mask layer?

You can remove a mask layer by deleting the layer. To delete the layer, click the name of the mask layer and then click 🗑. Deleting a mask layer will unmask all the layers below the mask layer.

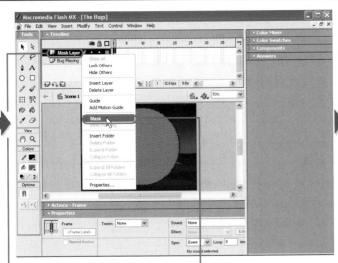

◆ **4** Right-click the name of the layer. A menu appears.

Note: On a Macintosh computer, press and hold down the Ctrl key as you click the name of the layer.

◆ **5** Click **Mask** to change the layer to a mask layer.

■ The objects on the layer you masked show through the filled area you created.

■ The mask layer displays the ⬤ icon. The layer you masked is indented below the mask layer and displays the 🦋 icon.

■ A lock icon (🔒) appears beside each layer. You can see the mask effect only when both layers are locked.

Note: To unlock the layers so you can make changes to the layers, see page 137.

CREATE A GUIDE LAYER

You can create a guide layer to help you position objects on the Stage. You can add any type of object, such as a line or shape, to a guide layer to help you draw and position objects on other layers.

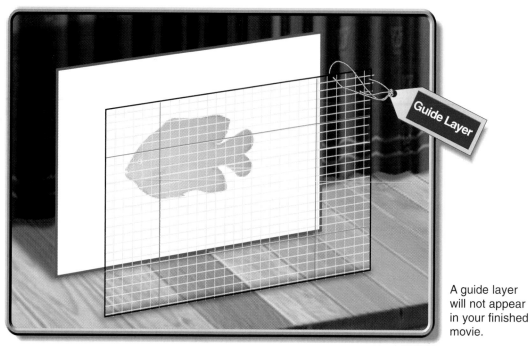

A guide layer will not appear in your finished movie.

CREATE A GUIDE LAYER

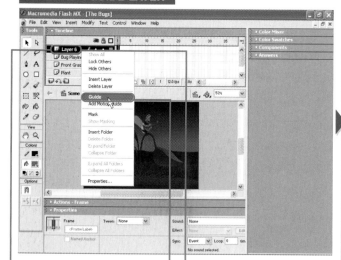

1 Click the name of the layer you want to use as a guide layer.

Note: To use a new layer as a guide layer, see page 132 to create a new layer.

2 Right-click the name of the layer. A menu appears.

Note: On a Macintosh computer, press and hold down the **Ctrl** *key as you click the name of the layer.*

3 Click **Guide** to change the layer to a guide layer.

■ A guide icon (🔧) appears beside the name of the guide layer.

■ You can draw objects on the guide layer that you can use to help you position objects on the Stage.

Note: You may want to lock the guide layer to make sure you do not accidentally make changes to the layer. To lock a layer, see page 137.

You can add a motion
guide layer that links
to another layer
containing objects
you want to
animate along
a specific path.

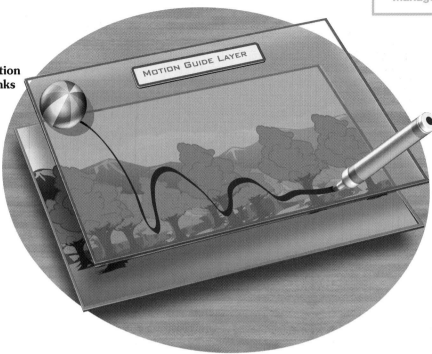

After you add a
motion guide layer,
you can draw the
path that you want
objects to follow
on the layer.

A motion guide
layer will not
appear in your
finished movie.

CREATE A MOTION GUIDE LAYER

1 Click the name of
the layer that contains
the object you want
to animate along a
specific path.

2 Click 🔧 to add a
new motion guide layer.

■ A new motion guide layer
appears. Motion guide
layers display the 🔧 icon.

■ The layer you selected
in step **1** appears indented
below the motion guide
layer.

*Note: For information on animating
with motion guides, see page 204.*

CHAPTER 7

Work With Imported Images

Read this chapter to learn how to import images into your Flash movie, fill objects with bitmap images and convert bitmap images to vector images.

IMPORT AN IMAGE

You can import images created in other programs into a Flash movie.

Flash can import many different types of images, including GIF, JPEG, Freehand and Adobe Illustrator images.

You can use an image-editing program to create images or use a scanner to scan images into your computer. You can also find images on the Internet or purchase collections of images on CDs at most computer stores.

IMPORT AN IMAGE

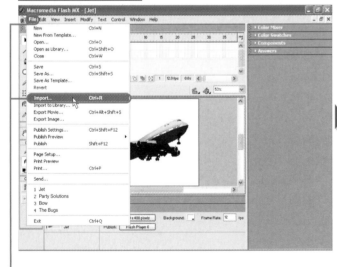

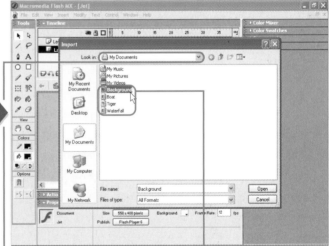

■1 Click **File**.

■2 Click **Import**.

■ The Import dialog box appears.

■ This area shows the location of the displayed files. You can click this area to change the location.

■3 Click the image you want to import.

Why can't I work with a GIF or JPEG image I imported into Flash the same way I can work with an imported Freehand or Adobe Illustrator image?

GIF and JPEG images are bitmap, or raster, images that consist of a grid of dots, called pixels. Images created in Freehand or Adobe Illustrator are vector images that consist of geometric lines and curves, called vectors. You can use Flash tools to work with vector images but not bitmap images. To work with a bitmap image, you must first break apart the image or convert the image to a vector image. To break apart a bitmap image, see page 152. To convert a bitmap image to a vector image, see page 156.

Can I import an image directly into the document's library?

If you do not want the image to appear on the Stage when you import the image, you can have Flash only save the image as a symbol in the document's library. To import an image into the document's library, perform steps 1 to 4 below, except select **Import to Library** in step 2. To use the library, see page 116.

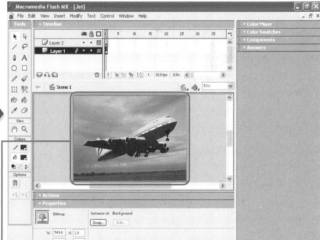

4 Click **Open** to import the image.

*Note: A dialog box may appear, allowing you to specify how you want to import the image. Click **OK** to accept the default settings Flash provides and import the image.*

■ Flash adds the image to the Stage.

Note: Flash may also add the image to the document's library. To view the library, see page 116.

BREAK APART A BITMAP IMAGE

You can break apart a bitmap image you imported into a document. Breaking apart a bitmap image allows you to use the tools included with Flash to work with the image.

BREAK APART A BITMAP IMAGE

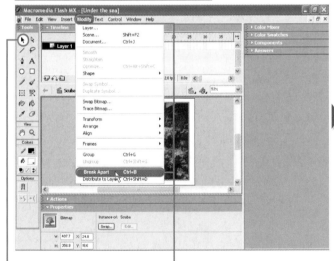

1 Click ▶ to be able to select a bitmap image on the Stage.

Note: To import a bitmap image, see page 150.

2 Click the bitmap image you want to break apart.

3 Click **Modify**.

4 Click **Break Apart** to break apart the bitmap image.

■ Flash breaks apart the bitmap image.

■ Small white dots cover the bitmap image to indicate that the image is broken apart.

You can fill an object on the Stage with a bitmap image.

Flash allows you to use a bitmap image to fill an object created with the Oval, Rectangle or Pen tool, as well as fill brush strokes created with the Brush tool.

FILL AN OBJECT WITH A BITMAP IMAGE

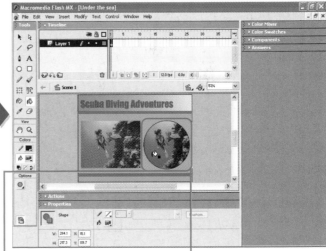

1 Break apart the bitmap image you want to use to fill an object. To break apart a bitmap image, see page 152.

2 Click 🖊 to be able to copy the bitmap image to the object you want to fill.

3 Click anywhere in the bitmap image to select the image (🖊 changes to 🪣).

4 Click inside the object you want to fill with the bitmap image.

■ Flash fills the object with the bitmap image.

Note: If the bitmap image is not large enough to fill the object, Flash repeats the image to fill the object.

153

CHANGE HOW A BITMAP IMAGE FILLS AN OBJECT

You can change the position and size of a bitmap image that fills an object. You can also rotate a bitmap image that fills an object.

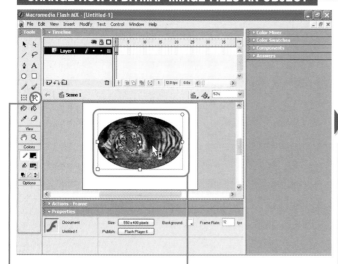

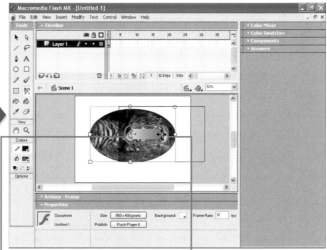

1 Click ⌖ to be able to change how a bitmap image fills an object.

Note: To fill an object with a bitmap image, see page 153.

2 Click the object that displays the bitmap image you want to change. A box with handles appears around the bitmap image.

REPOSITION A BITMAP IMAGE

3 To reposition the bitmap image within the object, position the mouse ⌖ over the center handle (○) in the box that surrounds the image (⌖ changes to ✛).

4 Drag the bitmap image to a new location inside the object.

■ A black outline indicates the new position of the bitmap image.

**Which handle should I use to resize a
bitmap image within an object?**

■ To change the width of the bitmap
image, drag the square handle on the
left side of the box.

■ To change the height of the bitmap
image, drag the square handle at the
bottom of the box.

■ To change the width and height of the
bitmap image at the same time, drag the
square handle at the bottom left corner
of the image.

**Can I slant a bitmap image within an
object?**

Yes. To slant, or skew, a bitmap image
within a shape, perform steps **1** and **2**
below to be able to change the bitmap
image. Position the mouse ◊ over one
of the circular handles (○) on the top or
right side of the box that surrounds the
image (◊ changes to ↕ or ↔). Then
drag the handle until the bitmap image
appears the way you want.

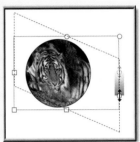

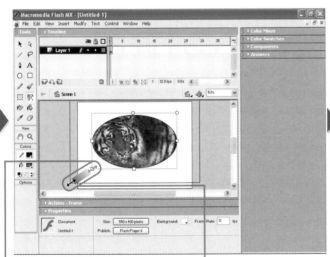

RESIZE A BITMAP IMAGE

5 To resize the bitmap
image within the object,
position the mouse ◊ over
a square handle (□) on the
box that surrounds the image
(◊ changes to ↗, ↔ or ↕).

6 Drag the handle
until the bitmap image
is the size you want.

■ A black outline
indicates the new size
of the bitmap image.

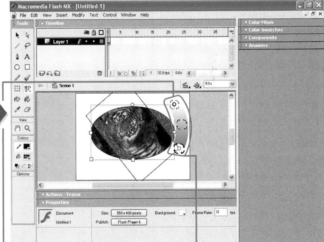

ROTATE A BITMAP IMAGE

7 To rotate the bitmap
image within the object,
position the mouse ◊ over
the top right handle (○) on
the box that surrounds the
image (◊ changes to ⟳
or ⟲).

8 Drag the handle until
the bitmap image appears
the way you want.

■ A black outline
indicates the new rotation
of the bitmap image.

CONVERT A BITMAP IMAGE TO A VECTOR IMAGE

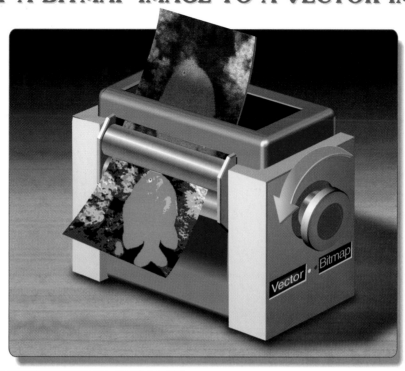

After importing a bitmap image into Flash, you can convert the image to a vector image.

Converting a bitmap image to a vector image allows you to use the tools in Flash to make changes to the image and may reduce the file size of the image.

CONVERT A BITMAP IMAGE TO A VECTOR IMAGE

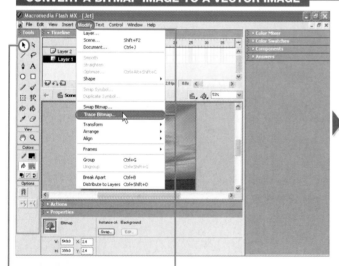

1 Click ▶ to be able to select a bitmap image on the Stage.

Note: To import a bitmap image, see page 150.

2 Click the bitmap image you want to convert to a vector image.

3 Click **Modify**.

4 Click **Trace Bitmap**.

■ The Trace Bitmap dialog box appears.

5 To specify when Flash will consider one pixel the same color as a neighboring pixel in the bitmap image, double-click this area and type a number between 0 and 500.

Note: When Flash compares two pixels, if the difference in the color values of the pixels is less than the number you specify, Flash considers the two pixels the same color. A higher number results in an image with fewer colors, less detail and a smaller file size.

What is the difference between a bitmap image and a vector image?

BITMAP 700K

VECTOR 50K

A bitmap image, also called a raster image, uses dots arranged in a grid pattern, called pixels, to define the details of the image. Resizing a bitmap image usually changes the file size of the image.

A vector image uses geometric lines and curves, called vectors, to define the details of the image. Vector images usually have a smaller file size than bitmap images. Resizing a vector image does not usually affect the file size of the image.

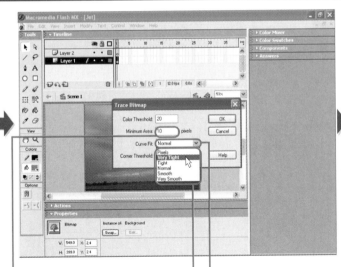

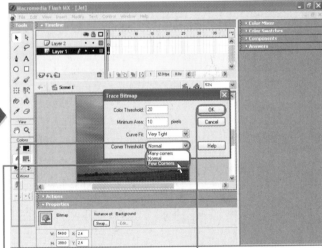

6 To specify the number of surrounding pixels Flash will consider when assigning a color to a pixel, double-click this area and type a number between 1 and 1000.

Note: A higher number results in an image with fewer colors, less detail and a smaller file size.

7 To specify how smoothly you want Flash to trace the curves of the image, click this area.

8 Click the curve option you want to use.

9 To specify how closely you want Flash to trace the corners of the image, click this area.

10 Click the corner option you want to use.

Note: The Many corners option will keep the sharp edges in the image. The Few Corners option smoothes out some edges.

11 Click **OK** to have Flash convert the bitmap image to a vector image.

■ Flash replaces the bitmap image with vector shapes that resemble the original bitmap image.

CHAPTER 8

Create Animations

In this chapter, you will learn how to work with frames and create frame-by-frame animations and movie clips.

INTRODUCTION TO FRAMES

You use frames to create animations for your Flash movie.

A movie consists of frames, each containing the content for a specific location in the movie. The total number of frames in a movie determines the total length of the movie.

Timeline

The Timeline allows you to organize and control the content of a movie. The Timeline is divided into frames. Frames appear in chronological order on the Timeline and each frame has a number. When you select a frame on the Timeline, the content of the frame appears on the Stage, displaying the events taking place at that point in the movie.

Keyframe

A keyframe is a special type of frame that indicates when you want a change to occur in a movie. For example, you can add a keyframe when you want to change the appearance or position of an object in a movie.

A keyframe with content in a movie displays a solid black dot (●) on the Timeline. A keyframe without content displays a hollow dot (○) on the Timeline.

Frames

Frames display exactly the same content as the previous keyframe on the Timeline. For example, if a keyframe displays a ball at a specific location, the frames that follow until the next keyframe will display the ball at the same location. The number of frames that follow a keyframe determine the amount of time the contents of the keyframe will appear in the movie. You can add or delete frames to increase or decrease the amount of time the contents of a keyframe will appear in the movie.

Frames with content in a movie appear gray on the Timeline. Frames without content appear white on the Timeline. The last frame at the end of a series of frames with the same content displays a hollow rectangle ([]) on the Timeline.

Frame-by-Frame Animation

Frame-by-frame animation creates the illusion of movement by changing the position or appearance of an object from frame to frame. When the movie is played, the object appears to move or change. Each time you want a change to occur in a movie, such as a car moving to a new location, you need to create a new keyframe.

ADD A KEYFRAME

You can add a special frame called a keyframe when you want a change to occur in your movie.

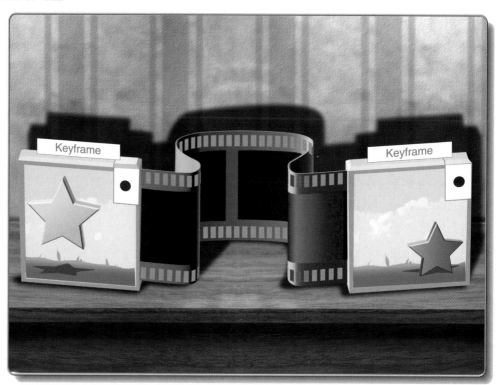

Keyframe

Keyframe

For example, you can add a keyframe when you want to change the appearance or position of an object in your movie.

When you add a keyframe, Flash copies the contents of the previous keyframe to the new keyframe. This allows you to easily make minor changes to the content of your movie. If you want to make major changes to your movie, add a blank keyframe.

ADD A KEYFRAME

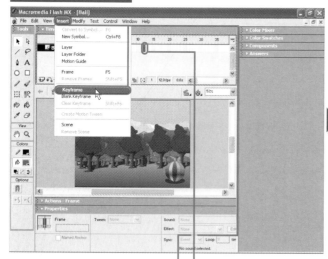

■ Flash automatically adds a blank keyframe to the first frame on the Timeline. Flash also includes hundreds of placeholder frames on the Timeline.

1 Click the frame on the Timeline where you want to add a keyframe. The frame is highlighted.

2 Click **Insert**.

3 Click **Keyframe**.

■ Flash adds a keyframe to the Timeline. A keyframe with content displays a black dot (●).

■ The keyframe displays the same content as the previous keyframe.

■ You can change the content of the new keyframe on the Stage to make a change to your movie.

What will the frames after a keyframe show?

When you add a keyframe, the content of all the frames between the new keyframe and the next keyframe will be the same as the new keyframe. For example, if you add a new keyframe at frame 20 and change the position of an object, frames 1 through 19 will display the object in the original position. Frames 20 to the next keyframe will display the object in the new position.

How do I remove a keyframe?

To remove a keyframe, you can first convert the keyframe to a regular frame and then delete the frame as you would delete any frame on the Timeline. To convert a keyframe, see page 167. To delete a frame, see page 165.

ADD A BLANK KEYFRAME

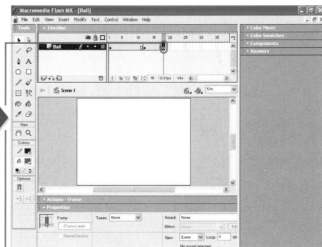

1 Click the frame on the Timeline where you want to add a blank keyframe. The frame is highlighted.

2 Click **Insert**.

3 Click **Blank Keyframe**.

■ Flash adds a blank keyframe. A blank keyframe displays a hollow dot (o).

■ You can add new content to the keyframe on the Stage to make a change to your movie.

Note: If the frame you selected in step 1 contained content, Flash removes the content from the frame to create the blank keyframe.

ADD A FRAME

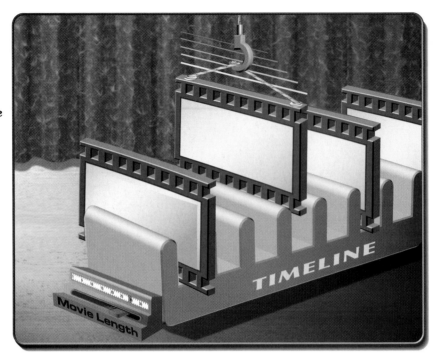

You can add a frame to the Timeline. Adding a frame will increase the length of the movie by one frame.

Adding a frame after a specific keyframe will increase the amount of time the content of the keyframe will appear in your movie.

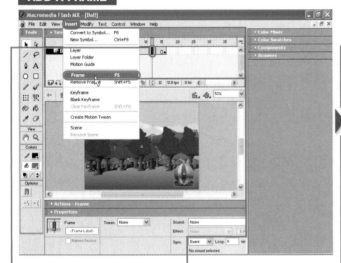

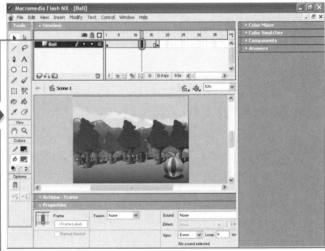

1 Click the location on the Timeline where you want to insert a new frame. The frame is highlighted.

Note: To add more than one frame, select one frame for each frame you want to add. To select multiple frames, see page 166.

2 Click **Insert**.

3 Click **Frame**.

■ Flash adds the frame to the Timeline. The frames to the right of the new frame move to make room for the new frame.

■ The new frame will display the same content as the previous keyframe.

DELETE A FRAME

You can delete a frame you no longer need from the Timeline. Deleting a frame will reduce the length of the movie by one frame.

Deleting a frame after a specific keyframe will reduce the amount of time the content of the keyframe will appear in your movie.

DELETE A FRAME

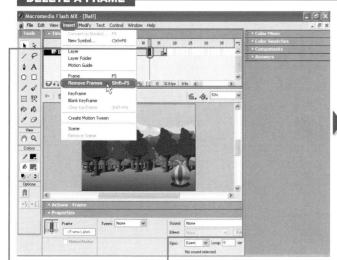

1 Click the frame you want to delete on the Timeline. The frame is highlighted.

Note: To delete more than one frame, select all the frames you want to delete. To select multiple frames, see page 166.

2 Click **Insert**.

3 Click **Remove Frames**.

■ Flash removes the frame you selected. The frames to the right of the deleted frame move to fill the space.

SELECT A FRAME

You can select a frame on the Timeline to display the contents of the frame on the Stage.

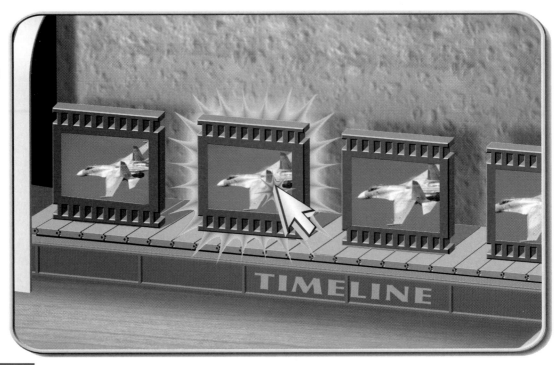

SELECT A FRAME

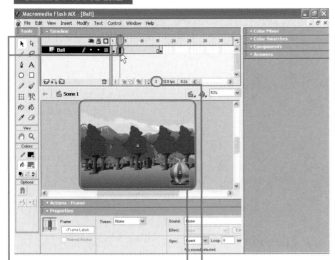

SELECT ONE FRAME

■1 Click the frame you want to select on the Timeline. The frame is highlighted.

■ The red playhead moves to the frame you selected.

■ This area displays the number of the currently selected frame.

■ The contents of the selected frame appear on the Stage. Flash automatically selects all the objects on the Stage.

SELECT MULTIPLE FRAMES

■1 Click the first frame you want to select on the Timeline.

■2 Press and hold down the Shift key as you click the last frame you want to select.

■ Flash selects all the frames between the two frames.

Note: To select frames that are not side by side, perform step 1 and then press and hold down the Ctrl key (Windows) or the ⌘ key (Macintosh) as you click each additional frame.

When you no longer want a change to occur in your movie, you can convert a keyframe to a regular frame on the Timeline.

When you convert a keyframe to a regular frame, the keyframe and all frames that follow to the next keyframe will display the contents of the previous keyframe.

You cannot convert the first keyframe in your movie to a regular frame.

CONVERT A KEYFRAME TO A FRAME

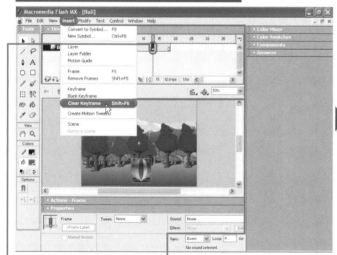

1 Click the keyframe you want to convert to a regular frame.

2 Click **Insert**.

3 Click **Clear Keyframe**.

■ The keyframe is converted to a frame. The keyframe you selected and all the frames that follow to the next keyframe display the contents of the previous keyframe.

■ Flash removes the dot (●) from the frame on the Timeline, indicating that the frame is no longer a keyframe.

CREATE A FRAME-BY-FRAME ANIMATION

You can create the illusion of movement by changing the position or appearance of an object from frame to frame. This type of animation is called frame-by-frame animation.

Each time you want a change to occur in your movie, such as a ball moving to a new location, you need to create a new keyframe.

CREATE A FRAME-BY-FRAME ANIMATION

1 Create a keyframe on the Timeline where you want the animation to start. A keyframe displays a dot (● or ○).

Note: To create a keyframe, see page 162.

2 Click the keyframe you created in step **1**. The frame is highlighted.

3 Add the object you want to animate to the Stage.

Note: To draw objects, see pages 26 to 37.

4 Create a keyframe on the Timeline where you want a change to occur in your movie.

Note: In this example, a change will occur in the movie after the movie plays for 10 frames.

5 Click the keyframe you created in step **4**. The frame is highlighted.

■ Flash copies the contents of the previous keyframe to the new keyframe so you can easily make changes to the object.

How can I adjust the amount of time each keyframe will play?

You can add or delete the frames after a keyframe to increase or decrease the amount of time the contents of the keyframe will play in the animation. Adding or deleting frames between keyframes is also useful when you want to reduce or increase the speed of the animation. To add a frame, see page 164. To delete a frame, see page 165.

Is there another way to move through the animation?

You can manually move the red playhead on the Timeline to scroll back or forth through the animation. Position the mouse over the playhead and then drag the playhead left or right to move through each frame in the animation.

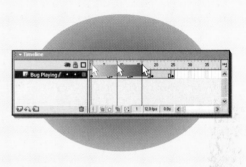

6 Change the contents of the keyframe. For example, you can move the object or change the object's appearance.

7 To complete the animation, repeat steps **4** to **6** until you create all the changes you want to occur in the movie.

TEST THE ANIMATION

1 To test your animation, click the first keyframe of the animation on the Timeline. The frame is highlighted.

2 Press the Enter key (Windows) or the Return key (Macintosh) to play the animation.

■ The animation plays on the Stage.

PREVIEW A MOVIE

You can preview a movie on the Stage or in the Flash Player.

You should regularly preview your movie to ensure the movie plays the way you expect, especially after you make a significant change to your movie.

Movie clips and buttons will function properly only when you preview the movie in the Flash Player.

PREVIEW A MOVIE

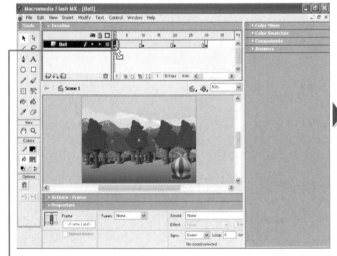

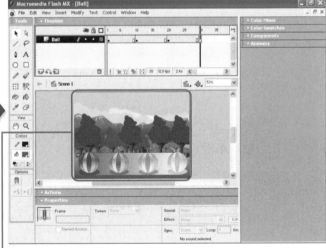

PREVIEW A MOVIE ON THE STAGE

1 Click the first frame on the Timeline. The frame is highlighted.

2 Press the Enter key (Windows) or the Return key (Macintosh) to play the movie.

■ The movie plays on the Stage.

Why does the Exporting Flash Movie window appear when I preview my movie in the Flash Player?

Each time you preview the movie in the Flash Player, Flash exports the movie and saves a copy of the movie in a new file format in the same location as your Flash movie file. For information on exporting a movie, see page 286. Flash does not export your movie when you preview the movie on the Stage.

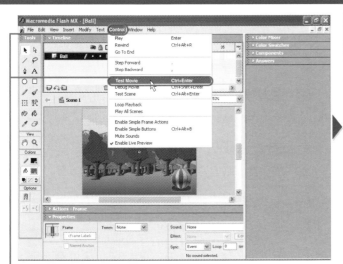

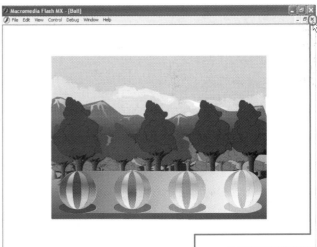

PREVIEW A MOVIE IN THE FLASH PLAYER

■ 1 Click **Control**.

■ 2 Click **Test Movie**.

■ The Exporting Flash Movie window briefly appears, showing the progress of exporting the movie.

■ Flash opens the Flash Player and plays the movie.

Note: The movie plays repeatedly until you stop the movie.

■ To stop or resume playing the movie at any time, press the Enter key (Windows) or the Return key (Macintosh).

■ 3 When you finish previewing the movie, click x (Windows) or ☐ (Macintosh) to close the Flash Player and return to the document.

MOVE A KEYFRAME

You can move a keyframe to a new location on the Timeline. Moving a keyframe allows you to control when a change will occur in your movie.

You can also move a keyframe to display the contents of a keyframe for a shorter or longer period of time.

MOVE A KEYFRAME

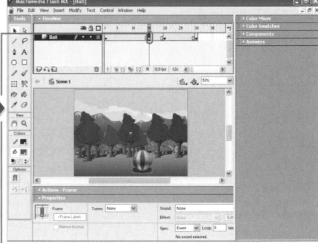

1 Click the keyframe you want to move. The keyframe is highlighted.

2 Position the mouse over the keyframe and then drag the keyframe left or right to a new location on the Timeline.

■ A gray box indicates the new location.

■ Flash moves the keyframe to the new location on the Timeline.

COPY A FRAME

You can copy a frame
to a new location on
the Timeline. Copying
a frame allows you to
display the contents
of the frame again in
your movie.

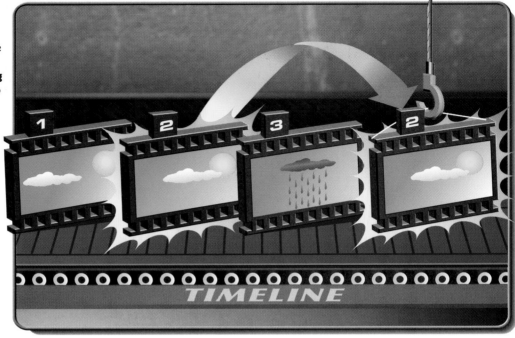

COPY A FRAME

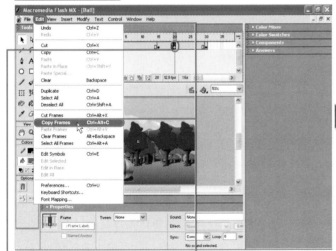

1 Click the frame you
want to copy. The frame
is highlighted.

*Note: To copy more than one
frame, select the frames you
want to copy. To select multiple
frames, see page 166.*

2 Click **Edit**.

3 Click **Copy Frames**.

4 Click the frame where
you want to place the
copy of the frame. The
frame is highlighted.

5 Click **Edit**.

6 Click **Paste Frames**.

■ Flash places a copy
of the frame in the frame
you selected.

*Note: Flash creates a new
keyframe for you in the frame
where you placed the copy.*

ADD A LABEL OR COMMENT TO A KEYFRAME

You can add a label or a comment to a keyframe. A label identifies a keyframe on the Timeline. A comment describes the contents or purpose of the keyframe.

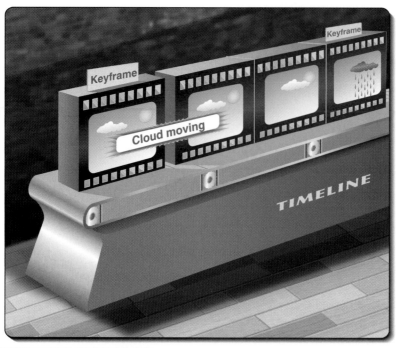

You can add a label or a comment to a keyframe, but you cannot add both.

Adding labels to keyframes is useful when adding actions to keyframes. For information on actions, see pages 250 to 265.

ADD A LABEL OR COMMENT TO A KEYFRAME

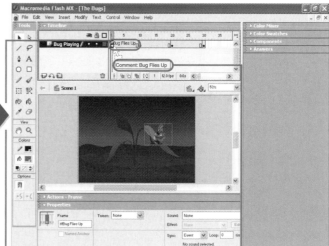

1 Click the keyframe you want to display a label or comment. The keyframe is highlighted.

2 Click this area and type the text for the label or comment. When adding a comment, type two slashes (//) before the text. Then press the Enter key (Windows) or the Return key (Macintosh).

Note: If the Frame Label area is not displayed, see page 16 to display the Property inspector.

■ The label or comment appears on the Timeline.

■ A keyframe with a label displays a flag (▶). A keyframe with a comment displays slashes (✔).

■ When you position the mouse ⟋ over a keyframe with a label or comment, the label or comment appears in a yellow box.

Note: To remove a label or comment from a keyframe, click the keyframe. Then select the text you typed in step 2 and press the Delete key.

REVERSE THE ORDER OF FRAMES

You can reverse
the order of a
series of frames
on the Timeline.

Reversing the order
of frames can help
you create interesting
effects in your movie.
For example, you can
create a series of
frames that show an
object increasing in
size, copy the frames
and then reverse
the copied frames
to show the object
decreasing in size.
To copy frames, see
page 173.

REVERSE THE ORDER OF FRAMES

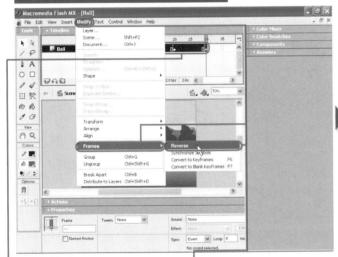

1 Select the frames you
want to play in reverse
order. To select multiple
frames, see page 166.

*Note: A keyframe must appear
at the beginning and end of the
frames you select.*

2 Click **Modify**.

3 Click **Frames**.

4 Click **Reverse**.

■ Flash reverses the
order of the frames.

CHANGE THE APPEARANCE OF FRAMES ON THE TIMELINE

You can customize how Flash displays frames on the Timeline.

You can have Flash display frames on the Timeline in various sizes, from tiny to large. You can also have Flash display the contents of each frame on the Timeline to help provide an overview of your animation.

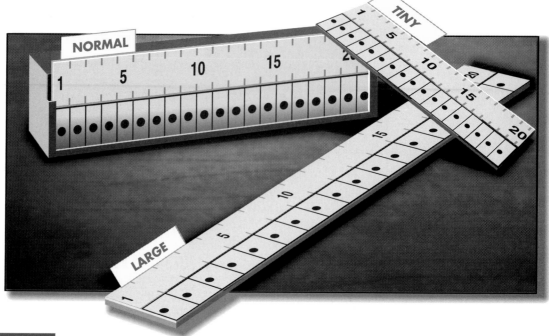

CHANGE SIZE OF FRAMES

1 Click 🖽 to display a list of options for the Timeline.

2 Click an option to specify the size you want to use for the frames on the Timeline.

■ A check mark (✔) appears beside the current size of the frames.

■ Flash changes the size of the frames on the Timeline.

Note: Selecting a smaller frame size allows you to display more frames on the Timeline at once.

■ To return to the original size of the frames, repeat steps 1 and 2, selecting **Normal** in step 2.

Are there any other changes I can make to the appearance of the Timeline?

You can decrease the height of the layers on the Timeline. This allows you to view more layers on the Timeline at once. To decrease the height of the layers, perform step 1 below to display a list of options for the Timeline and then click **Short**.

Why are some frames on the Timeline shaded gray?

Frames that contain content are shaded gray on the Timeline. This allows you to quickly see which frames contain content and which frames are empty. You can use the Tinted Frames option to turn the shading of frames on or off. Perform step 1 below to display a list of options for the Timeline and then click **Tinted Frames** to turn the option on or off.

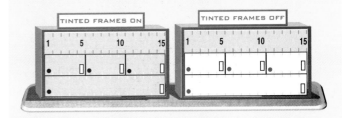

PREVIEW FRAME CONTENTS

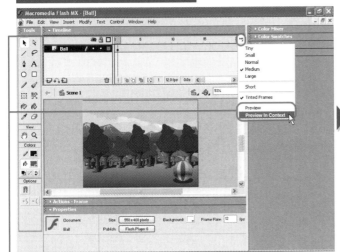

■1 Click ⊞ to display a list of options for the Timeline.

■2 Click the preview option you want to use.

Preview
Displays the contents of each frame.

Preview In Context
Displays a small version of the Stage for each frame.

■ In this example, Flash displays a small version of the Stage for each frame on the Timeline.

USE ONION SKINNING

You can use the onion skinning feature to display the contents of several frames on the Stage at once. Using onion skinning is useful when working with animations.

When viewing the contents of a specific frame, you can use the onion skinning feature to display the contents of the surrounding frames as dimmed or outlined objects. This allows you to work with one frame while viewing the appearance and location of objects in other frames.

USE ONION SKINNING

DISPLAY DIMMED FRAME CONTENTS

■1 Click the frame you want to display with surrounding frames.

■ The Stage displays the contents of the frame.

■2 Click 🔳 to display the dimmed contents of the surrounding frames.

■ Flash displays the dimmed contents of the surrounding frames on the Stage. You cannot make changes to the dimmed objects.

■ The onion skin markers on the Timeline indicate which frames are displayed on the Stage.

■ To no longer display the dimmed contents of the surrounding frames, click 🔳.

Can I display onion skinning for only one layer in my drawing?

To display the onion skinning effect for only one layer in your drawing, you can lock all the layers except the layer you want to display. This is useful when your movie has multiple layers that contain animation and you want to focus on the animation for a specific layer. To lock a layer, see page 137.

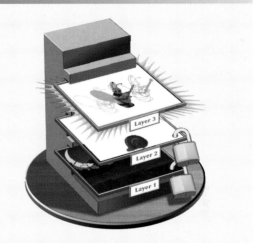

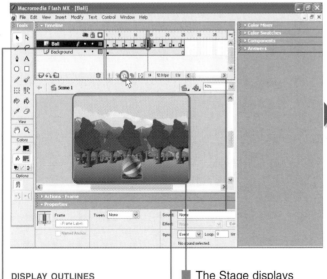

DISPLAY OUTLINES OF FRAME CONTENTS

■1 Click the frame you want to display with surrounding frames.

■ The Stage displays the contents of the frame.

■2 Click 🔲 to display the outlined contents of the surrounding frames.

■ Flash displays the outlined contents of the surrounding frames on the Stage. You cannot make changes to the outlined objects.

■ The onion skin markers on the Timeline indicate which frames are displayed on the Stage.

■ To no longer display the outlined contents of the surrounding frames, click 🔲.

CONTINUED ▶

USE ONION SKINNING

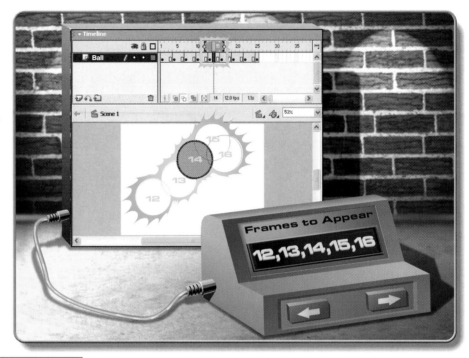

When using the onion skinning feature to display the contents of several frames at once, you can change the number of frames that are displayed on the Stage.

USE ONION SKINNING (CONTINUED)

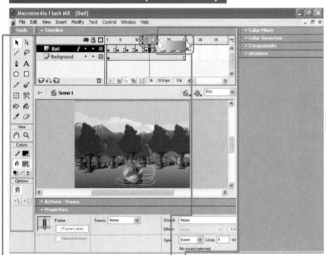

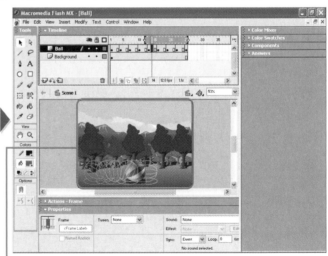

CHANGE THE NUMBER OF FRAMES DISPLAYED

■ When you are using the onion skinning feature, the onion skin markers on the Timeline indicate which frames are displayed on the Stage.

1 To display more or fewer frames on the Stage, position the mouse ⍝ over the Start (⟨) or End (⟩) onion skin marker.

2 Drag the mouse ⍝ left or right to display more or fewer frames on the Stage.

■ Flash changes the number of frames displayed on the Stage.

While using the onion skinning feature, can I change which frames are displayed?

While viewing frames in onion skin mode, you can select another frame that you want to display with the surrounding frames. To select a frame, click the frame on the Timeline. Flash moves the onion skin markers and displays the contents of the frames surrounding the frame you select.

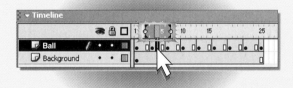

Can I quickly display all the frames in onion skin mode?

To quickly display all the frames in your drawing in onion skin mode, click below the Timeline and then click **Onion All**. You can click again and select **Onion 2** to return to the default setting.

EDIT MULTIPLE FRAMES

■ By default, you cannot make changes to the dimmed or outlined objects in the surrounding frames when using the onion skinning feature.

1 Click to be able to make changes to all the objects shown on the Stage.

■ Flash displays the contents of the surrounding frames as solid objects. You can now make changes to the contents of all the displayed frames.

■ If you no longer want to be able to make changes to multiple frames at once, click .

CREATE A MOVIE CLIP

You can create a movie clip that acts like a mini-movie in your document. A movie clip can be reused throughout a document and has its own Timeline.

Flash stores each movie clip you create in the library of the current document.

Creating movie clips allows you to better organize the frames in your document. Adding an animation directly to the document's Timeline usually requires multiple frames, while a movie clip uses only one frame.

CREATE A MOVIE CLIP

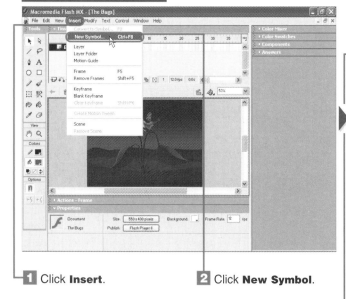

1 Click **Insert**.

2 Click **New Symbol**.

■ The Create New Symbol dialog box appears.

3 Type a name for the new movie clip.

4 Click **Movie Clip** to create a movie clip (○ changes to ●).

5 Click **OK** to add the new movie clip to the document's library.

What is the cross (+) that appears on the Stage in symbol-editing mode?

The cross (+) on the Stage indicates the center of your drawing. Flash uses this center point to determine how to position or change your movie clip on the Stage. To help ensure that your movie clip will appear the way you expect on the Stage, you should make sure the cross (+) appears at the center of your drawing when creating the movie clip.

How do I edit a movie clip?

After you add a movie clip to your movie, you can edit the movie clip the same way you would edit any symbol. Any changes you make to the movie clip will affect all instances of the movie clip in your document. To edit a symbol, see page 118.

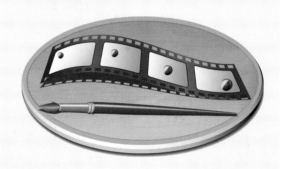

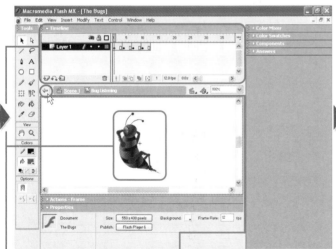

■ Flash switches to symbol-editing mode so you can create the movie clip.

■ This area displays the timeline for the movie clip.

6 Create the animation for the movie clip.

Note: In this example, we create a frame-by-frame animation that moves an object. To create a frame-by-frame animation, see page 168.

7 When you finish creating the movie clip, click ⟵ to return to the document.

■ The document reappears on the screen.

Note: The movie clip does not appear on the Stage.

■ You can now add the movie clip to your movie. To add a movie clip to a movie, see page 184.

ADD A MOVIE CLIP TO A MOVIE

After you create a movie clip, you can add the movie clip anywhere in your movie.

When you add a movie clip to the Stage, you are adding an instance of the movie clip that is stored in the document's library. Using a movie clip more than once in your movie will not increase the file size of the movie.

ADD A MOVIE CLIP TO A MOVIE

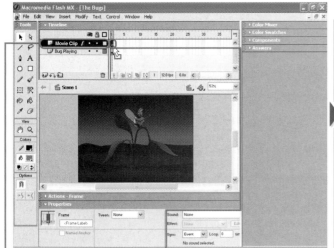

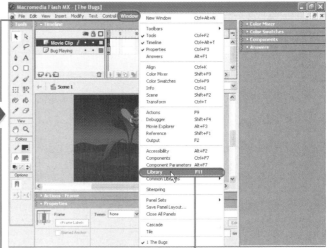

1 Add a new layer for the movie clip you want to add. To add a layer, see page 132.

2 On the layer you added, create a keyframe where you want a movie clip to start playing. To create a keyframe, see page 162.

3 Click the keyframe you created in step **2**. The frame is highlighted.

4 To display the library that stores the movie clips you can use in the document, click **Window**.

5 Click **Library**.

■ The Library panel appears.

How can I see how a movie clip will play in my movie?

You can see how a movie clip will play in your movie only when you preview the movie in the Flash Player. To preview a movie in the Flash Player, see page 171. When you view a movie clip on the Stage, Flash displays only the first frame of the movie clip.

Can I have a movie clip play only once in a movie?

When you play a movie, a movie clip will play repeatedly until the movie ends. To have a movie clip play only once, you can add a stop action to the last keyframe in the movie clip's Timeline. You can edit a movie clip the same way you edit a symbol. To edit a symbol, see page 118. To add a stop action to a keyframe, see page 250.

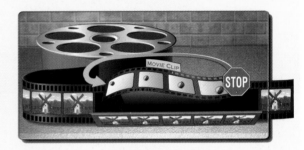

■ This area displays the items in the library. Movie clips display the 🎬 icon.

6 Click the name of the movie clip you want to add to your movie. The movie clip is highlighted.

■ This area displays the first frame of the movie clip.

7 To play the movie clip, click ▶.

8 To add the movie clip to the movie, position the mouse over the name of the movie clip.

9 Drag the movie clip to the location on the Stage where you want the movie clip to start playing.

■ The first frame of the movie clip appears on the Stage.

10 To close the Library panel, click ✕ (Windows) or ▢ (Macintosh).

Note: To delete a movie clip from your movie, click the movie clip on the Stage and press the Delete key.

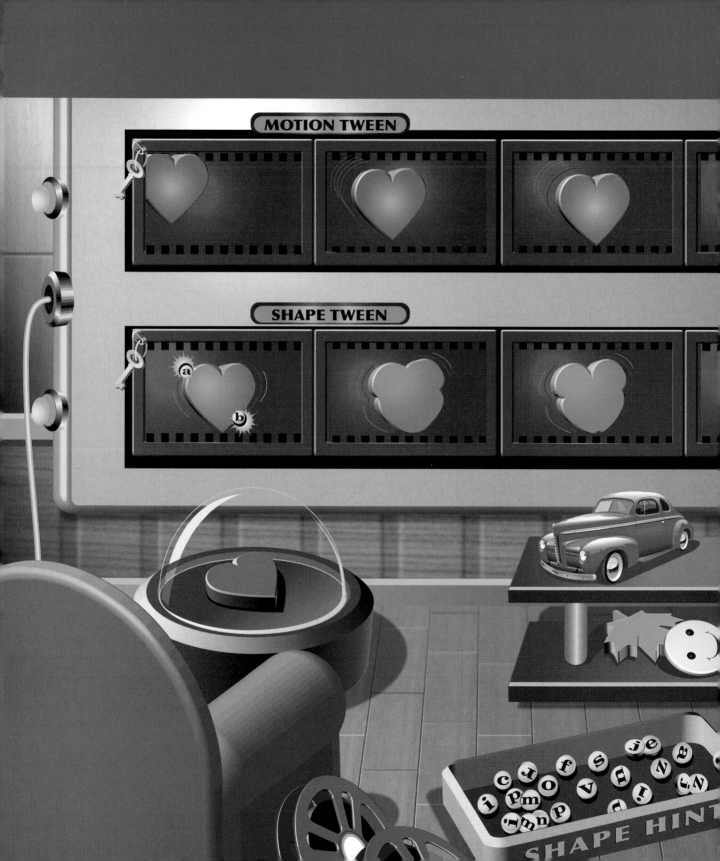

CHAPTER 9

Create Tweened Animations

Flash can help you create animations quickly and efficiently with tweening effects. In this chapter, you will learn how to create motion tweens and shape tweens.

MOVE AN OBJECT USING A MOTION TWEEN

You can create a motion tween to move an object from one location to another on the Stage.

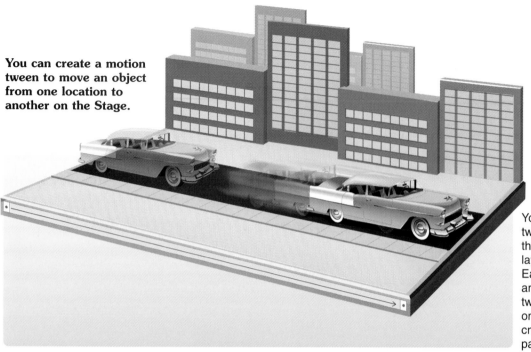

You cannot use a motion tween to move more than one object on a layer in your document. Each object you want to animate using a motion tween must be placed on a different layer. To create a new layer, see page 132.

MOVE AN OBJECT USING A MOTION TWEEN

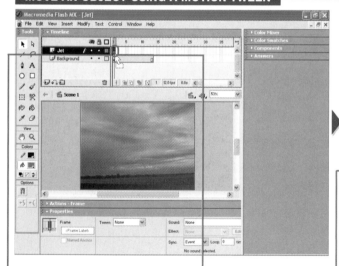

1 Create a keyframe that will display the object you want to move in its starting location.

Note: To create a keyframe, see page 162.

2 Click the keyframe you created in step **1**. The frame is highlighted.

3 Add the object to the Stage in the location where you want the object to appear first.

Note: You can only use a motion tween to animate symbol instances, text or grouped objects. To add a symbol instance to the Stage, see page 116. To add text to the Stage, see page 94. To group objects on the Stage, see page 74.

Why should I use a motion tween instead of creating a frame-by-frame animation?

Motion tweens help you create animations more quickly than frame-by-frame animations. When creating a motion tween, you do not need to create the movement in each frame of the animation as you would with a frame-by-frame animation. You can simply specify two keyframes that each display an object in a different position and then have Flash create the movement for the in-between frames. Motion tweens also require less file space than frame-by-frame animations.

Motion Tween   Frame-By-Frame

4 Create a keyframe that will display the object in its final location.

5 Click the keyframe you created in step **4**. The frame is highlighted.

6 Click ▶ to be able to move the object on the Stage.

7 To move the object to a different location, position the mouse ▷ over the selected object (▷ changes to ▶₊) and then drag the object to the final location.

8 Click the keyframe you created in step **1**. The frame is highlighted.

9 To create a motion tween that will move the object to the new location, click this area to display the available tweens.

Note: If the area is not displayed, see page 16 to display the Property inspector.

10 Click **Motion**.

CONTINUED ▶

MOVE AN OBJECT USING A MOTION TWEEN

When creating a motion tween, you can have the object speed up or slow down as it moves from one location to another.

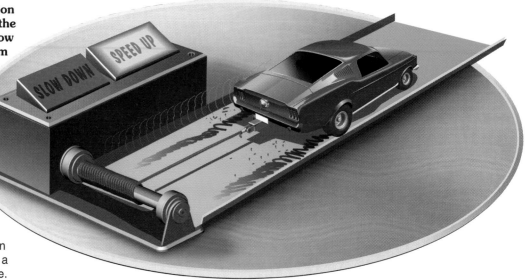

By default, Flash will keep the motion of the object constant. Adjusting the rate of change of the motion can help give the movement a more natural appearance.

■ The frames between the keyframes on the Timeline display an arrow (>———➤) and a light blue color to indicate the motion tween.

■ Flash creates the content for the frames between the two keyframes. Each frame displays the object in a slightly different position.

■11 To control the rate of change of the motion, double-click this area and type a value.

Note: Type a value from 1 to 100 to start the motion quickly and then slow down. Type a value from -1 to -100 to start the motion slowly and then speed up. Type a value of 0 to keep the motion constant.

Can I view the position of the object in multiple frames at the same time?

You can use the onion skinning feature to display the contents of multiple frames at once. This is useful when you want to work with an object in one frame while viewing the position of the object in the surrounding frames. To use the onion skinning feature, see page 178.

How do I change the movement of an object after creating a motion tween?

To change the movement of an object in a motion tween, you can click the frame where you want the movement to change and then reposition the object on the Stage. When you change the position of the object in an in-between frame, Flash converts the in-between frame to a keyframe and then adjusts the motion tween to include the new position of the object.

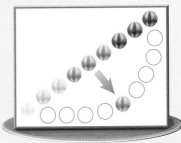

TEST THE ANIMATION

1 To test your animation, click the first keyframe of the motion tween on the Timeline. The frame is highlighted.

2 Press the Enter key (Windows) or the Return key (Macintosh) to play the animation.

■ The animation plays on the Stage.

REMOVE A MOTION TWEEN

1 Click the first keyframe of the motion tween on the Timeline. The frame is highlighted.

2 Click this area to display the available tweens.

Note: If the area is not displayed, see page 16 to display the Property inspector.

3 Click **None** to remove the motion tween.

ROTATE AN OBJECT USING A MOTION TWEEN

You can create a motion tween that will rotate or spin an object on the Stage.

When you create a motion tween, you need to create a keyframe that displays the object at its starting rotation and another keyframe that displays the object at its final rotation. Flash creates the content of the frames between the two keyframes to rotate the object.

Each object you want to rotate using a motion tween must be placed on a different layer in your document. To create a layer, see page 132.

ROTATE AN OBJECT USING A MOTION TWEEN

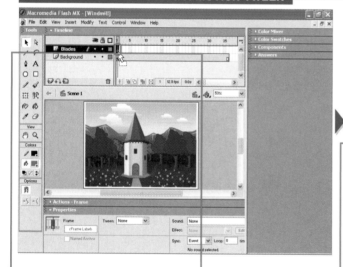

1 Create a keyframe that will display the object you want to rotate.

Note: To create a keyframe, see page 162.

2 Click the keyframe you created in step **1**. The frame is highlighted.

3 Add the object you want to rotate to the Stage.

Note: You can only use a motion tween to rotate symbol instances, text or grouped objects. To add a symbol instance to the Stage, see page 116. To add text to the Stage, see page 94. To group objects on the Stage, see page 74.

Can I have an object perform multiple movements using the same motion tween?

Yes. In addition to rotating, you can have an object perform another movement using the same motion tween. For example, you can have the object move to a new location on the Stage while rotating. After performing step 6 below, move the object to a different location on the Stage.

How do I change the length of time the animation will run?

After you create a motion tween to rotate an object, you can change the amount of time the object will be animated. You can add frames between the two keyframes of the motion tween to increase the animation time or delete frames to decrease the animation time. To add a frame, see page 164. To delete a frame, see page 165.

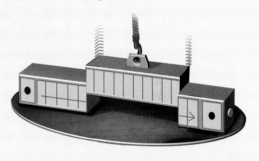

-4 Create a keyframe that will display the object in its final rotation.

-5 Click the keyframe you created in step 4. The frame is highlighted.

-6 If you want the object to appear at a different angle in the final keyframe, rotate the object.

Note: To rotate an object, see page 68.

-7 Click the keyframe you created in step 1. The frame is highlighted.

-8 To create a motion tween that will rotate the object, click this area to display the available tweens.

Note: If the area is not displayed, see page 16 to display the Property inspector.

-9 Click **Motion**.

CONTINUED

ROTATE AN OBJECT USING A MOTION TWEEN

When creating a motion tween that rotates an object, you can specify how you want the object to rotate.

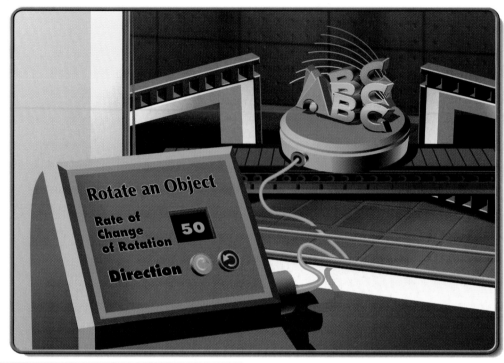

■ The frames between the keyframes on the Timeline display an arrow (>———→) and a light blue color to indicate the motion tween.

■ Flash creates the content for the frames between the two keyframes. Each frame displays the object at a slightly different angle.

10 To control the rate of change of the rotation, double-click this area and type a value.

Note: Type a value from 1 to 100 to start the rotation quickly and then slow down. Type a value from -1 to -100 to start the rotation slowly and then speed up. Type a value of 0 to keep the rotation constant.

How can I rotate an object?

CW

Rotates the object clockwise.

CCW

Rotates the object counterclockwise.

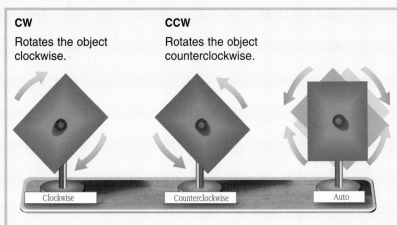

Clockwise

Counterclockwise

Auto

Auto

Rotates the object in the direction that requires the least amount of change. This option is useful when you want to rotate an object less than 360 degrees. The object will rotate only if you have set up the object to appear at a different angle in the final keyframe in your motion tween.

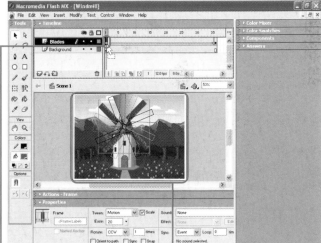

11 To select the way you want to rotate the object, click this area to display the rotation options.

12 Click the way you want to rotate the object.

Note: For information on the available rotation options, see the top of this page.

13 If you selected **CW** or **CCW** in step 12, double-click this area and type the number of times you want the object to rotate.

TEST THE ANIMATION

1 To test your animation, click the first keyframe of the motion tween on the Timeline. The frame is highlighted.

2 Press the Enter key (Windows) or the Return key (Macintosh) to play the animation.

■ The animation plays on the Stage.

RESIZE AN OBJECT USING A MOTION TWEEN

You can create a motion tween that will resize, or scale, an object on the Stage.

When you create a motion tween, you need to create a keyframe that displays the object at its starting size and another keyframe that displays the object at its final size. Flash creates the content of the frames between the two keyframes to change the size of the object.

Each object you want to resize using a motion tween must be placed on a different layer in your document. To create a layer, see page 132.

RESIZE AN OBJECT USING A MOTION TWEEN

1 Create a keyframe that will display the object you want to resize at its starting size.

Note: To create a keyframe, see page 162.

2 Click the keyframe you created in step **1**. The frame is highlighted.

3 Add the object you want to resize to the Stage.

Note: You can only use a motion tween to resize symbol instances, text or grouped objects. To add a symbol instance to the Stage, see page 116. To add text to the Stage, see page 94. To group objects on the Stage, see page 74.

What kind of effects can I create when resizing an object using a motion tween?

You can resize the object in different ways to create various effects. For example, increasing or decreasing the object's size both vertically and horizontally can make the object appear to be zooming out or in. You can change only the height to create the impression of the object growing taller or shorter or you can change only the width to show the object getting wider or narrower.

Can I have an object change in other ways when resizing the object using a motion tween?

In addition to resizing, you can display other changes to the object using the same motion tween. For example, you can also skew, or slant, the object. After performing step **9** below, position the mouse ⊳ over one of the lines surrounding the object (⊳ changes to ⇆ or ⏐). Then drag the mouse ⇆ until the object appears the way you want.

4 Create a keyframe that will display the object at its final size.

5 Click the keyframe you created in step **4**. The frame is highlighted.

6 Click ⊞ to be able to resize the object on the Stage.

7 Click the object on the Stage to select the object. A box with handles (■) appears around the object.

8 Position the mouse ⊳ over a handle (⊳ changes to ↖, ↗, ↕ or ↔).

9 Drag the handle until the object is the size you want.

CONTINUED

RESIZE AN OBJECT USING A MOTION TWEEN

You can control the rate at which Flash will resize the object using a motion tween.

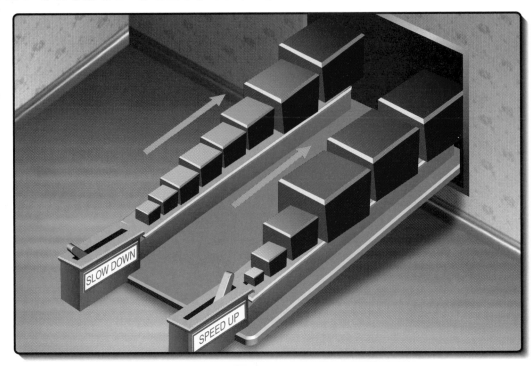

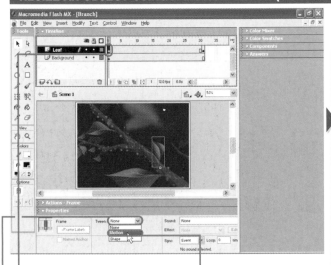

10 Click the keyframe you created in step **1** on page 196. The frame is highlighted.

11 To create a motion tween that will change the size of the object, click this area to display the available tweens.

Note: If the area is not displayed, see page 16 to display the Property inspector.

12 Click **Motion**.

■ The frames between the keyframes on the Timeline display an arrow (>——→) and a light blue color to indicate the motion tween.

13 When the Scale option is on, Flash creates the content for the frames between the two keyframes. Each frame displays the object at a slightly different size. To turn the Scale option on, click **Scale** (☐ changes to ☑).

Can I change the speed of the motion tween?

You can change the speed of the motion tween by inserting or deleting frames between the two keyframes of the motion tween. Adding frames will slow down the motion tween and increase the amount of time the animation will run. Removing frames will speed up the motion tween and cause the animation to run for a shorter time. To add a frame, see page 164. To delete a frame, see page 165.

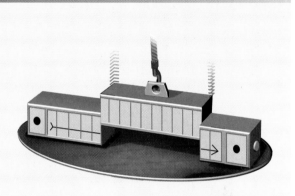

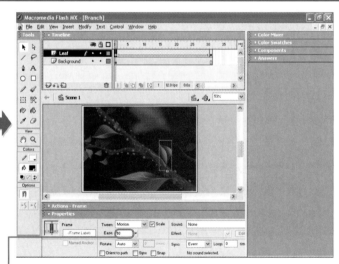

14 To control the rate of change of the animation, double-click this area and type a value.

Note: Type a value from 1 to 100 to start the change quickly and then slow down. Type a value from -1 to -100 to start the change slowly and then speed up. Type a value of 0 to keep the rate of change constant.

TEST THE ANIMATION

1 To test your animation, click the first keyframe of the motion tween on the Timeline. The frame is highlighted.

2 Press the Enter key (Windows) or the Return key (Macintosh) to play the animation.

■ The animation plays on the Stage.

CHANGE THE COLOR OF AN OBJECT USING A MOTION TWEEN

When creating a motion tween that will change the color of an object, you can specify the rate at which you want the color to change.

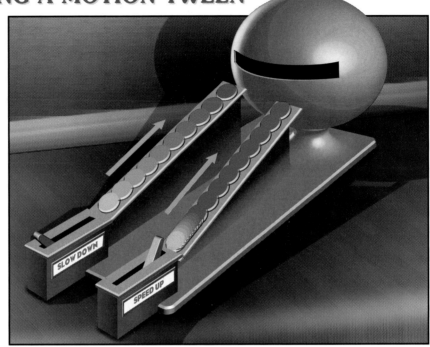

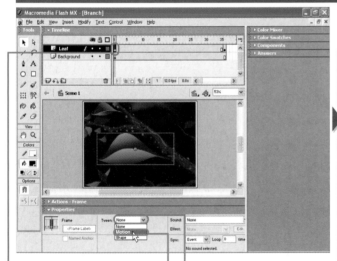

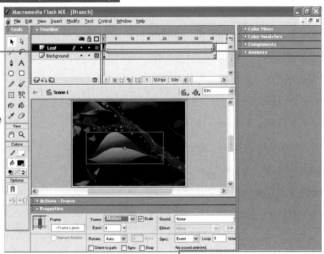

■9 Click the keyframe you created in step 1 on page 200. The frame is highlighted.

■10 To create a motion tween that will gradually change the color of the object, click this area to display the available tweens.

Note: If the area is not displayed, see page 16 to display the Property inspector.

■11 Click **Motion**.

■ The frames between the keyframes on the Timeline display an arrow (>——→) and a light blue color to indicate the motion tween.

■ Flash creates the content for the frames between the two keyframes. Each frame displays the object with a slightly different color.

**Can I have an object display another
change using the same motion tween?**

In addition to changing the color, you
can display other changes to the object
using the same motion tween. For
example, you can also have the object
move to another location on the Stage.
After performing step **8** on page 201,
move the object to a different location
on the Stage. Then perform steps **9** to
12 below.

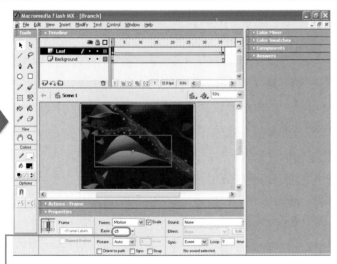

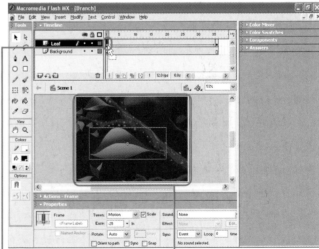

12 To control the rate of
change of the animation,
double-click this area
and type a value.

*Note: Type a value from 1 to
100 to start the change quickly
and then slow down. Type a
value from -1 to -100 to start
the change slowly and then
speed up. Type a value of 0
to keep the rate of change
constant.*

TEST THE ANIMATION

1 To test your animation,
click the first keyframe of
the motion tween on the
Timeline. The frame is
highlighted.

2 Press the `Enter` key
(Windows) or the
`Return` key (Macintosh)
to play the animation.

■ The animation plays
on the Stage.

MOVE AN OBJECT ALONG A PATH USING A MOTION TWEEN

You can create a motion tween that will make an object follow a path you draw.

An object can follow any type of path, such as a curve, a loop or a wave, even if the path goes off the Stage.

MOVE AN OBJECT ALONG A PATH USING A MOTION TWEEN

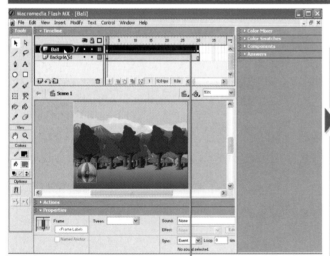

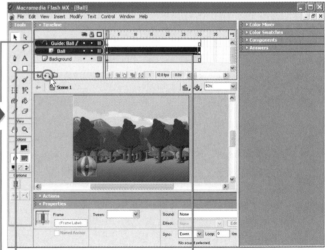

1 Create a motion tween that moves an object from one location to another.

Note: To create a motion tween, see page 188.

2 Click the name of the layer that contains the motion tween you created. The layer is highlighted.

Note: For more information on working with layers, see pages 132 to 143.

3 Click ⊹ to add a new motion guide layer.

■ A new motion guide layer appears. Motion guide layers display the ⊹ icon.

■ The layer that contains the motion tween appears indented below the motion guide layer. This indicates that the motion tween layer is linked to the motion guide layer.

204

How can I view the object's position in the last frame of the animation while I draw the path?

You can use the onion skinning feature to display the contents of multiple frames at once. This allows you to view the position of the object in each frame of the animation while you draw the path you want the object to follow. To use the onion skinning feature, see page 178.

After I create a path, how can I avoid accidentally changing the path?

To avoid changing a path accidentally, you can lock the motion guide layer that contains the path. You cannot make changes to objects on a locked layer. To lock a layer, see page 137.

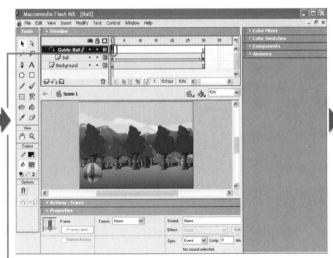

4 Create a keyframe on the motion guide layer directly above the first keyframe of the motion tween.

Note: To create a keyframe, see page 162.

5 To draw the path you want the object to follow, click the Pencil tool ( ).

Note: You can also use another tool, such as the Pen or Brush tool, to draw the motion path.

6 Position the mouse over the object you want to follow a path (changes to).

7 Drag the mouse to draw the path you want the object to follow.

Note: For more information on using the Pencil tool, see page 26.

CONTINUED ▶

MOVE AN OBJECT ALONG A PATH USING A MOTION TWEEN

When moving an object along a path, you can have Flash snap the object to the path and adjust the angle of the object as the object moves along the path.

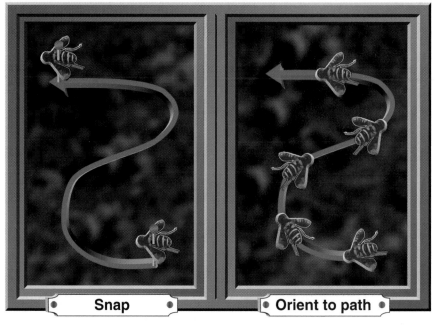

Snap

Orient to path

The **Snap** option automatically snaps the center of the object to the path.

The **Orient to path** option adjusts the angle of the object as the object moves along the path.

MOVE AN OBJECT ALONG A PATH USING A MOTION TWEEN (CONTINUED)

8 Click the first keyframe of the motion tween.

9 To automatically snap the center of the object to the motion path you created, click **Snap** (☐ changes to ☑).

*Note: If **Snap** is not displayed, see page 16 to display the Property inspector.*

10 To change the orientation of the object as the object moves along the path, click **Orient to path** (☐ changes to ☑).

Note: Changing the orientation of the object can make the movement look more natural.

When positioning an object at the end of a path, how can I find the center of the object?

A circle (⊕ or ○) appears at the center of an object to indicate the object's center. If you do not see the center of an object, click the Arrow tool (▶) and then click the object you want to find the center for. Then click the Free Transform tool (▦). You can use the circle to help you align the object's center with the end of the path.

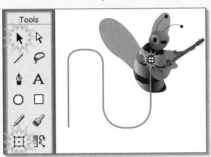

Can I manually change the angle of an object that moves along a path?

If Flash does not position the object the way you want, you can manually adjust the angle of the object on the path. Create a keyframe on the Timeline at the location where you want to change the angle of the object. To create a keyframe, see page 162. Then rotate the object until the object appears the way you want. To rotate objects, see page 68.

11 Click the last keyframe of the motion tween.

■ To ensure the object follows the path you created, the center of the object must align with the end of the path.

12 If the object's center does not align with the end of the path, click ▶ to be able to move the object.

13 To move the object, position the mouse ▶⊕ over the object and then move the object to the end of the path.

TEST THE ANIMATION

1 To test your animation, click the first keyframe of the motion tween on the Timeline. The frame is highlighted.

2 Press the `Enter` key (Windows) or the `Return` key (Macintosh) to play the animation.

■ The animation plays on the Stage.

TRANSFORM AN OBJECT USING A SHAPE TWEEN

You can create a shape tween that will transform one object into another object. Shape tweens create an effect that is similar to morphing.

When you create a shape tween, you need to create a keyframe that displays the original object and another keyframe that displays the final object. Flash creates the content of the frames between the two keyframes to transform the original object into the new object.

TRANSFORM AN OBJECT USING A SHAPE TWEEN

1 Create a keyframe that will display the object you want to transform into another object.

Note: To create a keyframe, see page 162.

2 Click the keyframe you created in step **1**. The frame is highlighted.

3 Draw the object you want to transform into another object.

4 Create a keyframe that will display the object you want the first object to transform into.

5 Click the keyframe you created in step **4**. The frame is highlighted.

6 Draw the object you want the first object to transform into.

How can I transform symbols, grouped objects or text using a shape tween?

To transform a symbol, grouped object or text, you must first break apart the symbol instance or text or ungroup the object. To break apart a symbol instance, see page 124. To break apart text, see page 108. To ungroup an object, see page 75.

Can I use a shape tween to transform more than one object on a layer?

You can use a shape tween to transform more than one object on a layer in your document, but the results of the shape tween can be unpredictable. To obtain more reliable results from your shape tween, you should place each object you want to transform on a different layer in your document. To create a layer, see page 132.

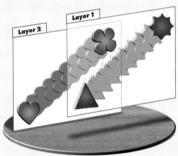

7 Click the keyframe you created in step 1. The frame is highlighted.

8 To create a shape tween that will transform the first object into the second object, click this area to display the available tweens.

Note: If the area is not displayed, see page 16 to display the Property inspector.

9 Click **Shape**.

■ The frames between the keyframes on the Timeline display an arrow (⟶) and a light green color to indicate the shape tween.

■ Flash creates the content for the frames between the two keyframes. Each frame displays the object with a slightly different shape.

CONTINUED

TRANSFORM AN OBJECT USING A SHAPE TWEEN

When creating a shape tween, you can specify the way you want the object to transform into another object.

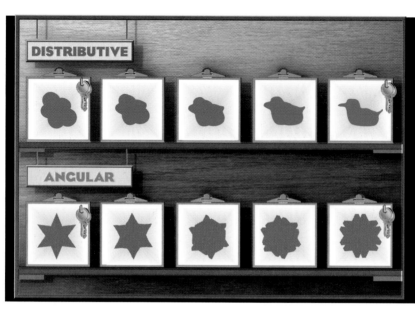

Distributive

Flash smoothes out the edges of the shape in the frames between the keyframes of the animation. This is useful when transforming irregular objects.

Angular

Flash maintains any corners and straight lines on the object in the frames between the keyframes of the animation. This is useful when transforming objects with clearly defined lines and angles.

TRANSFORM AN OBJECT USING A SHAPE TWEEN (CONTINUED)

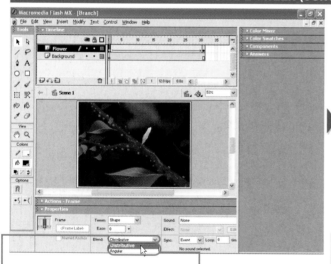

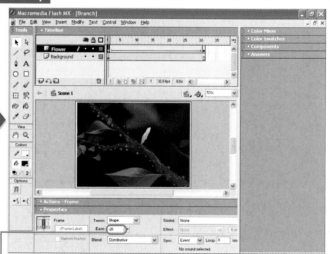

10 Click this area to specify the way you want the object to transform into another object.

11 Click the type of transformation you want to use.

12 To control the rate of change of the transformation, double-click this area and type an acceleration value.

Note: Type a value from 1 to 100 to start the transformation quickly and then slow down. Type a value from -1 to -100 to start the transformation slowly and then speed up. Type a value of 0 to keep the transformation constant.

**Can I have an object display another
change using the same shape tween?**

In addition to transforming the object,
you can display other changes to the
object using the same shape tween.
For example, you can have the object
move to another location on the Stage
while transforming. After performing
step **6** on page 208, move the object
to a different location on the Stage.

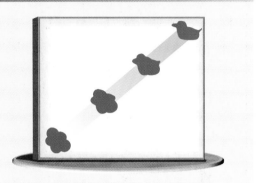

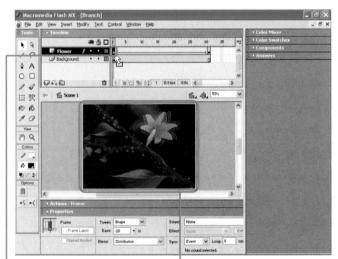

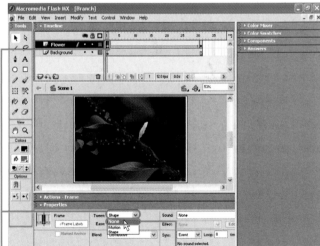

TEST THE ANIMATION

1 To test your animation,
click the first keyframe of
the shape tween on the
Timeline. The frame is
highlighted.

2 Press the Enter key
(Windows) or the
Return key (Macintosh)
to play the animation.

■ The animation plays
on the Stage.

REMOVE A SHAPE TWEEN

1 Click the first keyframe
of the shape tween on the
Timeline. The frame is
highlighted.

2 Click this area to display
the available tweens.

*Note: If the area is not displayed,
see page 16 to display the
Property inspector.*

3 Click **None** to remove
the shape tween.

USE SHAPE HINTS TO IMPROVE A SHAPE TWEEN

After you create a shape tween that transforms one object into another object, you can use shape hints to improve the transformation.

A shape hint helps Flash transform an object by identifying a location on the original object that corresponds with a location on the final object.

USE SHAPE HINTS TO IMPROVE A SHAPE TWEEN

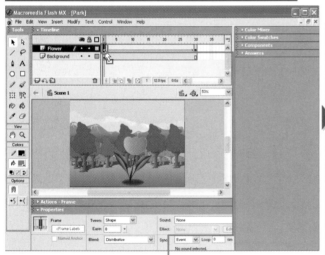

1 Create a shape tween that transforms one object into another object.

Note: To create a shape tween, see page 208.

2 Click the first keyframe in the shape tween. The frame is highlighted.

3 Click **Modify**.

4 Click **Shape**.

5 Click **Add Shape Hint**.

TEACH YOURSELF

Is there anything else I can do to improve a shape tween?

When using a shape tween to transform a complex object, you may want to consider creating several different shape tweens that will perform the transformation in small segments. Shorter shape tweens can provide more control over the way the object transforms and are usually simpler to work with than one large shape tween.

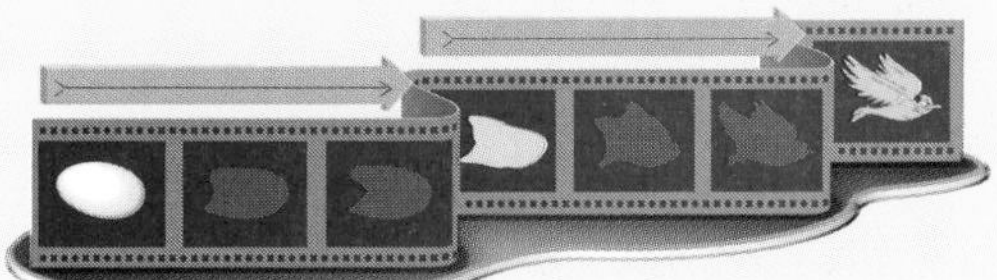

TEACH YOURSELF

Is there a faster way to add shape hints?

Yes. You can use your keyboard to quickly add shape hints. Click the first keyframe in the shape tween. On a Windows computer, press and hold down the Ctrl and Shift keys as you press the H key. On a Macintosh computer, press and hold down the ⌘ and Shift keys as you press the H key.

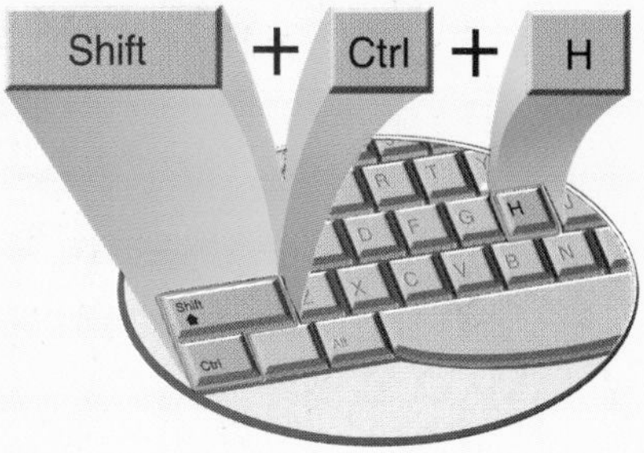

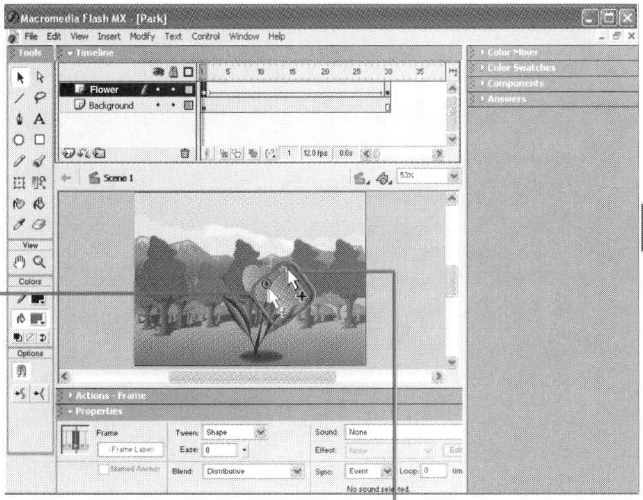

■ The shape hint appears in the middle of the object as a red circle, labeled with the letter 'a'.

6 To move the shape hint to a location on the object that will correspond to a location on the final object, position the mouse over the shape hint (changes to).

7 Drag the shape hint to the new location.

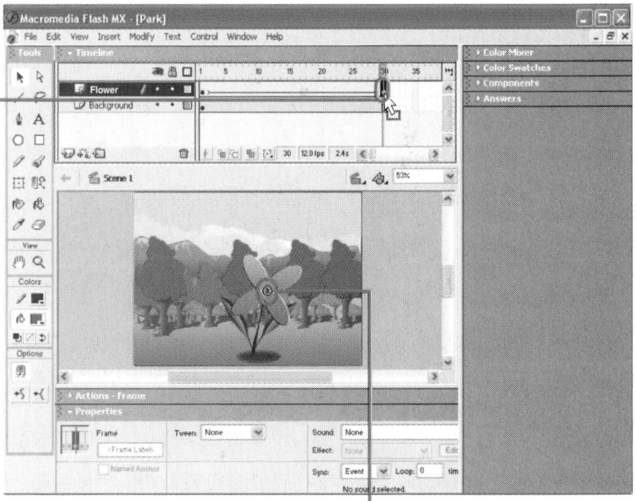

8 Click the last keyframe in the shape tween. The frame is highlighted.

■ A corresponding shape hint labeled with the letter 'a' appears in the middle of the object.

CONTINUED

USE SHAPE HINTS TO IMPROVE A SHAPE TWEEN

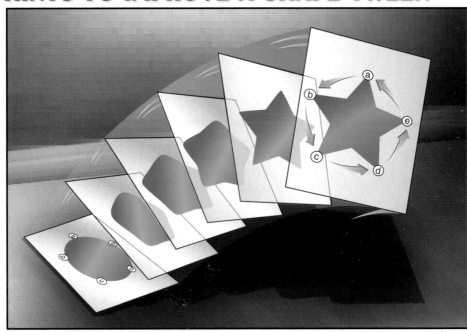

When using shape hints, you must position the shape hints in corresponding locations on the original and final shapes.

To achieve the best results from your shape hints, you should arrange the shape hints counterclockwise and in alphabetical order on both the original and final shapes of the animation.

USE SHAPE HINTS TO IMPROVE A SHAPE TWEEN (CONTINUED)

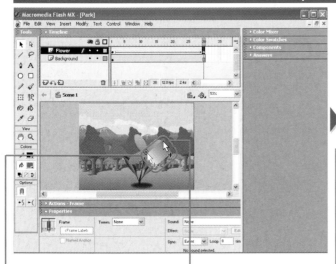

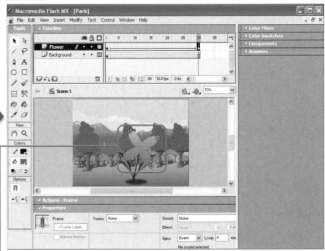

9 To move the shape hint to a location that corresponds with the shape hint you added to the original object, position the mouse over the shape hint (changes to).

10 Drag the shape hint to the corresponding location on the object.

Note: After you move the shape hint, the shape hint on the final object may change to green and the shape hint on the original object may change to yellow.

11 To add more shape hints to other areas on the original and final objects, repeat steps **2** to **10** for each shape hint you want to add.

Note: Flash labels the shape hints alphabetically from a to z. You can add up to 26 shape hints.

How can I quickly remove all the shape hints I added to the Stage?

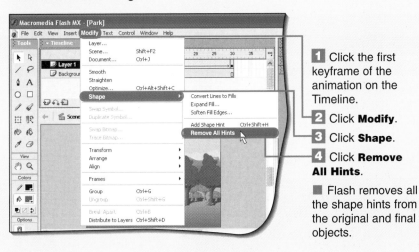

1 Click the first keyframe of the animation on the Timeline.

2 Click **Modify**.

3 Click **Shape**.

4 Click **Remove All Hints**.

■ Flash removes all the shape hints from the original and final objects.

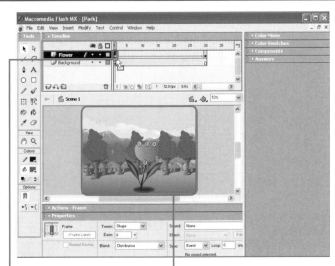

TEST THE ANIMATION

1 To test how the shape hints you added improve the animation, click the first keyframe of the shape tween on the Timeline. The frame is highlighted.

2 Press the Enter key (Windows) or the Return key (Macintosh) to play the animation.

■ The animation plays on the Stage.

Note: To fine-tune the animation, you can reposition the shape hints on the original and final objects.

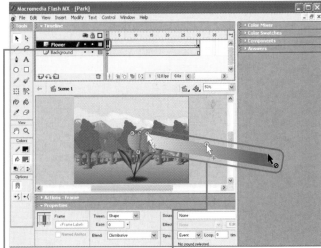

REMOVE A SHAPE HINT

1 Click the first keyframe of the shape tween on the Timeline. The frame is highlighted.

2 To remove a shape hint, position the mouse over the shape hint (changes to) and then drag the shape hint out of the work area.

■ Flash removes the shape hint. Flash also removes the corresponding shape hint from the object in the final keyframe.

CHAPTER 10

Add and Work With Scenes

Scenes help you organize your movie. This chapter shows you how to add, delete, rename, switch between, rearrange and preview scenes.

DELETE A

1 Click **Win**

2 Click **Sce**

ADD O[ ] REARRANGE SCENES

You can add s[ ]
to a movie to [ ]
organize the c[ ]
of the movie. [ ]
scene has its o[ ]
Timeline and S[ ]
You can also d[ ]
scene you no l[ ]
want to appea[ ]
movie.

You can rearrange
the scenes in a
movie. When you
play the movie,
the scenes will
play in the order
you specify.

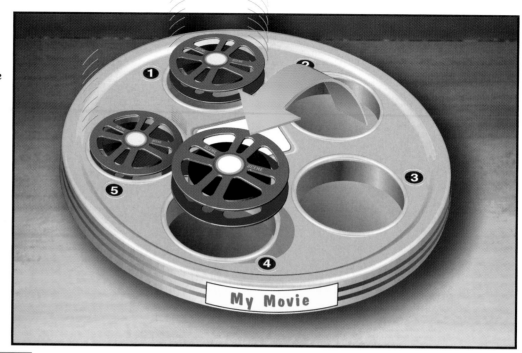

ADD A SCENE

1 Click Windo[ ]

2 Click Scene[ ]

REARRANGE SCENES

1 Click Window.

2 Click Scene.

■ The Scene panel
appears.

■ This area displays a
list of all the scenes in
the movie.

3 Position the mouse
over the name of the scene
you want to move and then
drag the scene up or down
to a new location in the list
of scenes.

Note: A line indicates where the
scene will appear in the list.

4 Click ⊠ (Windows)
or ☐ (Macintosh) to
close the Scene panel.

You can preview
a scene in the
Flash Player
to view all the
animation you
included in the
scene.

When you preview
a scene in the Flash
Player, Flash exports
the movie and saves
the movie as a new
file in the same
location as your
Flash document.
For information on
exporting a movie,
see page 286.

PREVIEW A SCENE

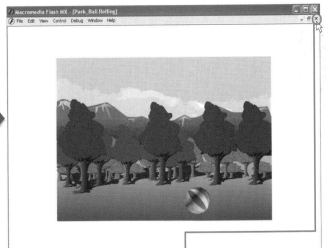

1 Click **Control**.

2 Click **Test Scene**.

■ The Exporting Flash
Movie dialog box briefly
appears, showing the
progress of exporting
the movie.

■ Flash opens the Flash
Player and plays the scene.

*Note: The scene plays repeatedly
until you stop the scene.*

■ To stop or resume playing
the scene at any time, press
the `Enter` key (Windows) or
the `Return` key (Macintosh).

3 When you finish
previewing the scene,
click ⊠ (Windows)
or ☐ (Macintosh) to
close the Flash Player.

*Note: To preview the current
scene on the Stage or preview
the entire movie in the Flash
Player, see page 170.*

CHAPTER 11

Add Buttons and Sounds

Read this chapter to find out how to add interactivity and interest to your movie by creating buttons and adding sounds.

CREATE A BUTTON

You can create an interactive button that changes in appearance when you position the mouse pointer over the button or click the button.

Flash stores each button you create in the document's library.

CREATE A BUTTON

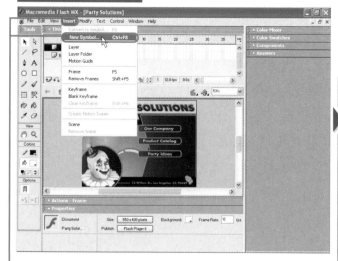

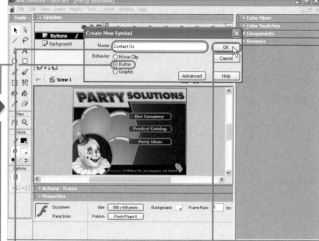

1 Click **Insert**.

2 Click **New Symbol**.

■ The Create New Symbol dialog box appears.

3 Type a name for the new button.

4 Click **Button** to create a button (○ changes to ◉).

5 Click **OK** to create the button.

What are the four states of a button?

Flash provides four states that you can use to specify how a button will look and work.

Up	**Over**
Shows the initial appearance of a button, before a user positions the mouse over the button or clicks the button. 	Shows the appearance of a button when a user positions the mouse over the button. 
Down	**Hit**
Shows the appearance of a button when a user clicks the button.	Represents the area a user can click to select the button. The graphic for the Hit state will not appear in your movie. 

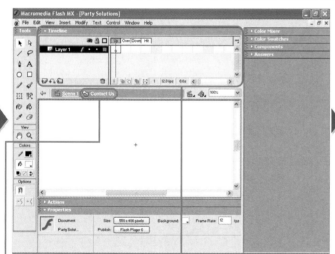

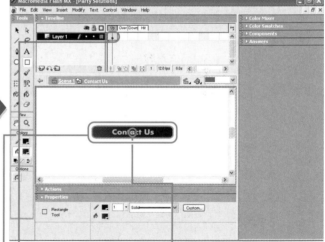

■ Flash opens in symbol-editing mode.

■ The name of the button you are creating appears in this area.

■ This area displays the Timeline for the button. The Timeline displays a frame for each of the button's states.

Note: For information on the states of a button, see the top of this page.

6 Click the **Up** frame. The frame is highlighted.

Note: Flash automatically creates a keyframe for the Up button state.

7 Create the graphic you want the button to display when the mouse ⬚ is not positioned over the button.

Note: To draw objects, see pages 26 to 37. To import a graphic, see page 150.

■ The crosshair (+) in the middle of the Stage indicates the center of the drawing area.

CONTINUED ▸

CREATE A BUTTON

You can make changes to the graphic for a button in each button state.

For example, you can change the color or shape of a button graphic for each button state.

CREATE A BUTTON (CONTINUED)

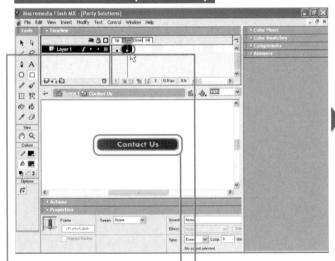

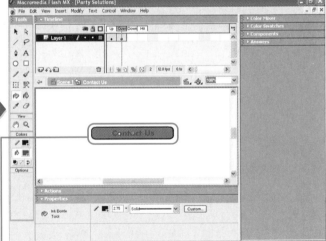

8 To specify the way you want the button to appear for another button state, create a keyframe for the button state. To create a keyframe, see page 162.

9 Click the keyframe you created in step **8**. The frame is highlighted.

■ Flash copies the graphic from the previous button state to the new keyframe so you can easily make changes to the graphic.

10 Change the graphic for the button to specify the appearance of the button for this button state. For example, you can change the color of the graphic.

Can I have a button display a different graphic for each button state?

Yes. You can use a different graphic for each button state rather than making changes to a single graphic for each state. To add a new graphic to a button state, create a blank keyframe in the frame for the state. You can then draw or import the graphic you want to use in the blank keyframe. To add a blank keyframe, see page 163.

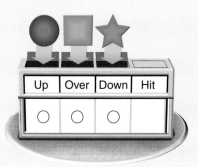

How can I create an animated button?

You can create an animated button by adding a movie clip to the Up, Over or Down frame for a button. To add a movie clip to a button frame, create a blank keyframe in the frame for the button state you want to display the movie clip. You can then add a movie clip to the blank keyframe as you would add a movie clip to any keyframe in your movie.

To add a blank keyframe, see page 163. To add a movie clip, see page 184.

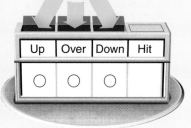

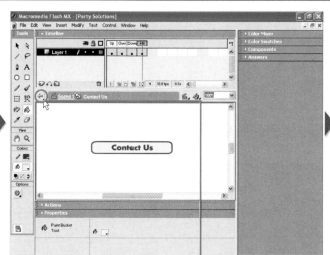

11 To change the graphic for the other button states, repeat steps **8** to **10** for each button state.

12 When you finish creating the button, click to return to the document.

■ The document reappears on the screen.

■ Flash adds the button to the document's library.

Note: The button does not appear on the Stage.

■ You can now add the button to your movie. To add a button to a movie, see page 230.

ADD A BUTTON TO A MOVIE

After you create a button, you can add the button anywhere in your movie.

When you add a button stored in the library to a movie, you create an instance of the button. Using a button more than once in your movie will not increase the file size of the movie.

ADD A BUTTON TO A MOVIE

1 Create a keyframe where you want to add a button. To create a keyframe, see page 162.

2 Click the keyframe you created in step **1**. The frame is highlighted.

3 To display the library for the current document, click **Window**.

4 Click **Library**.

■ The Library panel appears.

■ This area displays the items in the library. Buttons display the 🖘 icon.

5 Click the name of the button you want to add to your movie. The name of the button is highlighted.

■ This area displays the appearance of the button's Up state.

How do I remove a button from the Stage?

To remove a button from the Stage, click ▶ and then click the button. Then press the Delete key.

Can I delete a button from the document's library?

Yes. Perform steps 3 and 4 on page 230 to display the Library panel. Click the name of the button you want to delete and then click 🗑 in the Library panel. Click **Delete** in the confirmation dialog box that appears. When you delete a button from the library, Flash also deletes all the instances of the button in your movie.

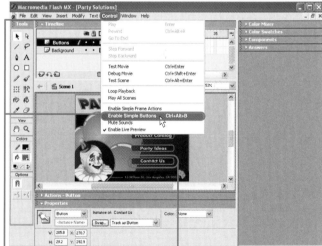

■ To preview the appearance of the button's other states, click ▶.

6 To add the button to the movie, position the mouse ▷ over the name of the button.

7 Drag the button to the location on the Stage where you want the button to appear.

■ An instance of the button appears on the Stage.

8 To close the Library panel, click ✕ (Windows) or ▨ (Macintosh).

TEST A BUTTON

1 To be able to test a button to ensure the button works as you intended, click **Control**.

2 Click **Enable Simple Buttons**.

3 To test a button, position the mouse 🖑 over the button and click the button to test the button states.

Note: When you finish testing a button, repeat steps 1 and 2 to disable simple buttons so you can once again select and work with buttons on the Stage.

IMPORT A SOUND

You can import a sound file into Flash so you can play the sound in your movie.

You can obtain sounds on the Internet, purchase collections of sounds at computer stores or record your own sounds using a sound recording program.

IMPORT A SOUND

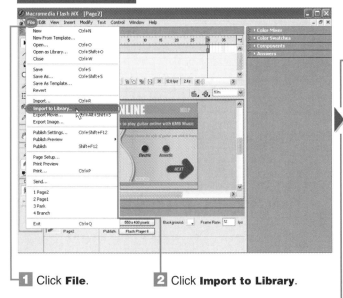

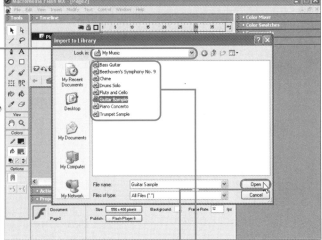

1 Click **File**.

2 Click **Import to Library**.

■ The Import to Library dialog box appears.

■ This area shows the location of the displayed files. You can click this area to change the location.

3 Click the sound file you want to import.

4 Click **Open** to import the sound file.

What types of sound files can I import?

When using a Windows computer, you can import WAV or MP3 sound files. When using a Macintosh computer, you can import AIFF or MP3 sound files. If you have QuickTime 4 or later installed on your computer, you can import WAV, AIFF or MP3 sound files, regardless of whether you use a Windows or Macintosh computer. You can obtain QuickTime at computer stores or at the www.apple.com/quicktime Web site.

Is there anything I should keep in mind when importing sound files?

When importing sound files, you should keep in mind that adding sound files to a movie can significantly increase the file size of the movie. You should try to use sounds with small file sizes whenever possible. For example, MP3 sound files have smaller file sizes than WAV or AIFF sound files, since MP3 sound files are compressed.

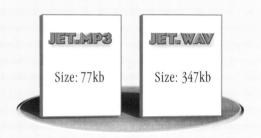

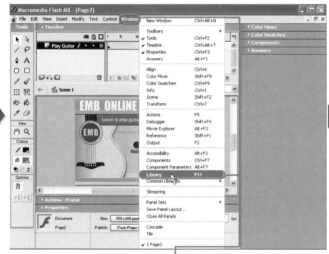

■ Flash imports the sound file and adds the sound file to the document's library.

■ You can now add the sound file to your movie. To add a sound to a movie, see page 234.

VIEW THE SOUND FILE IN THE LIBRARY

1 To display the library for the current document, click **Window**.

2 Click **Library**.

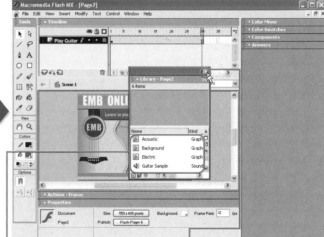

■ The Library panel appears.

■ This area displays the items in the library. Sound files you have imported display the ◀ icon.

3 To close the Library panel, click ✕ (Windows) or ▊ (Macintosh).

ADD A SOUND TO A MOVIE

You can add a sound to a movie to have a sound effect, background music or narration play in the movie.

ADD A SOUND TO A MOVIE

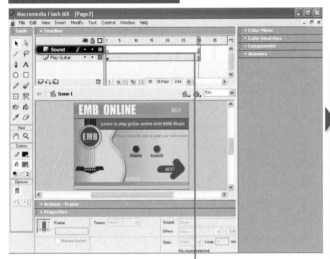

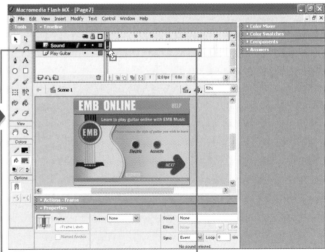

■ Before you can add a sound to a movie, you must import the sound you want to use. To import a sound, see page 232.

1 Add a new layer for the sound you want to add. To add a layer, see page 132.

Note: Creating a new layer for each sound you add to your movie will help you organize your sounds.

2 Create a keyframe on the sound layer where you want a sound to start playing. To create a keyframe, see page 162.

3 Click the keyframe you created in step **2**. The frame is highlighted.

**Does Flash include
sounds I can add to
my movie?**

Yes. Flash provides
a sounds library that
contains sounds you
can use in your movies.

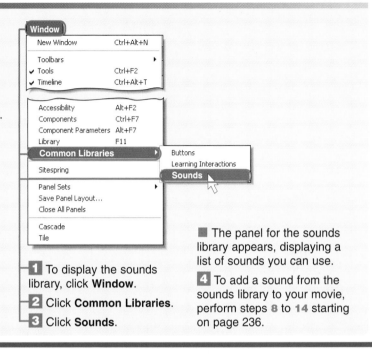

-1 To display the sounds
library, click **Window**.

-2 Click **Common Libraries**.

-3 Click **Sounds**.

■ The panel for the sounds
library appears, displaying a
list of sounds you can use.

4 To add a sound from the
sounds library to your movie,
perform steps 8 to 14 starting
on page 236.

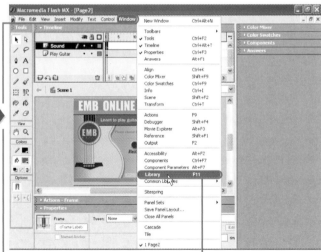

-4 To display the library
that stores the sounds you
have imported into the
document, click **Window**.

5 Click **Library**.

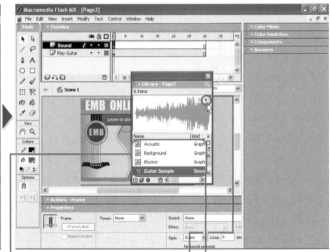

■ The Library panel appears.

■ This area displays the
items in the library. Sounds
display the ◄ icon.

6 Click the name of the
sound you want to add to
your movie. The sound is
highlighted.

-7 To play the sound,
click ▶.

CONTINUED ▶

ADD A SOUND TO A MOVIE

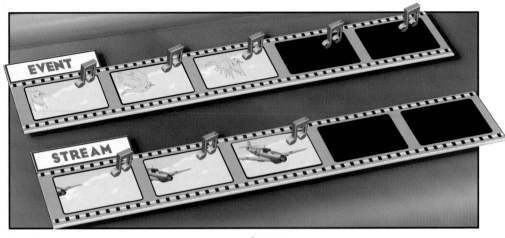

When adding a sound to a movie, you can specify the way you want Flash to synchronize the sound in the movie.

You can choose the Event or Stream synchronization option.

Event

Synchronizes the beginning of the sound with a keyframe and plays the entire sound, even if the sound continues playing after the movie ends. The Event option is useful for brief sounds.

Stream

Synchronizes the entire sound with the frames in a movie, so the movie plays at the same speed as the sound. When the movie stops playing, the sound also stops. The Stream option is useful for long sounds, such as background music or narration.

ADD A SOUND TO A MOVIE (CONTINUED)

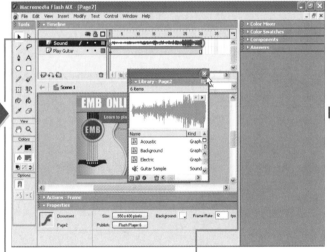

■8 To add the sound to the movie, position the mouse Ⓚ over the name of the sound.

■9 Drag the sound to the Stage.

■ A graphical representation of the sound appears on the Timeline.

Note: A graphical representation of the sound does not appear on the Stage.

■10 To close the Library panel, click ☒ (Windows) or ▨ (Macintosh).

TEACH YOURSELF
TY

How do I remove a sound from my movie?

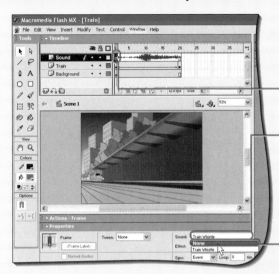

1 Click the keyframe that contains the sound you want to remove.

2 Click the Sound area in the Property inspector. The Sound area displays the name of the sound.

Note: If the Sound area is not displayed, see page 16 to display the Property inspector.

3 Click **None** to remove the sound.

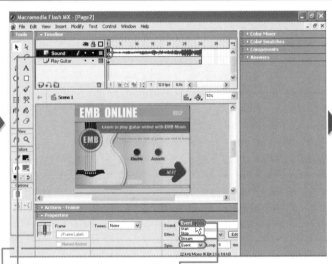

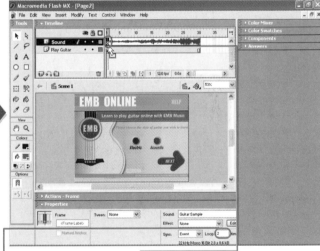

11 Click the keyframe you added the sound to. The frame is highlighted.

12 Click this area to display a list of the available synchronization options.

Note: If the area is not displayed, see page 16 to display the Property inspector.

13 Click **Event** or **Stream** to select the synchronization option you want to use.

Note: For information on the Start and Stop synchronization options, see page 242.

14 If you want the sound to play more than once, double-click this area and type the number of times you want the sound to play.

*Note: If you selected **Stream** in step **13**, playing the sound more than once will increase the file size.*

TEST A SOUND

1 To test the sound you added to a movie, click the first keyframe on the Timeline.

2 Press the Enter key (Windows) or the Return key (Macintosh).

■ When the movie reaches the frame that contains the sound, the sound will play.

ADD A SOUND EFFECT

After adding a sound to your movie, you can add a sound effect to change the way the sound plays in your movie.

Flash offers several sound effects that you can choose from. You can also create your own custom sound effect.

Adding a sound effect to a sound in your movie will not affect any other instances of the sound in the movie.

ADD A SOUND EFFECT

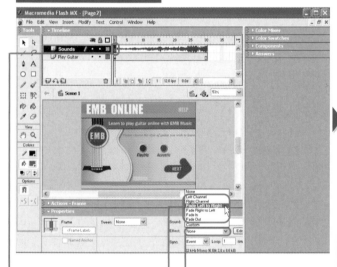

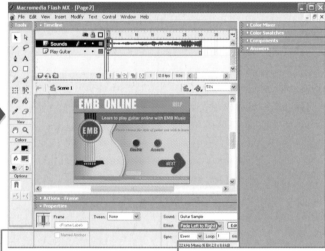

1 Click the keyframe that contains the sound you want to add a sound effect to. The frame is highlighted.

2 Click this area to display a list of the available sound effects.

Note: If the area is not displayed, see page 16 to display the Property inspector.

3 Click the sound effect you want to use.

■ The sound effect you selected appears in this area.

■ To test the sound effect, click the keyframe that contains the sound on the Timeline and then press the `Enter` key (Windows) or the `Return` key (Macintosh) to play the movie with the sound.

What are the sound effects that Flash offers?

Flash offers six sound effects you can choose from to quickly change the way a sound plays in your movie.

Sound Effect	Description
Left Channel	Plays the sound only in the left speaker.
Right Channel	Plays the sound only in the right speaker.
Fade Left to Right	Moves the sound from the left speaker to the right speaker.
Fade Right to Left	Moves the sound from the right speaker to the left speaker.
Fade In	Gradually increases the volume of the sound.
Fade Out	Gradually decreases the volume of the sound.

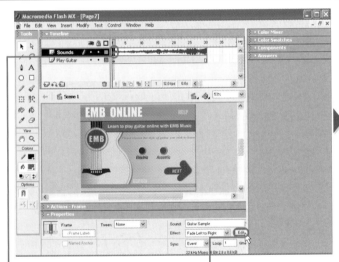

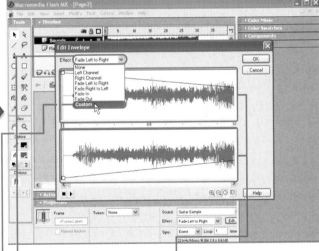

CREATE A CUSTOM SOUND EFFECT

1 Click the keyframe that contains the sound you want to add a custom sound effect to. The frame is highlighted.

2 Click **Edit**.

Note: If the Edit button is not displayed, see page 16 to display the Property inspector.

■ The Edit Envelope dialog box appears.

3 Click this area to display a list of the available sound effects.

4 Click **Custom** to create a custom sound effect.

■ These areas display a graphical representation of the sound that will play for the left and right channels.

Note: The left and right channels determine the sound that plays in the left and right speakers.

CONTINUED

ADD A SOUND EFFECT

When creating a custom sound effect for a sound, you can adjust the volume of different parts of the sound and change the length of the sound.

Although Flash allows you to perform simple sound editing tasks, Flash is not a sound editing program. To perform more advanced tasks, you should use a full-featured sound editing program, such as Sonic Foundry's Sound Forge.

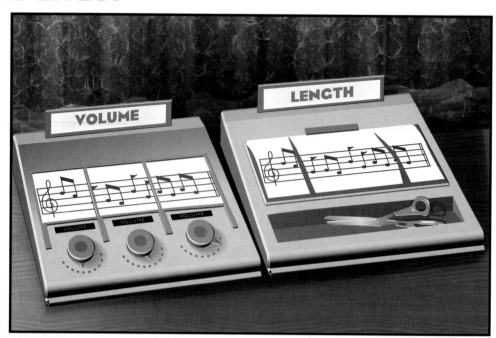

ADD A SOUND EFFECT (CONTINUED)

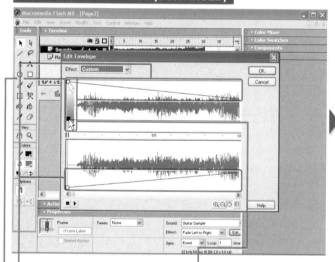

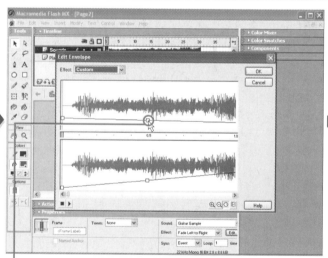

■ Thin black lines indicate the volume of the sound for each channel. The handles (□) on the lines allow you to adjust the volume.

5 To adjust the volume for a specific portion of the sound in a channel, position the mouse ▹ over a handle (□).

6 Drag the handle (□) up or down to raise or lower the volume of the sound in the channel.

Note: Adjusting the volume in one channel will not affect the volume in the other channel.

7 To add another handle (□) to adjust the volume for a different portion of the sound, click the location in the sound where you want to add the handle.

Note: Flash allows you to use up to 8 handles in each channel. When you add a handle in one channel, Flash automatically adds a corresponding handle to the other channel.

**How can I remove a sound effect I
added to a sound in my movie?**

1 Click the keyframe that
contains the sound you want
to remove a sound effect
from on the Timeline.

2 This area displays the
name of the sound effect you
added to the sound. Click
this area to display a list of
sound effects.

*Note: If the area is not displayed,
see page 16 to display the Property
inspector.*

3 Click **None** to remove the
sound effect from the sound.

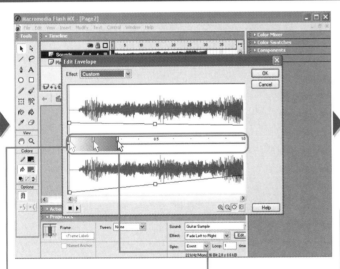

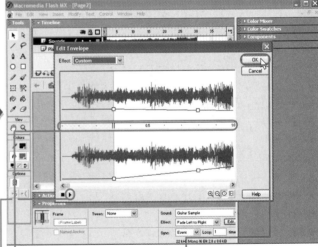

■ The white area on the
ruler indicates the length of
the sound. The sliders ([])
allow you to change the start
and end points of the sound.

8 To change the length
of the sound, position the
mouse ↳ over a slider ([]).

9 Drag the slider to
the right or left until it
appears where you
want to start or stop
the sound.

■ The white area on the
ruler moves to line up with
the new position of the
slider ([]). Flash will not
play the portion of the
sound that appears outside
the white area.

10 To play the sound with
all the changes you made,
click ▶ to play the sound.

*Note: You can click ■ to stop
playing the sound at any time.*

11 Click **OK** to confirm
all your changes.

START AND STOP SOUNDS

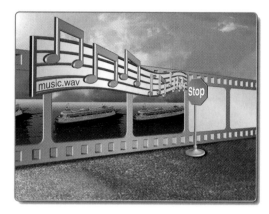

After adding a sound to your movie, you can add start and stop sounds to have the sound play again or stop playing.

Start Sound

Specifies where you want a sound to start playing again. The sound plays again only if the first instance of the sound has finished playing. This prevents the sounds from overlapping.

Stop Sound

Specifies where you want a sound to stop playing. For example, if your sound is longer than your animation, you may want to stop the sound from playing when your animation ends. A stop sound will stop all instances of the sound that are currently playing.

START A SOUND

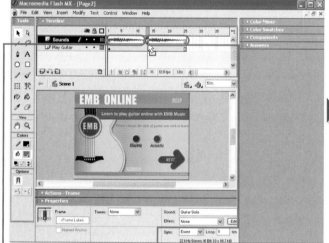

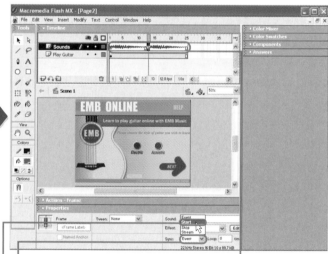

■1 Add a sound to your movie where you want the sound to start playing. To add a sound to your movie, see page 234.

■2 To specify where you want the sound to play again, add the same sound you added in step 1 to the keyframe in your movie where you want the sound to play again.

■3 Click the keyframe where you added the sound in step 2. The frame is highlighted.

■4 Click this area to display a list of the available synchronization options.

Note: If the area is not displayed, see page 16 to display the Property inspector.

■5 Click **Start**.

■ When the movie plays and reaches the first sound, the sound will play. When the movie reaches the start sound, the sound will play again only if the first sound has finished playing.

Note: To test sounds in your movie, see page 237.

How do I remove a start or stop sound I added to my movie?

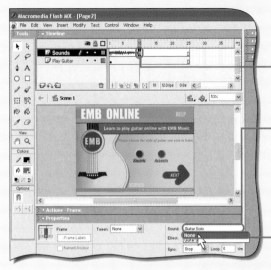

1 To remove a start or stop sound, click the keyframe that contains the start or stop sound.

2 Click the Sound area in the Property inspector. The Sound area displays the name of the sound.

Note: If the Sound area is not displayed, see page 16 to display the Property inspector.

3 Click **None** to remove the start or stop sound.

STOP A SOUND

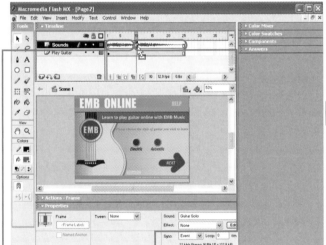

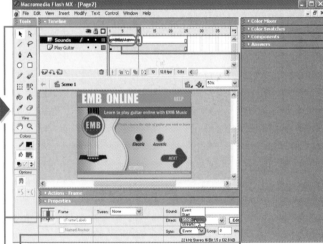

1 Add a sound to your movie where you want the sound to start playing. To add a sound to your movie, see page 234.

2 To specify where you want the sound to stop playing, add the same sound you added in step **1** to the keyframe in your movie where you want the sound to stop playing.

3 Click the keyframe where you added the sound in step **2**. The frame is highlighted.

4 Click this area to display a list of the available synchronization options.

Note: If the area is not displayed, see page 16 to display the Property inspector.

5 Click **Stop**.

■ A rectangle (🔲) appears in the keyframe to indicate that the frame contains a stop sound.

■ When the movie plays and reaches the first sound, the sound will play. When the movie reaches the stop sound, the sound will stop playing.

Note: To test sounds in your movie, see page 237.

ADD SOUNDS TO A BUTTON

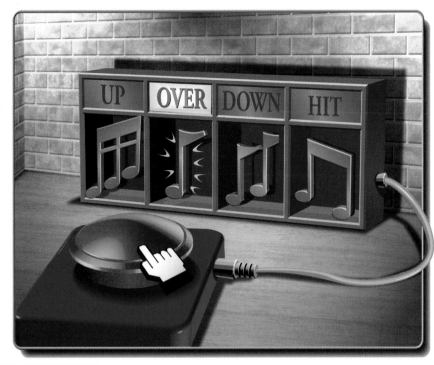

You can add sounds to a button to add interactivity and flair to the button.

Up - The sound plays when a user moves the mouse 🔓 away from the button.

Over - The sound plays when a user positions the mouse 🖐 over the button.

Down - The sound plays when a user clicks the button.

Hit - The sound plays when a user releases the mouse button after clicking within the active button area.

ADD SOUNDS TO A BUTTON

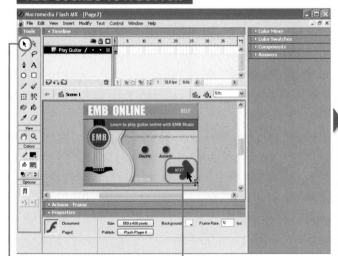

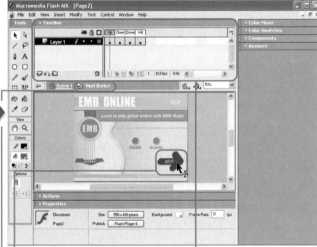

■ Before adding sounds to a button, make sure you import the sounds you want to use into Flash. To import sounds, see page 232.

1 Click 🔧 to be able to select a button on the Stage.

Note: To create a button, see page 226.

2 Double-click the button you want to add sounds to.

■ The button opens in symbol-editing mode. All other objects on the Stage are dimmed.

■ When you are working in symbol-editing mode, the name of the button you are editing appears in this area.

■ This area displays the button's Timeline. The Timeline displays a frame for each of the button's states.

Note: For information on the states of a button, see the top of this page.

Does Flash offer any pre-made buttons I can use?

Yes. Flash includes a buttons library that contains buttons you can use in your movies.

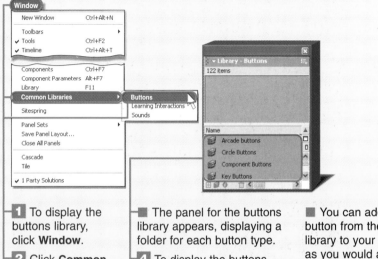

■ **1** To display the buttons library, click **Window**.

2 Click **Common Libraries**.

3 Click **Buttons**.

■ The panel for the buttons library appears, displaying a folder for each button type.

4 To display the buttons in a folder, double-click ![folder] beside the name of the folder.

■ You can add a button from the buttons library to your movie as you would add any button. To add a button, see page 230.

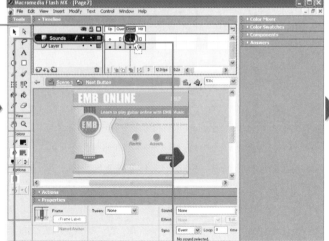

3 Add a new layer for the sounds you want to add to the button. To add a layer, see page 132.

4 Create a keyframe on the sound layer that corresponds to the button state you want to add a sound to.

Note: Flash automatically adds a keyframe to the Up button state. To create a keyframe, see page 162.

5 Click the keyframe you created in step **4**. The frame is highlighted.

6 To display the library for the current document, click **Window**.

7 Click **Library**.

■ The Library panel appears.

CONTINUED

245

ADD SOUNDS TO A BUTTON

After adding a sound to a button, you can test the button to preview how the sound will play.

When you add a sound to a button, Flash automatically adds the sound to every instance of the button in your movie.

ADD SOUNDS TO A BUTTON (CONTINUED)

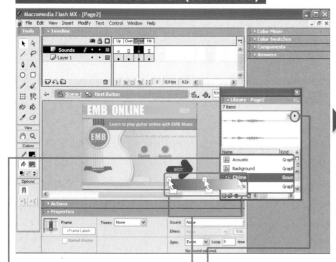

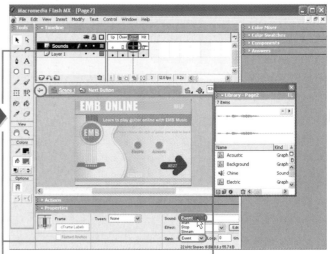

■ This area displays the items in the library. Sounds display the 🔊 icon.

8 Click the name of the sound you want to add to the button. The sound is highlighted.

9 To play the sound, click ▶.

10 To add the sound to the button, position the mouse ⇖ over the name of the sound.

11 Drag the sound to the Stage.

■ A graphical representation of the sound appears on the Timeline.

12 Click the keyframe you created in step **4**. The frame is highlighted.

13 Click this area to display a list of the available synchronization options.

Note: If the area is not displayed, see page 16 to display the Property inspector.

14 Click **Event**.

Note: To add a sound to another button state, repeat steps 4 to 14 starting on page 245.

15 To return to the document, click ⮌.

How do I remove a sound I added to a button?

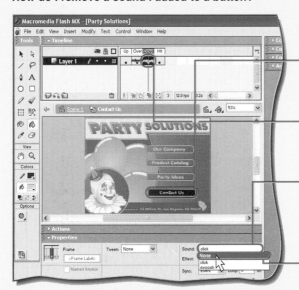

1 Double-click the button in your document to open the button in symbol-editing mode.

2 On the sound layer, click the keyframe for the button state you want to remove the sound from.

3 Click the Sound area in the Property inspector.

Note: If the Sound area is not displayed, see page 16 to display the Property inspector.

4 Click **None** to remove the sound.

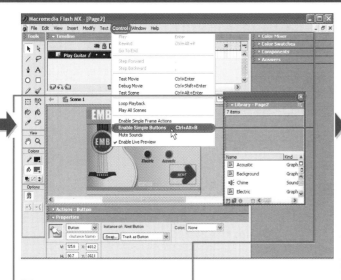

■ The document reappears on the screen.

16 To close the Library panel, click ☒ (Windows) or ▨ (Macintosh).

TEST A BUTTON

1 To be able to test the sounds you added to a button, click **Control**.

2 Click **Enable Simple Buttons**.

3 To test a button, position the mouse 🖑 over the button, move the mouse 🖑 away from the button or click the button to play the sound you added to the button.

Note: When you finish testing a button, repeat steps 1 and 2 to disable simple buttons so you can once again select and work with buttons on the Stage.

Go to Frame 33

Go To
Stop
Play Sounds
Load Movie
Get URL

GO TO
FRAME
27

CHAPTER 12

Add Flash Actions

An action tells Flash to perform a specific task. This chapter shows you how to add an action to your movie to perform tasks such as jumping to a specific frame or scene in the movie or stop playing all sounds in the movie.

STOP AND PLAY A MOVIE

You can assign the stop action to a button or keyframe in your movie.

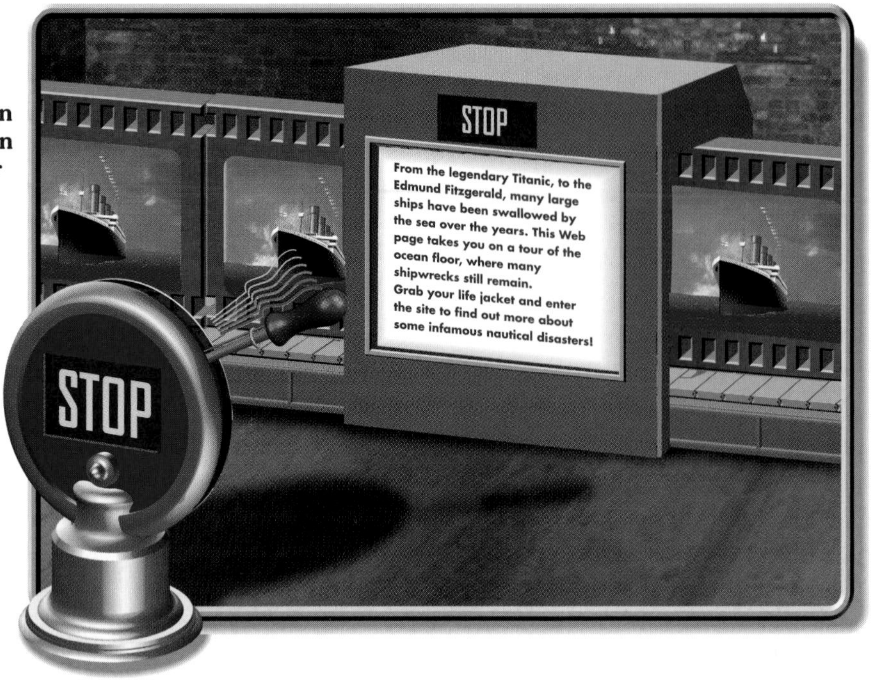

Assigning the stop action to a button allows users to click the button to stop your movie. For example, if a keyframe in your movie displays a lot of text, you can create a Stop button that users can click to stop the movie while they read the text.

When you add the stop action to a keyframe, Flash will automatically stop the movie when the movie reaches that frame.

STOP A MOVIE

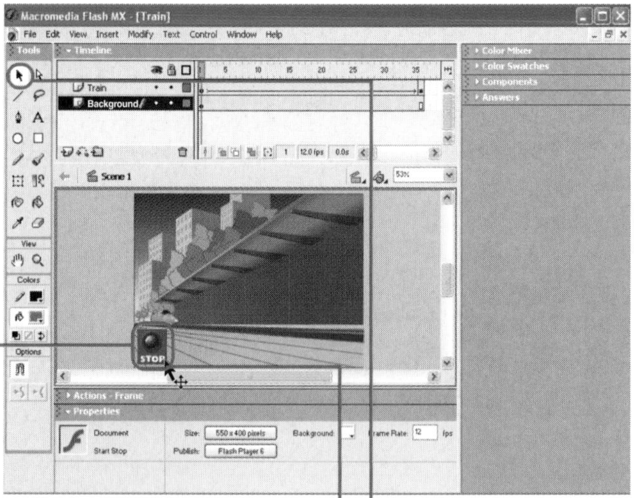

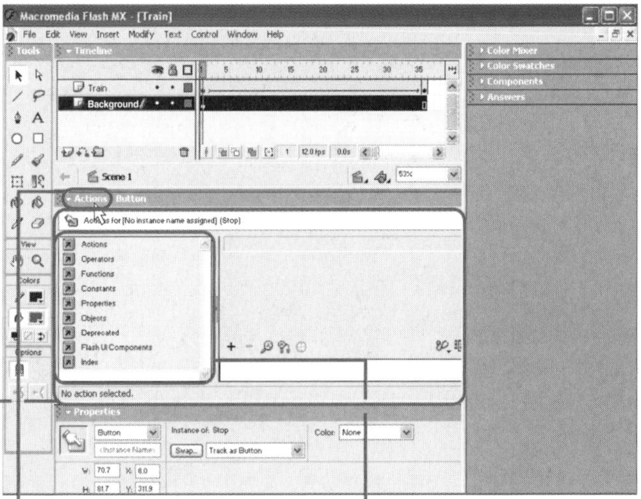

1 Create a button that you want users to click to stop the movie. Then add the button to the Stage.

Note: To create a button, see page 226. To add a button to the Stage, see page 230.

2 Click the selection arrow to be able to select the button.

3 Click the button.

■ To add a stop action to a keyframe, click the keyframe. To create a keyframe, see page 162.

4 Click **Actions** to display the Actions panel.

Note: If Actions is not displayed, see page 17 to display the Actions panel.

■ The Actions panel appears.

*Note: To hide the Actions panel at any time so you can once again view the Stage, click **Actions** again.*

■ This area displays the available actions, organized by category.

How can I prevent my movie from starting automatically?

You can assign the stop action to the first keyframe in your movie to prevent the movie from starting automatically when a user opens the movie. You can then create a Play button that users can click to start the movie when they are ready to view the movie. To create a Play button, see page 252.

Should I create a new layer for the stop action I am assigning to a keyframe?

To keep your Timeline more organized, you can create a layer for all the actions you plan to add to keyframes in your movie, such as the stop action. This will make it easier to later find actions you want to edit. Keeping all the actions in your movie on the same layer can also help you manage your actions and ensure that the actions occur in the correct order. To add a new layer to the Timeline, see page 132.

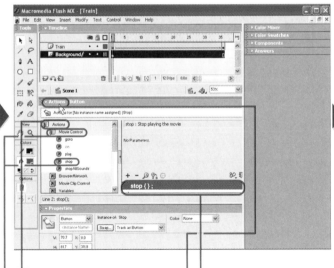

5 Click **Actions**.

6 Click the **Movie Control** category to display the actions in the category.

7 Double-click **stop** to assign the action to the button or keyframe you selected.

■ Flash adds the action to the list of actions for the button or keyframe in this area.

8 Click **Actions** to close the Actions panel.

■ If you added the stop action to a keyframe, a small 'a' appears in the keyframe, indicating that the keyframe contains an action.

Note: To test the stop action you added to a button or keyframe, see page 171 to preview the movie in the Flash Player.

■ To create a Play button that users can click to continue playing the movie, see page 252.

CONTINUED

STOP AND PLAY A MOVIE

You can add the play action to a button in your movie so users will be able to click the button to play the movie.

For example, if you created a Stop button that users can click to stop the movie, you can create a Play button that users can click to continue playing the movie.

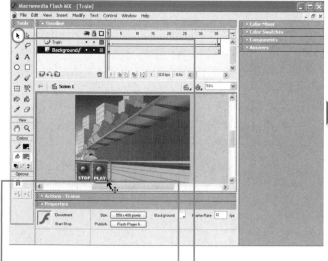

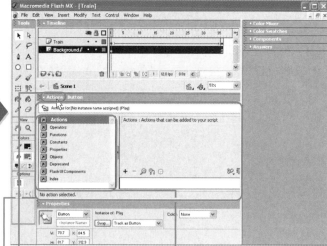

1 Create a button that you want users to click to play the movie. Then add the button to the Stage.

Note: To create a button, see page 226. To add a button to the Stage, see page 230.

2 Click ► to be able to select the button.

3 Click the button.

4 Click **Actions** to display the Actions panel.

Note: If Actions is not displayed, see page 17 to display the Actions panel.

■ The Actions panel appears.

*Note: To hide the Actions panel at any time so you can once again view the Stage, click **Actions** again.*

■ This area displays the available actions, organized by category.

252

Can I assign a play or stop action to a movie clip I added to my movie?

Yes. You can assign a play or stop action to a movie clip to control the way the movie clip will play during your movie. Double-click the movie clip on the Stage to display the timeline for the movie clip. You can then add a play or stop action to a button in the movie clip as you would add a play or stop action to a button in the main movie. To add a movie clip to your movie, see page 184.

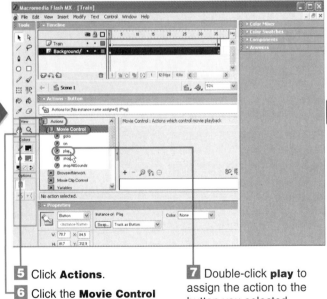

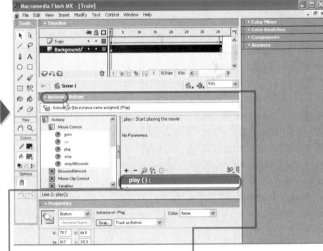

5 Click **Actions**.

6 Click the **Movie Control** category to display the actions in the category.

7 Double-click **play** to assign the action to the button you selected.

■ Flash adds the action to the list of actions for the button in this area.

8 Click **Actions** to close the Actions panel.

Note: To test the play action you added to the button, see page 171 to preview the movie in the Flash Player.

253

JUMP TO A SPECIFIC FRAME OR SCENE IN A MOVIE

You can use the goto action to have a movie jump to another frame or scene in the movie. You can add the goto action to a button or keyframe.

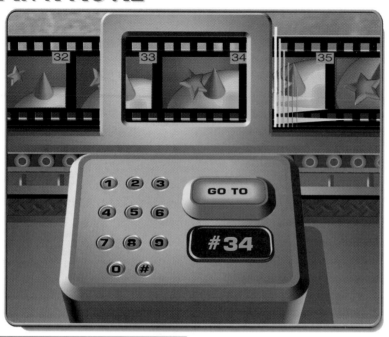

When you add the goto action to a button, users can click the button to jump to a specific frame or scene in your movie.

When you add the goto action to a keyframe, Flash will automatically jump to a specific frame or scene in your movie when the movie reaches the keyframe.

JUMP TO A SPECIFIC FRAME OR SCENE IN A MOVIE

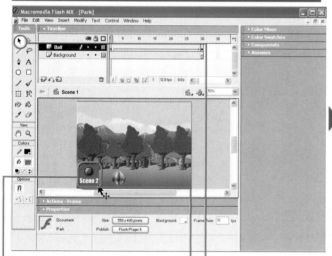

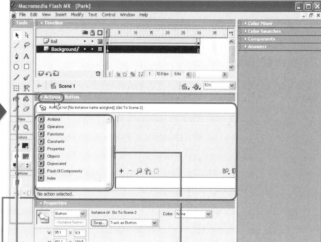

1 Create a button that you want users to click to jump to a specific frame or scene in your movie. Then add the button to the Stage.

Note: To create a button, see page 226. To add a button to the Stage, see page 230.

2 Click ⬚ to be able to select the button.

3 Click the button.

■ To add the goto action to a keyframe, click the keyframe. To create a keyframe, see page 162.

4 Click **Actions** to display the Actions panel.

Note: If Actions is not displayed, see page 17 to display the Actions panel.

■ The Actions panel appears.

*Note: To hide the Actions panel at any time so you can once again view the Stage, click **Actions** again.*

■ This area displays the available actions, organized by category.

254

What is a scene?

A scene is a segment of a movie that has its own Timeline and Stage. Scenes help you better organize and review the contents of a long movie by breaking up the movie into more manageable segments. For example, when creating a movie that contains 100 frames, you can create two scenes that will each contain 50 frames of the movie. To create scenes, see page 218.

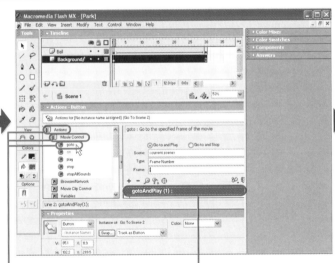

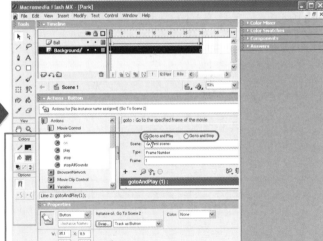

■5 Click **Actions**.

■6 Click the **Movie Control** category to display the actions in the category.

■7 Double-click **goto** to assign the action to the button or keyframe you selected.

■ Flash adds the action to the list of actions for the button or keyframe in this area.

■8 Click an option to specify what you want to occur after the movie jumps to another frame or scene (○ changes to ◉).

Go to and Play
Continue playing the movie.

Go to and Stop
Stop playing the movie.

CONTINUED ▶

JUMP TO A SPECIFIC FRAME OR SCENE IN A MOVIE

When assigning the goto action to a movie, you need to specify which frame or scene in the movie you want to jump to.

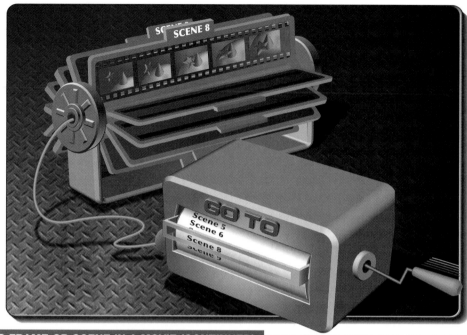

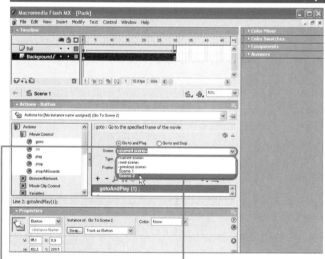

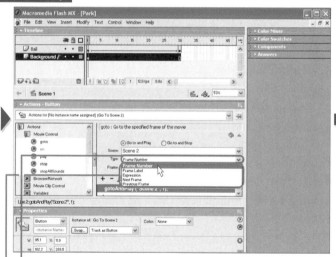

9 If you want the movie to jump to another scene, click ⊽ or ⊼ in this area to display the scene options.

Note: You can hide the toolbox to provide more room on the screen for the Actions panel. See page 14 to hide the toolbox.

10 Click the scene you want the movie to jump to.

Note: If you selected <next scene> or <previous scene> in step 10, skip to step 14.

11 To select how you want to specify where you want the movie to jump to, click this area.

12 Click the option you want to use.

Note: You can use the frame number or frame label to specify where you want the movie to jump to. For more information on frame labels, see page 174. You can also choose to have the movie jump to the next or previous frame. The Expression option is for advanced users.

256

Do I need to create the scene I want the movie to jump to before assigning a goto action?

No. If you know the name of a scene you intend to create in your movie, you can type the name of the scene in the Scene area of the Actions panel instead of performing steps **9** and **10** below. When you later create the scene, you should make sure the name of the scene exactly matches the name you specified in the goto action.

Can I edit or delete a goto action?

Yes. If you later make changes to the frames or scenes in your movie, you can edit the action to update the information you entered for the action. You can also delete a goto action you no longer need. To edit an action, see page 264. To delete an action, see page 265.

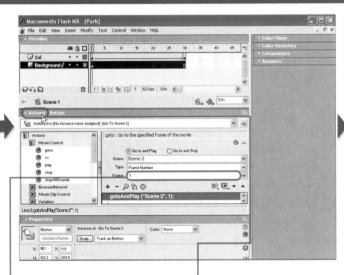

13 If you selected **Frame Number** or **Frame Label** in step **12**, click this area and type the number or label of the frame you want the movie to jump to.

14 Click **Actions** to close the Actions panel.

■ If you added the goto action to a keyframe, a small 'a' appears in the keyframe, indicating that the keyframe contains an action.

Note: To test the goto action you added to a button or keyframe, see page 171 to preview the movie in the Flash Player.

LINK A BUTTON TO A WEB PAGE

You can assign the getURL action to a button so users will be able to click the button to display a specific Web page.

For example, you can create Company Information, Product Catalog and Press Release buttons that will display corresponding Web pages in your company's Web site.

LINK A BUTTON TO A WEB PAGE

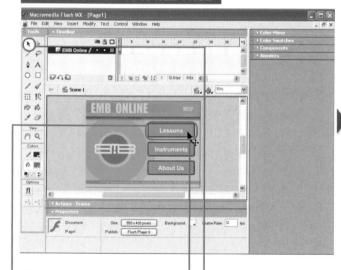

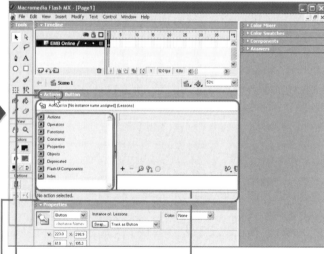

1 Create a button that you want users to click to display a Web page. Then add the button to the Stage.

Note: To create a button, see page 226. To add a button to the Stage, see page 230.

2 Click ▶ to be able to select the button on the Stage.

3 Click the button to select the button.

4 Click **Actions** to display the Actions panel.

Note: If Actions is not displayed, see page 17 to display the Actions panel.

■ The Actions panel appears.

*Note: To hide the Actions panel at any time so you can once again view the Stage, click **Actions** again.*

■ This area displays the available actions, organized by category.

Which option should I choose when specifying where I want a linked Web page to open?

If you want the linked Web page to open in the current Web browser window, you should choose the **_self** option in step **10**. To have the linked Web page open in a new Web browser window, choose the **_blank** option. If your Web site contains frames, you can choose the **_parent** option to open the linked Web page in the parent of the current frame or the **_top** option to open the Web page in the top-level frame of the current Web browser window.

How can I create a button that users can click to quickly send an e-mail message?

Perform steps **1** to **8** below, except type **mailto:** followed by the e-mail address of the person you want to receive the message in step **8**. For example, type **mailto:lindsay@abc.com** to have users send an e-mail message to lindsay@abc.com when they click the button. Then perform step **11** below.

lindsay@abc.com

E-MAIL US!

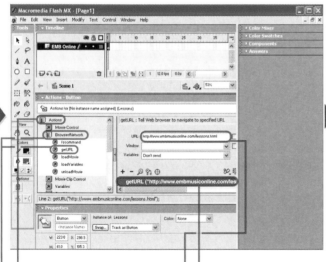

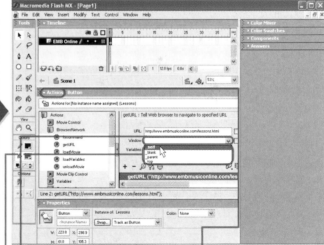

5 Click **Actions**.

6 Click the **Browser/Network** category to display the actions in the category.

7 Double-click **getURL** to assign the action to the button you selected.

■ Flash adds the action to the list of actions for the button in this area.

8 Click this area and type the location and name of the Web page on your computer or the address of the Web page on the Internet that you want to link the button to.

9 To select where you want the Web page to open, click 🔽 (Windows) or 🔽 (Macintosh) in this area.

10 Click the option you want to use.

Note: For information on the available options, see the top of this page.

11 Click **Actions** to close the Actions panel.

Note: To test the getURL action you added to the button, see page 171 to preview the movie in the Flash Player.

LOAD A MOVIE INTO THE CURRENT MOVIE

You can use the loadMovie action to load a movie into the current movie. The loadMovie action allows you to play two movies at once by superimposing the loaded movie on top of the current movie. You can add the loadMovie action to a button or a keyframe.

When you add the loadMovie action to a button, users can click the button to load another movie into the current movie.

When you add the loadMovie action to a keyframe, Flash will automatically load another movie into the current movie when the current movie reaches the keyframe.

LOAD A MOVIE INTO THE CURRENT MOVIE

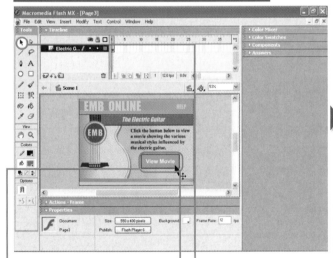

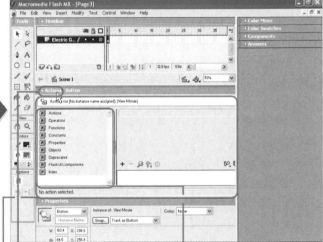

1 Create a button that you want users to click to load a movie into the current movie. Then add the button to the Stage.

Note: To create a button, see page 226. To add a button to the Stage, see page 230.

2 Click ▶ to be able to select the button.

3 Click the button.

■ To add the loadMovie action to a keyframe, click the keyframe. To create a keyframe, see page 162.

4 Click **Actions** to display the Actions panel.

Note: If Actions is not displayed, see page 17 to display the Actions panel.

■ The Actions panel appears.

*Note: To hide the Actions panel at any time so you can once again view the Stage, click **Actions** again.*

■ This area displays the available actions, organized by category.

Why would I load a movie into another movie?

Loading a movie into another movie can help reduce the file size of a large movie so the movie downloads faster. Instead of creating one large movie, you can create several small movies that you load into a main movie. The main movie can include buttons that users can select to play the additional movies.

How can I allow a user to stop playing a movie I loaded into the current movie?

You can create a button that users can click to stop playing a movie you loaded into the current movie. To create the button, perform steps **1** to **7** below, except double-click **unloadMovie** in step **7**. Then double-click the number in the **Location** area and type the number for the level that contains the loaded movie.

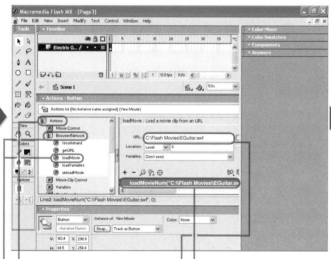

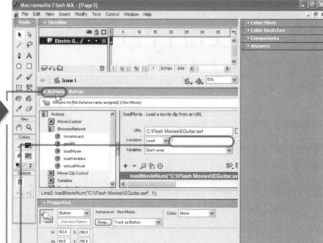

5 Click **Actions**.

6 Click the **Browser/Network** category to display the actions in the category.

7 Double-click **loadMovie** to assign the action to the button or keyframe you selected.

■ Flash adds the action to the list of actions for the button or keyframe in this area.

8 Click this area and type the location and name of the Flash movie file on your computer or the Web that you want to load into the current movie.

9 To play the movie on top of the current movie, double-click this area and type **1**.

*Note: If you want the movie to replace the current movie, type **0**.*

10 Click **Actions** to close the Actions panel.

■ If you added the loadMovie action to a keyframe, a small 'a' appears in the keyframe, indicating that the keyframe contains an action.

Note: To test the loadMovie action you added to a button or keyframe, see page 171 to preview the movie in the Flash Player.

STOP PLAYING ALL SOUNDS

You can use the stopAllSounds action to stop all sounds that are currently playing in a movie at once. You can add the stopAllSounds action to a button or a keyframe.

Sounds can provide sound effects, background music or narration for a movie. To add sounds to a movie, see page 234.

When you add the stopAllSounds action to a button, users can click the button to turn off all the sounds in a movie but still continue to view the movie.

When you add the stopAllSounds action to a keyframe, all sounds will stop playing when the movie reaches the frame. The movie will continue to play.

STOP PLAYING ALL SOUNDS

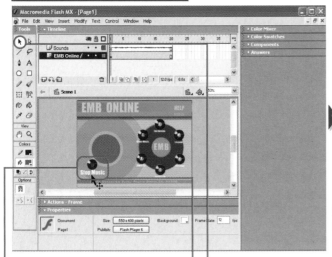

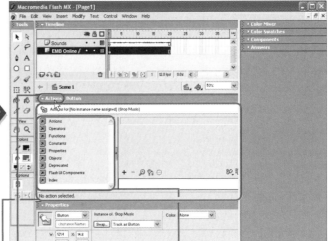

■1 Create a button that you want users to click to stop all sounds in the movie. Then add the button to the Stage.

Note: To create a button, see page 226. To add a button to the Stage, see page 230.

■2 Click 🔾 to be able to select the button.

■3 Click the button.

■ To add the stopAllSounds action to a keyframe, click the keyframe. To create a keyframe, see page 162.

■4 Click **Actions** to display the Actions panel.

Note: If Actions is not displayed, see page 17 to display the Actions panel.

■ The Actions panel appears.

*Note: To hide the Actions panel at any time so you can once again view the Stage, click **Actions** again.*

■ This area displays the available actions, organized by category.

How can I stop a specific sound that is playing in my movie?

You can add a Stop sound to stop a specific sound that is playing in your movie. The other sounds in the movie will continue to play. To add a Stop sound, see page 243.

When I previewed my movie, why did the sounds start playing again after I stopped them using the stopAllSounds action?

The stopAllSounds action stops all the sounds that are currently playing in your movie, but will not prevent the sounds from playing again when the movie plays again. When you preview the movie, the sounds will start playing again each time the movie plays.

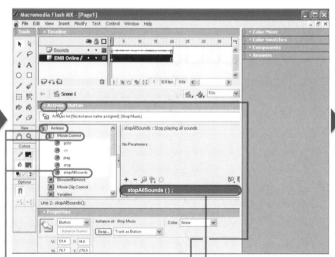

■ -**5** Click **Actions**.

■ -**6** Click the **Movie Control** category to display the actions in the category.

■ -**7** Double-click **stopAllSounds** to assign the action to the button or keyframe you selected.

■ Flash adds the action to the list of actions for the button or keyframe in this area.

■ -**8** Click **Actions** to close the Actions panel.

■ If you added the stopAllSounds action to a keyframe, a small 'a' appears in the keyframe, indicating that the keyframe contains an action.

Note: To test the stopAllSounds action you added to a button or keyframe, see page 171 to preview the movie in the Flash Player.

EDIT AN ACTION

You can change the information you entered when you added an action to a button or keyframe in a movie.

For example, you can change the Web page that will appear when users click a button you added the getURL action to.

EDIT AN ACTION

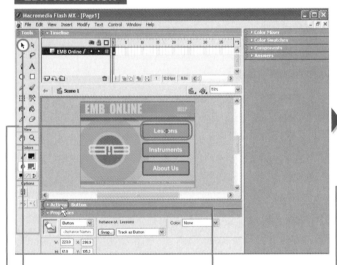

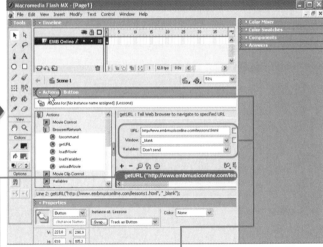

■1 To edit an action you added to a button, click ▶ to be able to select the button.

■2 Click the button.

■ To edit an action you added to a keyframe, click the keyframe. A keyframe that contains an action displays a small 'a'.

■3 Click **Actions** to display the Actions panel.

Note: If Actions is not displayed, see page 17 to display the Actions panel.

■ The Actions panel appears.

■ This area displays the actions you have added to the button or keyframe.

■4 Click the action you want to edit. The action is highlighted.

Note: You can hide the toolbox to provide more room on the screen for the Actions panel. See page 14 to hide the toolbox.

■ This area displays the information you entered for the action.

■5 Make the desired changes for the action.

■6 Click **Actions** to close the Actions panel.

DELETE AN ACTION

If you no longer want an action to occur when users click a button or when a movie reaches a specific keyframe, you can delete the action from the button or keyframe.

DELETE AN ACTION

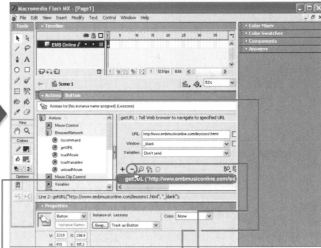

1 To remove an action you added to a button, click ![arrow] to be able to select the button.

2 Click the button.

■ To remove an action you added to a keyframe, click the keyframe. A keyframe that contains an action displays a small 'a'.

3 Click **Actions** to display the Actions panel.

Note: If Actions is not displayed, see page 17 to display the Actions panel.

■ The Actions panel appears.

■ This area displays the actions you have added to the button or keyframe.

4 Click the action you want to delete. The action is highlighted.

Note: You can hide the toolbox to provide more room on the screen for the Actions panel. See page 14 to hide the toolbox.

5 Click ![minus] to delete the action.

■ The action disappears from the list of actions.

6 Click **Actions** to close the Actions panel.

CHAPTER 13

Distribute Flash Movies

Read this chapter to find out about the many ways that Flash allows you to publish your movie for others to view. This chapter will also teach you how to test, preview and print your movie.

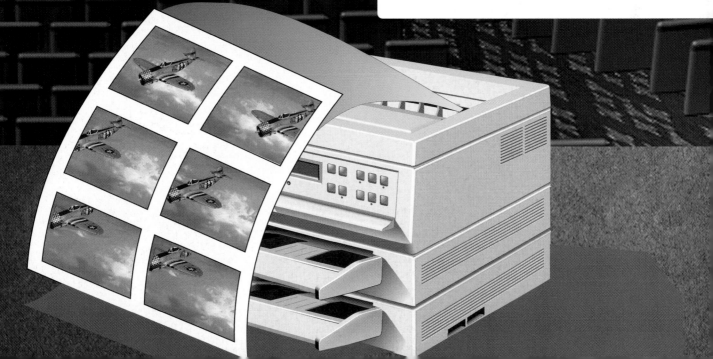

OPTIMIZE A MOVIE

You can optimize a movie to reduce its file size so the movie will download and play more quickly.

When you publish a movie, Flash automatically performs some optimization on the movie, such as detecting objects that appear more than once in the movie and placing the objects in the published movie file only once.

Optimize Lines

When drawing lines and objects, try to limit the number of dashed and dotted lines, which create larger files than solid lines. Lines you create with the Pencil tool require less file space than lines you create with the Brush tool.

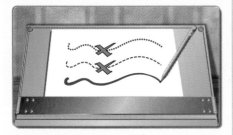

Optimize Filled Objects

When filling objects with color, try to use gradients sparingly. Objects filled with gradients require much more file space than objects filled with solid colors. A gradient is two or more colors that blend from one color to another.

Optimize Fonts

You should try to minimize the number of fonts and font styles in your movie. Using too many different fonts and font styles in a movie increases the file size.

Use Symbols

You should use symbols for every object in your movie that appears more than once. Instances of symbols require less file space than individually drawn objects. If you want an object to appear in different colors, create multiple instances of the symbol and then change the color of each instance rather than creating a new object each time. Change the transparency of symbol instances in your movie sparingly since this can slow down the playback of your movie.

Optimize Animations

Try to limit the amount of change that takes place between keyframes in a movie, since too many changes between keyframes can reduce the playback speed of the movie. For example, if an object rotates and changes size, color and transparency between two keyframes, consider making only one or two of the changes. Also, try to avoid using bitmap images in animations. You should use bitmap images only as background images or stationary images in your movie.

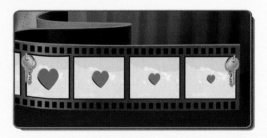

Use Tweened Animations

Whenever possible, use tweened animations instead of frame-by-frame animations, since frame-by-frame animations require more file space in a movie. For example, instead of creating each frame to show an object moving in a movie, create the first and last frames and use a motion tween to have Flash create the in-between frames of the animation for you.

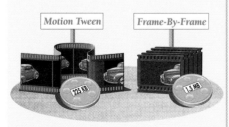

Use Movie Clips

Instead of creating a complicated or long animation on the main Timeline of your movie, consider using several movie clips, which act like mini-movies in your main movie.

Optimize Sounds

When using sounds in your movie, use MP3 sounds whenever possible. MP3 sounds have a much smaller file size and offer better sound quality than other types of sounds.

TEST MOVIE DOWNLOAD PERFORMANCE

You can test a movie you plan to deliver over the Internet to determine if any of the frames may cause the movie to slow down during playback.

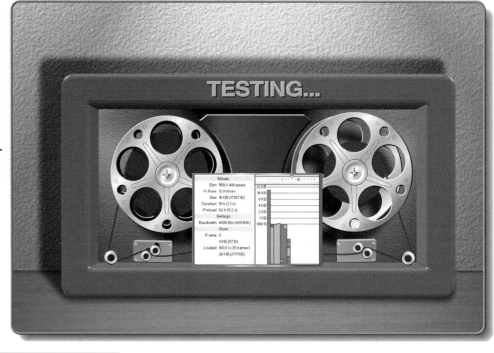

Testing the download performance of a movie allows you to determine which frames may contain too much data to download efficiently.

TEST MOVIE DOWNLOAD PERFORMANCE

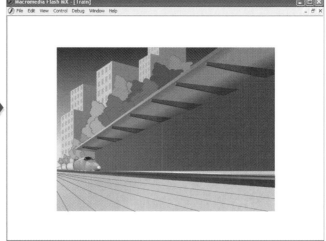

■1 Click **Control**.

■2 Click **Test Movie**.

■ The Exporting Flash Movie dialog box briefly appears, showing the progress of exporting the movie.

■ The Flash Player opens and plays the movie.

Note: The movie plays repeatedly until you stop the movie.

■ To stop or resume playing the movie at any time, press the [Enter] key (Windows) or the [Return] key (Macintosh).

Note: To close the Flash Player and return to the document at any time, click [×] (Windows) or [ ] (Macintosh).

Can I test the download performance of a single scene in my movie?

To test how the current scene in your movie will download on the Internet, perform steps **1** to **4** below, except select **Test Scene** in step **2**. Testing a scene allows you to analyze the download performance of a specific scene without testing the entire movie. For information on scenes, see pages 218 to 223.

How can I reduce the file size of the frames in my movie?

If you find that frames in your movie may cause problems during playback because the frames contain too much data, you may need to reduce the file size of the frames. For example, you may want to use tweened animations instead of frame-by-frame animations. For more information on reducing the file size of your frames, see page 268.

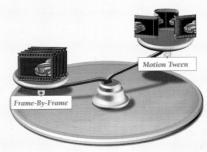

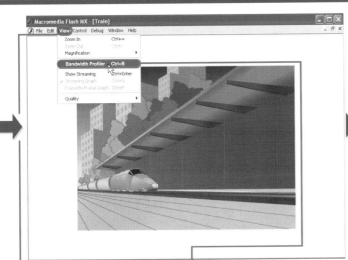

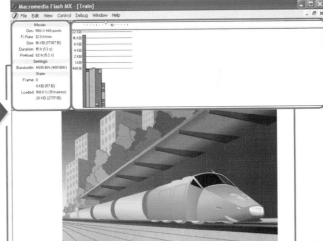

3 To display the Bandwidth Profiler to help you determine if any frames in your movie might cause the movie to slow down during playback, click **View**.

4 Click **Bandwidth Profiler**.

■ A check mark (✔) appears beside Bandwidth Profiler when the Bandwidth Profiler is displayed.

■ The Bandwidth Profiler appears.

*Note: To close the Bandwidth Profiler at any time, repeat steps **3** and **4**.*

■ This area displays information about the movie, such as the size and duration of the movie.

■ This area displays a graph that shows the download performance of each frame in the movie.

CONTINUED ▶

TEST MOVIE DOWNLOAD PERFORMANCE

You can test the download performance of a movie at different download speeds. You can also change the view of the Bandwidth Profiler graph.

Testing the movie at different download speeds allows you to determine how your movie will play on computers that use different types of connections to the Internet.

TEST MOVIE DOWNLOAD PERFORMANCE (CONTINUED)

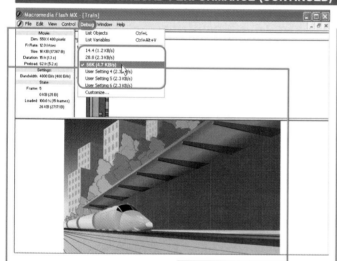

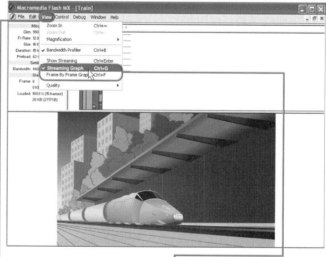

SELECT A DOWNLOAD SPEED

1 Click **Debug**.

2 Click the download speed at which you want to test the movie.

■ A check mark (✔) appears beside the currently selected download speed.

■ Flash changes the graph in the Bandwidth Profiler to reflect the new download speed you selected.

CHANGE VIEW OF GRAPH

1 Click **View**.

2 Click the view of the graph you want to use.

■ A check mark (✔) appears beside the current view of the graph.

How can I see the progress of the download?

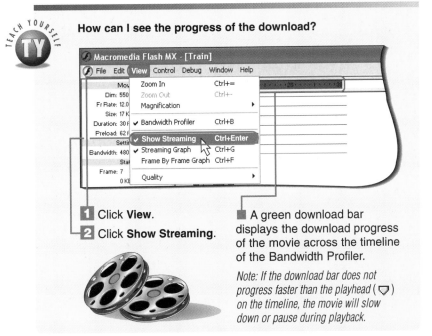

1 Click **View**.

2 Click **Show Streaming**.

■ A green download bar displays the download progress of the movie across the timeline of the Bandwidth Profiler.

Note: If the download bar does not progress faster than the playhead (▽) on the timeline, the movie will slow down or pause during playback.

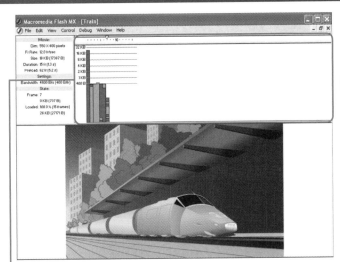

STREAMING GRAPH

■ The graph shows the amount of time each frame takes to download. Each alternating block of light and dark gray on the graph represents a frame in the movie. The width of each block indicates how long a frame takes to download.

Note: Frames that download quickly appear stacked in a single time unit. Frames that take longer to download stretch over several time units.

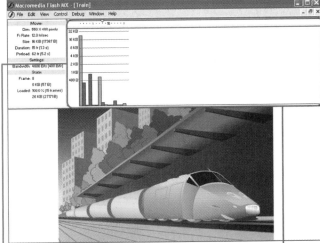

FRAME BY FRAME GRAPH

■ The graph shows the amount of data in each frame. Each bar represents a frame in the movie. The height of each bar indicates the amount of data in a frame.

■ If a bar extends above the red line in the graph, the movie will pause until the frame's data finishes downloading.

PUBLISH A MOVIE AS A FLASH MOVIE FILE

You can publish a movie as a Flash movie file for other people to view.

You can distribute copies of your Flash movie file to colleagues, friends or family members. To view your Flash movie file, a user's computer must have the Flash Player installed. Users can obtain the Flash Player at the www.macromedia.com Web site.

PUBLISH A MOVIE AS A FLASH MOVIE FILE

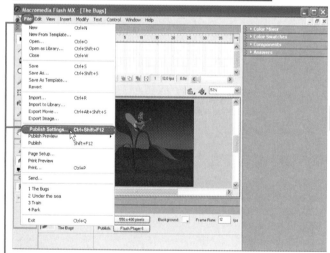

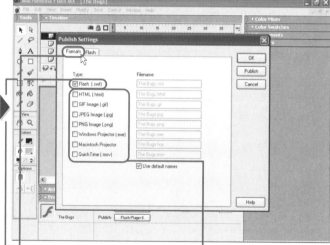

1 Click **File**.

2 Click **Publish Settings**.

■ The Publish Settings dialog box appears.

3 Click the **Formats** tab.

■ Flash automatically displays a check mark (✔) beside the Flash format so you can publish a movie as a Flash movie file. If a check mark is not displayed, click the format (☐ changes to ☑).

■ If you do not want to publish your movie in any other formats, make sure a check mark (✔) does not appear beside any other formats. To remove a check mark (✔), click the format.

Can I use a Flash movie file in other movies?

You can use a Flash movie file in other movies you create. For example, you may want to create a button in another movie that a user can click to play the Flash movie file. You can use the loadMovie action to insert your Flash movie file into another movie. To load a movie into another movie, see page 260.

How do I play a movie I published as a Flash movie file?

Flash saves the Flash movie file in the same location as your Flash document. You can locate the file on your computer and double-click the file to open the Flash Player and play the file. A Flash movie file displays the ⬡ icon.

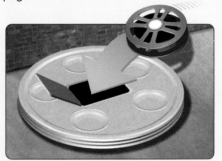

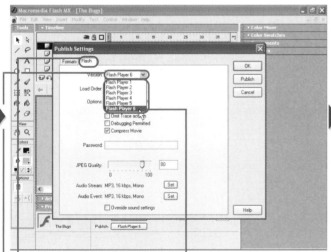

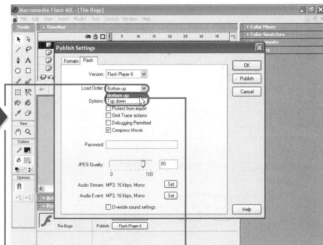

4 Click the **Flash** tab to specify the settings for your Flash movie file.

5 To specify the version of the Flash Player you want your movie to be compatible with, click this area.

6 Click the version of the Flash Player you want your movie to be compatible with.

Note: If you select an earlier version of the Flash Player, some features in your movie that are specific to Flash 6 may not work.

7 To specify the order in which you want Flash to load the layers in the movie when a user plays the movie over a slow connection, click this area.

8 Click the order in which you want to load the layers.

*Note: **Bottom up** loads the lowest layers first. **Top down** loads the top layers first.*

CONTINUED

PUBLISH A MOVIE AS A FLASH MOVIE FILE

You can have Flash create a report that shows the amount of data each frame in your movie contains.

The report Flash creates can help you find frames that may slow down the movie during playback. Flash will save the report in the same location as the current Flash document.

PUBLISH A MOVIE AS A FLASH MOVIE FILE (CONTINUED)

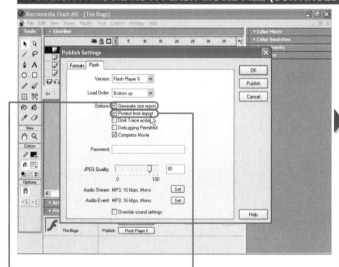

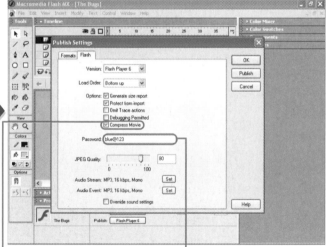

9 This option creates a report that lists the amount of data in each frame in the movie. To turn the option on (☑) or off (☐), click the option.

10 This option prevents other people from importing your movie into their Flash program. To turn the option on (☑) or off (☐), click the option.

11 This option compresses the movie to reduce the file size and download time of the movie. To turn the option on (☑) or off (☐), click the option.

Note: A compressed movie file can only play on a computer that has Flash Player 6 installed.

12 If you selected **Protect from import** in step **10**, you can click this area and type a password that users can enter to be able to import your movie into their Flash program.

Can I change the Flash movie after I publish the movie?

You cannot edit the published Flash file but you can edit the Flash document on your computer to make changes to your movie. After making changes to the movie, you can quickly republish the movie with the previous settings you specified. To quickly republish the movie, click the **File** menu and then click **Publish**. Flash will replace the previously published Flash movie file with the new file you publish.

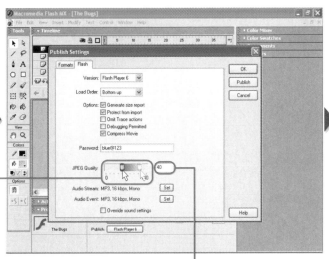

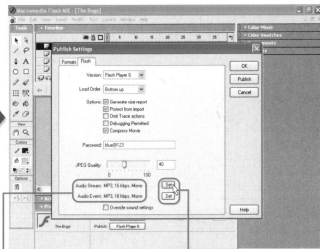

13 To adjust the quality of the JPEG images in your movie, drag this slider (◻) to the left or right to decrease or increase the image quality.

■ This area displays the quality setting.

Note: Lower quality settings result in the highest amount of compression and the smallest file sizes.

■ This area displays the current sound settings for stream and event sounds in your movie.

Note: For information on stream and event sounds, see page 236.

14 To change the settings for stream or event sounds in your movie, click **Set** beside the appropriate type of sound.

■ The Sound Settings dialog box appears.

CONTINUED ▶

PUBLISH A MOVIE AS A FLASH MOVIE FILE

When publishing a movie as a Flash movie file, you can specify the sound settings you want to use for the movie.

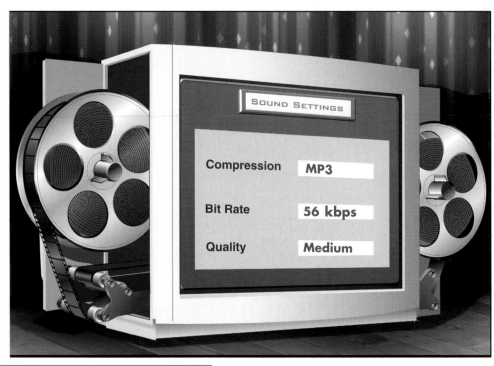

SOUND SETTINGS

Compression	MP3
Bit Rate	56 kbps
Quality	Medium

PUBLISH A MOVIE AS A FLASH MOVIE FILE (CONTINUED)

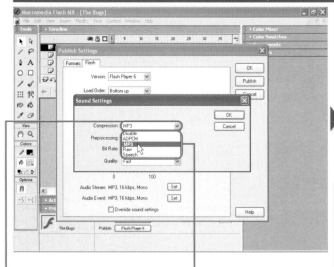

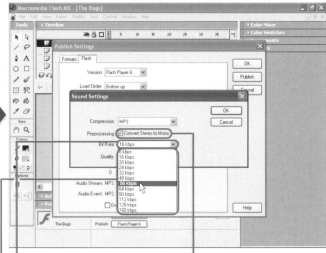

15 To select the compression method you want to use for the type of sound you selected, click this area.

16 Click the compression method you want to use.

*Note: The options in the dialog box change to reflect the compression method you selected. If you selected **Disable** to turn off all sounds, skip to step **22**.*

17 To specify a bit rate for the sounds, click this area.

18 Click the bit rate you want to use.

*Note: If you selected **ADPCM**, **Raw** or **Speech** in step **16**, you can specify a sample rate instead.*

19 This option converts stereo sounds to mono sounds. To turn the option on (☑) or off (☐), click the option.

*Note: This option is not available if you selected **Speech** in step **16** or a bit rate setting lower than 20 kbps in step **18**.*

What sound compression options are available for my movie?

Disable - Turns off the sound for the published movie.

ADPCM - Useful for short sounds, such as a click.

MP3 - Useful for longer sounds, such as music.

Raw - Does not compress the sounds in the movie. This option uses a large amount of file space.

Speech - Useful for spoken sounds, such as narration.

Which bit rate should I choose?

A high bit rate results in better quality sound but increases the file size of your movie. A low bit rate produces low quality sound, but decreases the movie's file size. You may want to choose a mid-range bit rate between 32 and 64 kbps and then adjust the bit rate until you find an acceptable quality and file size.

160 kbps
(High sound quality, larger file size)

8 kbps
(Low sound quality, smaller file size)

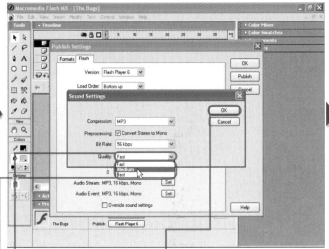

20 To specify a quality for the sounds, click this area.

21 Click the sound quality option you want to use.

*Note: This option is not available if you selected **Raw** or **Speech** in step 16. If you selected **ADPCM**, you can specify the ADPCM bits instead of the sound quality.*

22 Click **OK** to confirm the sound settings you specified.

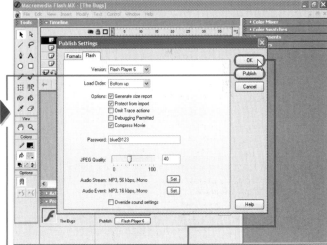

23 Click **Publish** to publish your movie with the settings you selected.

Note: If you do not want to publish your movie now, but you want to save the settings you specified, skip to step 24.

■ Flash publishes the movie and places the movie file in the same location that stores the current Flash document.

24 Click **OK** to confirm your changes.

PUBLISH A MOVIE ON A WEB PAGE

You can publish a Flash movie that will display on a Web page. Displaying a Flash movie on a Web page allows people on the Internet or your company's intranet to view the movie.

When you publish a Flash movie for display on a Web page, Flash creates the Web page that will display the movie and the Flash Player file that will appear on the Web page.

PUBLISH A MOVIE ON A WEB PAGE

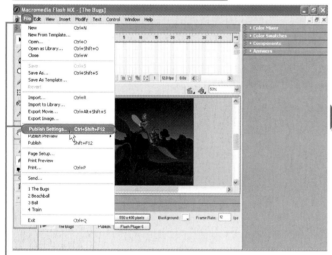 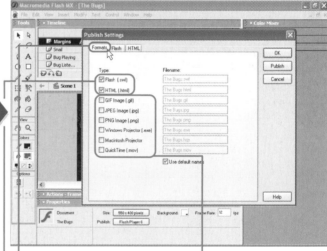

■1 Click **File**.

■2 Click **Publish Settings**.

■ The Publish Settings dialog box appears.

■3 Click the **Formats** tab.

■ Flash automatically displays a check mark (✔) beside the Flash and HTML formats so you can publish a Flash movie on a Web page. If a check mark is not displayed, click the format (☐ changes to ☑).

■ If you do not want to publish your movie in any other formats, make sure a check mark (✔) does not appear beside any other formats. To remove a check mark (✔), click the format.

After I set my Flash movie to pause when it appears on the Web page, how will users be able to start playing my movie?

If you turned on the **Paused At Start** option in step 8 below, you can create a button in your movie that users can click to start playing the Flash movie. To create a Play button, see page 252.

Users can also right-click (Windows) or **Control**-click (Macintosh) the movie on the Web page to display a list of options and then click **Play** to start playing the movie.

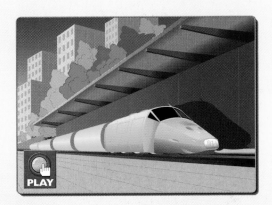

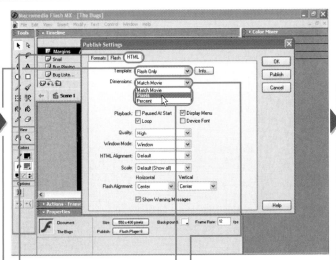

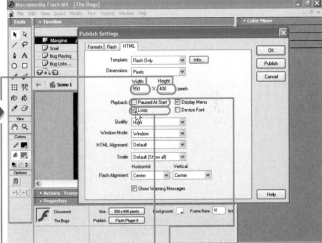

4 Click the **HTML** tab to specify the settings for the Web page.

■ The Flash Only template creates a Web page to display your Flash movie.

5 To specify the size of your movie on the Web page, click this area.

6 Click the movie size option you want to use.

Note: You can have the movie on the Web page match the size of the original movie or you can specify a movie size in pixels or as a percentage of a Web browser window.

7 If you selected **Pixels** or **Percent** in step 6, double-click these areas and type the number of pixels or the percentage of a Web browser window for the width and height of your movie.

8 This option starts the movie after a user clicks a button in the movie or chooses the Play option from a shortcut menu. To turn the option on (☑) or off (☐), click the option.

9 This option plays the movie repeatedly. To turn the option on (☑) or off (☐), click the option. **CONTINUED**

PUBLISH A MOVIE ON A WEB PAGE

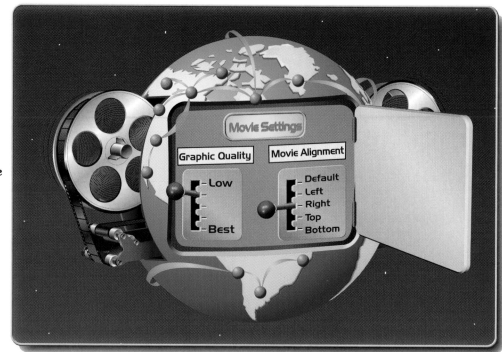

When publishing a
movie on a Web page,
you can select the
settings you want to
use for the movie,
such as the quality of
the graphics and the
alignment of the movie
in the Web browser
window.

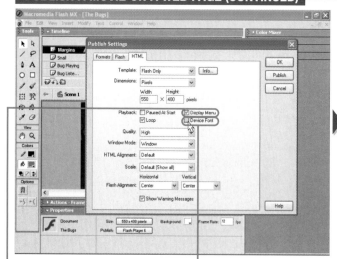

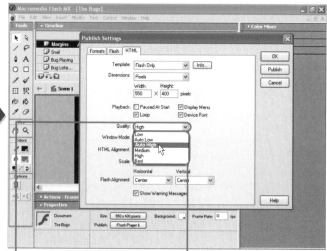

10 This option displays a
shortcut menu of playback
options when a user right-clicks
(Windows) or **Control**-clicks
(Macintosh) the movie on the
Web page. To turn the option
on (☑) or off (☐), click the
option.

11 This option allows a
Windows computer to
substitute fonts in your
movie that are not installed
on a user's computer
with anti-aliased, or
smooth-edged, system
fonts. To turn the option
on (☑) or off (☐), click
the option.

12 To specify the quality
of the graphics you want
to use in your movie,
click this area.

13 Click the graphic quality
option you want to use.

*Note: For information on the
graphic quality options, see the
top of page 283.*

Which graphic quality option should I choose for my movie?

The graphic quality options allow you to specify whether playback speed or graphic quality is more important for your movie. Selecting the **Low** or **Auto Low** option provides a lower graphic quality, but a faster playback speed. The **Auto High** and **Medium** options attempt to balance the graphic quality and playback speed. The **High** and **Best** options display the best graphic quality, but may decrease playback speed.

How do I make the Web page and Flash movie available for other people to view?

After Flash creates the Web page that will display the movie and the Flash Player file that will appear on the Web page, you can transfer the files to a computer that stores Web pages, called a Web server. Once you publish the files to a Web server, the Web page and Flash movie will be available for other people to view. For more information on publishing a Web page, contact your network administrator or Internet service provider.

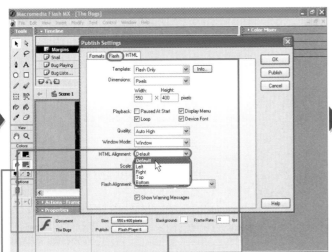

14 To specify the way you want to align your movie in a Web browser window, click this area.

15 Click the alignment option you want to use.

Note: You can align your movie along the left, right, top or bottom of a Web browser window. The Default option centers the movie in a Web browser window.

16 Click the **Flash** tab to specify the settings for the movie that will play on the Web page.

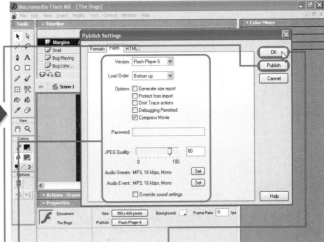

■ This area displays the settings for the movie.

Note: To change the settings for the movie, perform steps 5 to 22 starting on page 275.

17 Click **Publish** to publish your movie with the settings you selected.

■ Flash publishes the movie and creates the Web page that will display the movie. Flash places the files in the same location that stores the current Flash document.

18 Click **OK** to confirm your changes.

PUBLISH A MOVIE AS A PROJECTOR FILE

You can create a projector file that allows you to play a Flash movie on most computers, even if a computer does not have Flash installed.

Creating a projector file is useful for showing a Flash movie during a presentation or sending a Flash movie in an e-mail message.

PUBLISH A MOVIE AS A PROJECTOR FILE

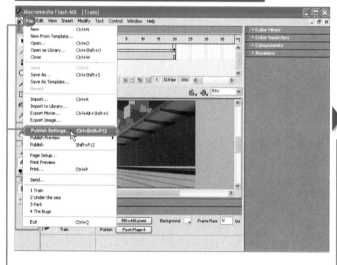

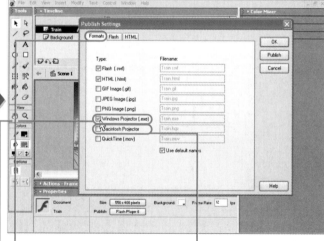

■1 Click **File**.

■2 Click **Publish Settings**.

■ The Publish Settings dialog box appears.

■3 Click the **Formats** tab.

■4 To create a projector file that runs on a Windows computer, click **Windows Projector** (☐ changes to ☑).

■ To create a projector file that runs on a Macintosh computer, click **Macintosh Projector** (☐ changes to ☑).

How can I rename the projector file?

If you do not want to use the name that Flash provides for the projector file, you can change the name. Perform steps **1** and **2** on page 284 to display the Publish Settings dialog box and click **Use default names** (☑ changes to ☐). You can then drag the mouse ⌶ over the name you want to change and type a new name for the projector file.

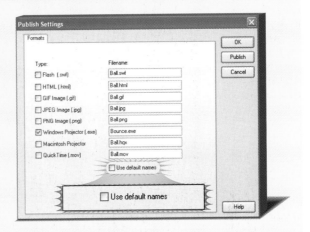

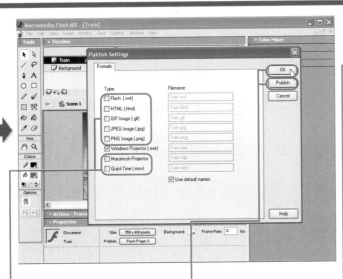

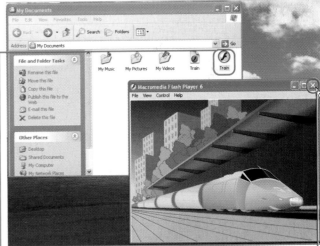

■ If you do not want to publish the movie in any other formats, make sure a check mark (✔) does not appear beside any other formats. To remove a check mark (✔), click the format.

5 Click **Publish** to create the projector file.

■ Flash places the projector file in the same location that stores the current Flash document.

6 Click **OK** to confirm your changes.

PLAY A PROJECTOR FILE

1 Locate the projector file on your computer.

2 Double-click the projector file to play the movie.

■ The Flash Player opens and the movie plays repeatedly.

3 When you finish playing the movie, click ☒ (Windows) or ☐ (Macintosh) to close the Flash Player.

EXPORT A MOVIE

EXPORT A MOVIE

Animated GIF   EPS   Adobe Illustrator

You can export a movie in a specific file format so you can use the movie in other programs.

Flash can export a movie in a variety of file formats, such as the Animated GIF, EPS and Adobe Illustrator file formats.

When you export a movie, interactive elements, such as buttons and actions, may not export properly.

EXPORT A MOVIE

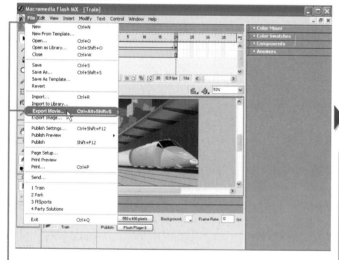

1 Click **File**.

2 Click **Export Movie**.

■ The Export Movie dialog box appears.

3 Type a name for the file that will contain your exported movie.

■ This area shows the location where Flash will store the file. You can click this area to change the location.

What is the difference between exporting and publishing a Flash movie?

When you export a movie, you can choose from many more file types than are available for publishing a movie. Also, unlike when you publish a movie, Flash does not store the settings for the file format you selected with the Flash document when you export a movie. For more information on publishing a movie, see pages 274 to 285.

Can I export a single frame of my movie?

Yes. Exporting a single frame is useful if you want to use an image from your movie in another document. To export a frame of your movie, click the frame on the Timeline that you want to export. Then perform steps **1** to **7** below, except select **Export Image** in step **2**.

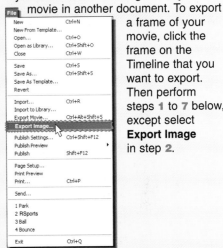

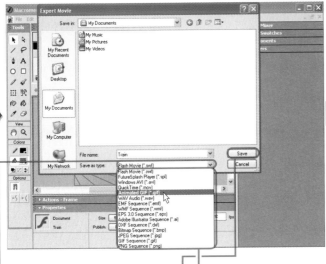

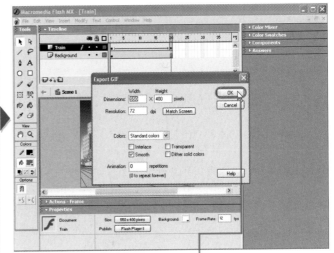

4 To select the format you want to use for the file, click this area to display the available file formats.

5 Click the file format you want to use.

6 Click **Save** to save the file.

■ A dialog box may appear, allowing you to specify the settings for the file.

Note: The available settings depend on the file format you selected in step 5.

7 Click **OK** to accept the default settings Flash provides and export the movie in the file format you specified.

Note: Another dialog box may appear, depending on the file format you selected in step 5. To continue, click OK.

PREVIEW A PUBLISHED MOVIE

You can
preview how
a movie will
appear after
you publish
the movie.

Before previewing
a published movie,
you should select the
format and settings
you want to use to
publish the movie. To
select the format and
settings for a movie,
see pages 274 to 285.

PREVIEW A PUBLISHED MOVIE

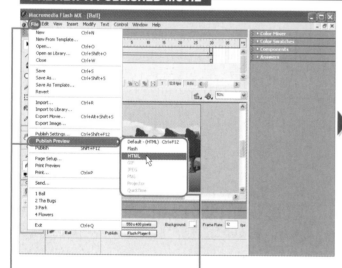

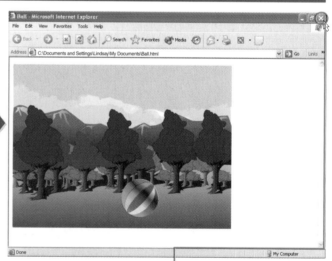

1 Click **File**.

2 Click **Publish Preview**.

3 Click the way you
want to preview the
published movie.

*Note: The available options
depend on the formats you
selected for the movie.*

■ Flash starts the
appropriate program
and the movie plays.

■ In this example, a
Web browser opens
and plays the Flash
movie on a Web page.

4 When you finish playing
the movie, click ☒ (Windows)
or ☐ (Macintosh) to close
the movie.

PRINT A MOVIE

You can produce
a paper copy of
a Flash movie.
Printing a Flash
movie is useful
if you want to
review the movie.

Before printing
a movie, make
sure your printer
is turned on and
contains paper.

PRINT A MOVIE

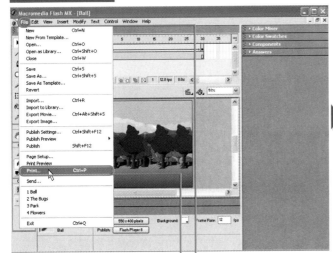

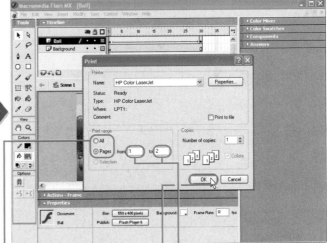

■ Before printing a movie,
you should set the print
options to specify the way
you want the frames in
the movie to appear on a
printed page. To set print
options, see page 290.

1 Click **File**.

2 Click **Print**.

■ The Print dialog box
appears.

3 Click the print
option you want to use
(○ changes to ◉).

All - Prints every page
in the movie.

Pages - Prints the
pages you specify.

4 If you selected **Pages**
in step **3**, type the first page
you want to print. Press the
`Tab` key and then type the
last page you want to print.

5 Click **OK** (Windows) or
Print (Macintosh) to print
the movie.

SET PRINT OPTIONS FOR A MOVIE

You can set the print options to specify the way you want the frames in a movie to appear on a printed page.

Margins

Determine the amount of space between the printed information and the edges of the paper.

Orientation

Determines the direction that information prints on each page.

Frames

Determines whether Flash prints only the first frame or all the frames in the movie.

SET PRINT OPTIONS FOR A MOVIE

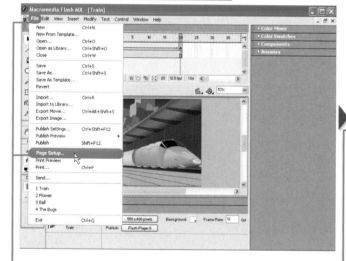

1 Click **File**.

2 Click **Page Setup**.

■ The Page Setup dialog box appears.

*Note: On a Macintosh computer, click **Print Margins** in step 2 to display the Print Margins dialog box.*

3 To change a margin, double-click the number in the box for the margin and then type a new margin.

4 To specify a page orientation, click the page orientation you want to use (○ changes to ◉).

5 To specify the frames you want to print, click this area.

6 Click an option to print only the first frame or all the frames in the movie.

Layout

  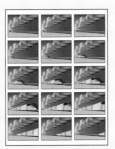 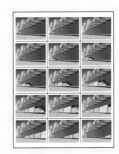 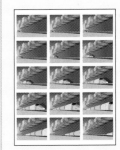

Actual Size

Prints each frame at full size.

Fit On One Page

Reduces or enlarges each frame to fill the print area of the page.

Storyboard - Boxes

Prints a small version of each frame outlined in a box.

Storyboard - Grid

Prints a small version of each frame within a grid.

Storyboard - Blank

Prints a small version of only the content of each frame.

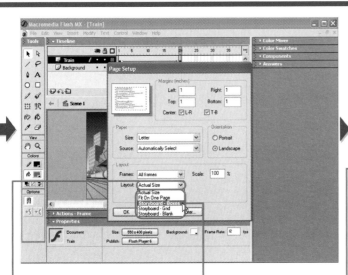

7 To specify how you want the frames to appear on each printed page, click this area.

8 Click the layout you want to use.

9 If you selected a **Storyboard** option in step 8, these areas show the number of frames that will print across each page and the amount of space between each frame. To change the information, double-click the number in an area and type a new number.

*Note: If you selected **Actual Size** in step 8, you can change the percentage by which you want to reduce or enlarge the printed frames.*

10 Click **OK** to confirm your changes.

Action

An action instructs Flash to perform a specific task when an event occurs. For example, you can add an action to a frame to move to another location in the movie or to stop playing the movie.

Anchor Points

Anchor points define the position and shape of an object.

Bandwidth

Bandwidth describes the rate at which information can transfer over a network connection. You can use the Bandwidth Profiler to test a movie you plan to deliver over the Internet to determine if the movie will transfer efficiently.

Bitmap Image

A bitmap image uses dots, called pixels, arranged in a grid pattern to define the details of the image. Bitmap images are also known as raster images.

Button

A button is an interactive object that changes in appearance or performs an action when you position the mouse pointer over the button or click the button.

Color Palette

A color palette is a set of colors available in a document. By default, each Flash document has a color palette of 216 colors.

Export

Exporting a Flash movie allows you to save the movie in a specific file format so you can use the movie in another program. You can export a Flash movie in a variety of file formats, such as Animated GIF, EPS and Adobe Illustrator file formats.

Fill

A fill is the color or pattern inside a shape. A fill can exist with or without an outlined border.

Flash Movie File

A Flash movie file allows you to play a Flash movie in the Flash Player. You can also use a Flash movie file in other movies you create or distribute copies of the file so other people to view. A Flash movie file uses the .swf extension and displays the (Windows) or (Mac) icon.

Frame Rate

Frame rate is measured in frames per second and determines how many frames appear each second. A higher frame rate creates a better quality movie but allows computers to play the movie properly. If the frame rate is too low, the movie may appear choppy.

294

CHAPTER 14

Glossary

This chapter helps you become more familiar with the terms often used in Flash.

Flash Player

The Flash Player is an application you can use to play Flash movie files. People who want to view a Flash movie file must have the Flash Player installed on their computers. Macromedia Flash MX includes the Flash Player application.

Frame

A frame stores the content, such as graphics or sound, for a specific location in a movie. The total number of frames in a movie determines the total length of the movie.

Frame-by-Frame Animation

Frame-by-frame animation creates the illusion of movement by slightly changing the position or appearance of an object in each frame. When the movie is played the object appears to move or change.

Guide Layer

A guide layer helps you draw and position objects on other layers. A guide layer will not appear in the finished movie.

Guides

Guides are lines you can place on the screen to help you draw and position objects more precisely. Guides will not appear in the finished movie.

Importing

Importing lets you use a file created in another program in your Flash document.

Gradient

A gradient is two or more colors that blend from one color to another. A linear gradient blends colors from one side of a shape to another. A radial gradient blends colors from the center point of a shape to the outer edges.

Grid

The grid is a set of overlapping horizontal and vertical lines that appear on the Stage. You can use the grid to help you draw and position objects more precisely.

Grouped Objects

Flash treats grouped objects as a single unit. For example, you can select all the objects in a group with a single mouse click.

Action

An action instructs Flash to perform a specific task when an event occurs. For example, you can add an action to a frame to move to another location in the movie or to stop playing the movie.

Anchor Points

Anchor points define the position and shape of an object.

Bandwidth

Bandwidth describes the rate at which information can transfer over a network connection. You can use the Bandwidth Profiler to test a movie you plan to deliver over the Internet to determine if the movie will transfer efficiently.

Bitmap Image

A bitmap image uses dots, called pixels, arranged in a grid pattern to define the details of the image. Bitmap images are also known as raster images.

Button

A button is an interactive object that changes in appearance or performs an action when you position the mouse pointer over the button or click the button.

Color Palette

A color palette is a set of colors available in a Flash document. By default, each Flash document provides a color palette of 216 colors.

Export

Exporting a Flash movie allows you to save the movie in a specific file format so you can use the movie in another program. You can export a Flash movie in a variety of file formats, such as Animated GIF, EPS and Adobe Illustrator file formats.

Fill

A fill is the color or pattern inside a shape. A fill can exist with or without an outlined border.

Flash Movie File

A Flash movie file allows you to play a Flash movie in the Flash Player. You can also use a Flash movie file in other movies you create or distribute copies of the file for other people to view. A Flash movie file uses the .swf extension and displays the (Windows) or (Mac) icon.

Flash Player

The Flash Player is an application you can use to play Flash movie files. People who want to view a Flash movie file must have the Flash Player installed on their computers. Macromedia Flash MX includes the Flash Player application.

Frame

A frame stores the content, such as graphics or sound, for a specific location in a movie. The total number of frames in a movie determines the total length of the movie.

Frame-by-Frame Animation

Frame-by-frame animation creates the illusion of movement by slightly changing the position or appearance of an object in each frame. When the movie is played, the object appears to move or change.

Frame Rate

Frame rate is measured in frames per second (fps) and determines how many frames of a movie will play each second. A higher frame rate produces a better quality movie but slower computers may not be able to play the movie properly. If the frame rate is set too low, the movie may appear choppy.

Gradient

A gradient is two or more colors that blend from one color to another. A linear gradient blends colors from one side of a shape to another. A radial gradient blends colors from the center point of a shape to the outer edges.

Grid

The grid is a set of overlapping horizontal and vertical lines that appear on the Stage. You can use the grid to help you draw and position objects more precisely.

Grouped Objects

Flash treats grouped objects as a single unit. For example, you can select all the objects in a group with a single mouse click.

Guide Layer

A guide layer helps you draw and position objects on other layers. A guide layer will not appear in the finished movie.

Guides

Guides are lines you can place on the screen to help you draw and position objects more precisely. Guides will not appear in the finished movie.

Import

Importing transfers a file created in another program into a Flash document.

Keyframe

A keyframe is a special type of frame that indicates when you want a change to occur in a movie.

Layer

A layer is like a piece of transparent paper containing a specific part of your drawing. When you stack all the layers on top of each other, you can view the entire drawing. Layers help you organize the artwork in your document.

Library

The library of the current document stores all the symbols that you can use in the document.

Mask Layer

A mask layer hides parts of a drawing on an underlying layer to create special effects in the movie.

Motion Guide Layer

A motion guide layer helps you move an object along a specific path. You can draw the path on the motion guide layer that you want an animated object on another layer to follow. A motion guide layer will not appear in the finished movie.

Motion Tween

A motion tween is an animation sequence that moves or changes an object. To create a motion tween, you specify two keyframes that each display an object in a different location, rotation, size or color and then have Flash create the animation for the in-between frames.

Movie Clip

A movie clip is a reusable animation that acts like a mini-movie in a document. A movie clip has its own timeline.

Onion Skinning

Onion skinning allows you to clearly view the contents of one frame while the contents of the surrounding frames are displayed as dimmed or outlined objects.

Panel

A panel allows you to create and work with items in a document. Each panel allows you to perform specific tasks. Examples of commonly used panels include the Actions panel and the Color Mixer.

Playhead

The red playhead on the Timeline indicates the frame that is currently displayed on the Stage.

Projector File

A projector file allows you to play a Flash movie on most computers, even if the computer does not have Flash installed. Creating a projector file is useful for showing a Flash movie during a presentation or sending a Flash movie in an e-mail message.

Property Inspector

The Property inspector allows you to view and change settings for an object or your movie. The options available in the Property inspector depend on the item selected in the toolbox, on the Timeline or on the Stage.

Rulers

The rulers can help you draw and position objects on the Stage more precisely.

Scene

A scene is a segment of a movie that has its own Timeline and Stage. Scenes help you better organize and review the contents of a long movie by breaking up the movie into more manageable segments.

Shape Tween

A shape tween is an animation sequence that transforms one object into another object by creating an effect that is similar to morphing. To create a shape tween, you specify two keyframes that each display an object in a different shape and then have Flash create the animation for the in-between frames.

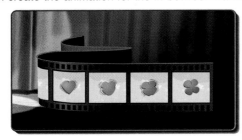

Stage

The Stage is the area where you create, change and view the content of a movie.

Symbol

A symbol is an object that you create once in a document and can reuse throughout the document. Flash stores each symbol you create in the library of the current document. Using symbols reduces a document's file size by allowing you to store an object only once as a symbol and then use instances of the symbol throughout your document.

Symbol Instance

A symbol instance is an occurrence of a symbol. When you add a symbol to the Stage, you are adding an instance of the symbol.

Timeline

The Timeline allows you to organize and control the content of a movie. The Timeline contains layers that help organize the artwork in a movie and frames that store the content for specific locations in a movie.

Toolbox

The toolbox contains tools that you can use to create and work with objects in Flash.

Vector Image

A vector image uses geometric lines and curves, called vectors, to define the details of the image.

Work Area

The work area surrounds the Stage. Objects you place in the work area will not appear in the finished movie.

INDEX

INDEX

INDEX

Read Less – Learn More™

Visual

Simplified®

Simply the Easiest Way to Learn

For visual learners who are brand-new to a topic and want to be shown, not told, how to solve a problem in a friendly, approachable way.

All *Simplified®* books feature friendly Disk characters who demonstrate and explain the purpose of each task.

Title	ISBN	U.S. Price
America Online Simplified, 3rd Ed. (Version 7.0)	0-7645-3673-7	$24.99
Computers Simplified, 5th Ed.	0-7645-3524-2	$27.99
Creating Web Pages with HTML Simplified, 2nd Ed.	0-7645-6067-0	$27.99
Excel 97 Simplified	0-7645-6022-0	$27.99
Excel 2002 Simplified	0-7645-3589-7	$27.99
FrontPage 2000 Simplified	0-7645-3450-5	$27.99
FrontPage 2002 Simplified	0-7645-3612-5	$27.99
Internet and World Wide Web Simplified, 3rd Ed.	0-7645-3409-2	$27.99
Microsoft Excel 2000 Simplified	0-7645-6053-0	$27.99
Microsoft Office 2000 Simplified	0-7645-6052-2	$29.99
Microsoft Word 2000 Simplified	0-7645-6054-9	$27.99
More Windows 98 Simplified	0-7645-6037-9	$27.99
Office 97 Simplified	0-7645-6009-3	$29.99
Office XP Simplified	0-7645-0850-4	$29.99
PC Upgrade and Repair Simplified, 2nd Ed.	0-7645-3560-9	$27.99
Windows 98 Simplified	0-7645-6030-1	$27.99
Windows Me Millennium Edition Simplified	0-7645-3494-7	$27.99
Windows XP Simplified	0-7645-3618-4	$27.99
Word 2002 Simplified	0-7645-3588-9	$27.99